# Film Study Collections

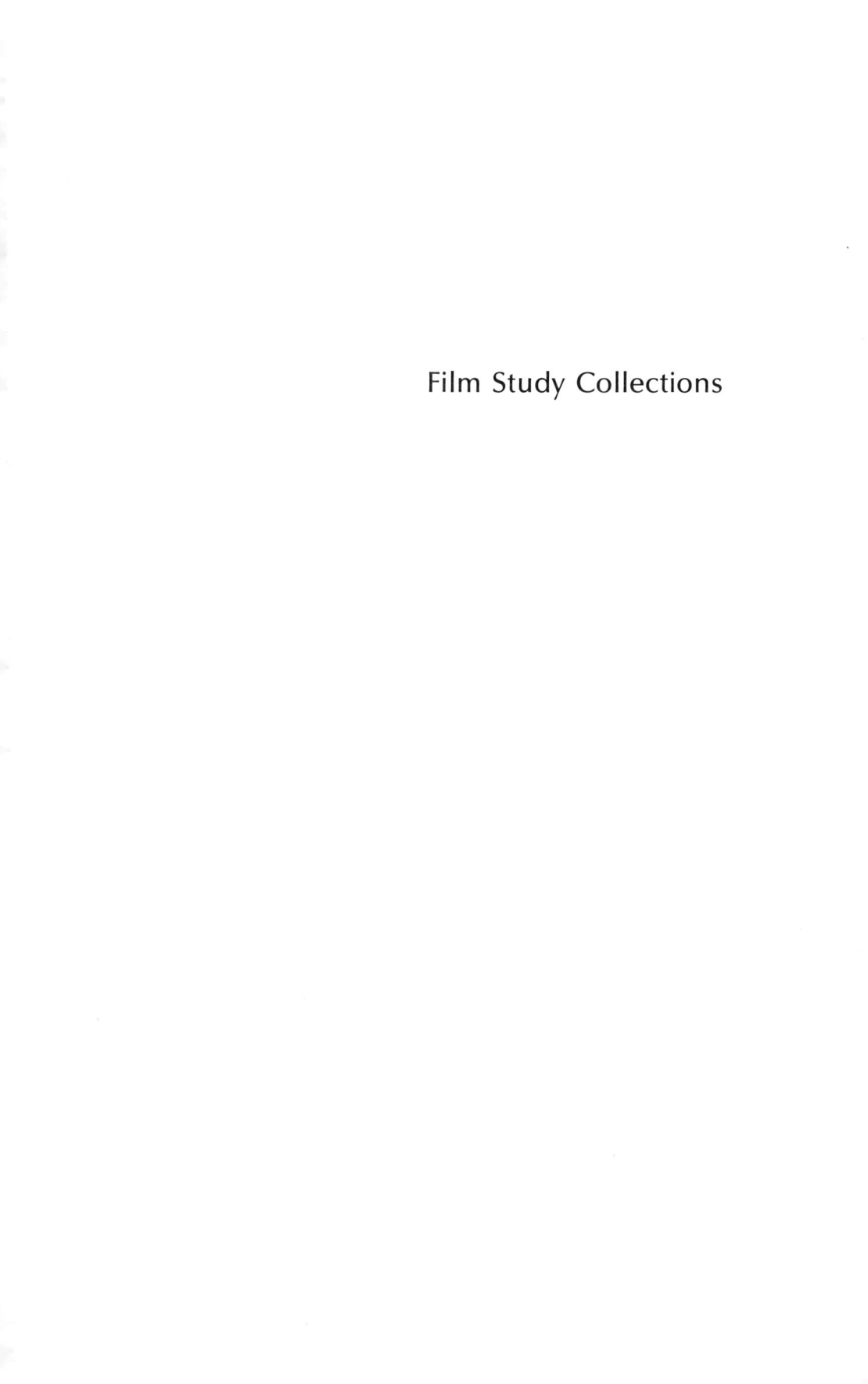

UNGAR FILM LIBRARY
Stanley Hochman, General Editor

Academy Awards: An Ungar Reference Index
  *Compiled and introduced by Richard Shale*
American History/American Film: Interpreting the Hollywood Image
  *Edited by John E. O'Connor and Martin A. Jackson*
The Classic American Novel and the Movies
  *Edited by Gerald Peary and Roger Shatzkin*
Costume Design in the Movies
  *Elizabeth Leese*
Faulkner and Film
  *Bruce F. Kawin*
Fellini the Artist
  *Edward Murray*
The Modern American Novel and the Movies
  *Edited by Gerald Peary and Roger Shatzkin*
On the Verge of Revolt: Women in American Films of the Fifties
  *Brandon French*
Ten Film Classics
  *Edward Murray*
Tennessee Williams and Film
  *Maurice Yacowar*

OTHER FILM BOOKS

The Age of the American Novel: The Film Aesthetic of Fiction between the Two Wars
  *Claude-Edmonde Magny*
The Cinematic Imagination: Writers and the Motion Pictures
  *Edward Murray*
A Library of Film Criticism: American Film Directors
  *Edited by Stanley Hochman*
Nine American Film Critics
  *Edward Murray*

# FILM STUDY COLLECTIONS

## A Guide to Their Development and Use

### by NANCY ALLEN
Research assistance, Laura Drasgow
Cataloging chapter, Michael Gorman

FREDERICK UNGAR PUBLISHING CO.
New York

Copyright © 1979 by Frederick Ungar Publishing Co., Inc.
Printed in the United States of America
Designed by Jacqueline Schuman

Library of Congress Cataloging in Publication Data

Allen, Nancy, 1950–
  Film study collections.

  Includes bibliographies and index.
  1. Libraries—Special collections—Film
literature.  I. Title.
Z688.F54A44     001.55'3     78-20935
ISBN 0-8044-2001-7


DEDICATION:
To my best friends

# Acknowledgments

Thanks go to:

Michael Gorman, for editing the first draft of the text and for preparing the chapter on cataloging and classification;

Laura Drasgow, for being such an able and hardworking research assistant;

Anne Schlosser and other members of the staff and faculty of the American Film Institute for allowing me to use portions of material prepared for the Film/TV Documentation Workshop, Summer 1978;

Bob Carringer of the Unit for Cinema Studies, and the faculty and staff of the Undergraduate Library for offering encouragement and support;

Vera Carroll, for help with bibliographic accuracy;

Ruth Burnham and Jytte Millan for typing;

The many librarians who spent their time and effort supplying information describing their library holdings;

The University of Illinois, for supporting the research involved in the preparation of this book by granting sabbatical time and research assistance;

Frederick Ungar Publishing Co., for believing that libraries and library material are important to the study of film.

# Contents

Introduction    xi

1. Film Study and Its Evolution    3
2. Monograph Series    11
3. Collection Development—Retrospective    17
4. Collection Development—Current    22
5. Selecting Periodicals    27
    A Core Collection of Frequently Indexed Film
        Periodical Titles    28
    Trade Magazines    33
    New Periodicals    34
    Foreign Language Periodicals    35
    Related Areas    37
    Indexes Examined for Journals Frequently Covered    38
6. Evaluation of Published Material    39
    Reference Books    40
    Nonreference or Circulating Books    44
7. Nonprint Material    50
    Nonprint Material and Copyright    55
8. Scripts    58
9. Bookstores and Film Memorabilia Dealers    63
    United States    64
    International    68
10. Major U.S. Archives    71
11. Reference Services    79
    A Reference Collection—109 Sources    81
    Reference Referral    93
    Data Base Searching    97
    National and Regional Film Information Sources    101
    Regional Film Study Centers    104

ix

12. Instruction to Library Users   106
    Basic Library Instruction   107
    A Specific Presentation for Library Users   108
13. Cataloging and Classification of Film Study Material (by Michael Gorman)   113
14. Survey of Film Study Libraries   124
    Summary Results of the Survey   126

Appendix A: Publishers' Addresses   169

Appendix B: Libraries Holding Screenplays   178

Topics Index   179

Collections Index   183

Works Cited Index   188

# INTRODUCTION

As the study of film history, techniques, and theory continues to develop as an important part of the curricula of high schools, colleges, and universities, both public and academic libraries are increasingly called upon to support cinema research. Film books are also popular for leisure reading, and are prime choices in browsing collections in all libraries. In addition, because film magazines appear in general periodical indexes, requests for readings from these magazines increase all the time. All in all, libraries have a lot to do in order to satisfy the need for information on that major element of twentieth-century culture—the movies.

The demand for and success of film literature has caused a boom in film publishing. The film student, teacher, and librarian have a mass of material to choose from. New periodicals, bibliographies, indexes, catalogs, biographies, and filmographies appear every month. Librarians are bombarded by advertisements for films, filmstrips, records, and slide sets. In the last ten years, and especially in the last five, the available amount of material on cinema has become increasingly difficult for the librarian to understand and control.

In an attempt to clarify the situation, this guide offers a description of the literature broken down by form and subject. It suggests resources to satisfy the needs of different kinds of library patrons and helps the librarian and scholar to find those resources. It investigates existing collections of cinema resources and aids the librarian in making the best use of them.

There are some limitations in the scope of this guide. For example, its basic focus is on English language material. In addition, the directory of resources in academic libraries contains entries primarily for U.S. schools listed in the 1978 edition of the American Film Institute's *Guide to College Courses in Film and Television*[1] as offering degree programs in film.

Some of the vocabulary used in this guide needs definition. The

---

[1] *The American Film Institute Guide to College Courses in Film and Television*. Edited by Dennis R. Bohnenkamp and Sam L. Grogg, Jr. 3rd ed. Princeton, N.J.: Peterson's Guides Publications for the American Film Institute, 1978.

definitions of monographs, serials, monograph series, and periodicals used here are as follows:

A *monograph* is a separate treatise on a single subject or class of subjects.

A *serial* is a publication issued in successive parts, usually appearing at regular intervals, intended to be continued indefinitely.

A *series* is a set of volumes related to each other, usually by subject matter, generally issued by the same publisher in a uniform style, and usually with a collective title.

A *periodical* is a serial with a distinctive title appearing at regular intervals more often than once a year. It contains writings by several contributors.

*Nonprint material,* by broad definition, is material presented in nonbook form. It includes films, filmstrips, photographs, artwork, realia, audio recordings, video recordings, etc. "Nonprint" may also include microforms, since like many other materials for projection, they require machinery for use. In addition, some definitions of "nonprint" include manuscript material.

Two other important definitions on source material are:

*Primary resources* are manuscripts, records, or documents used by an author to prepare a book or other compilation.

*Secondary sources* are material in the compilation of which primary sources have been used.

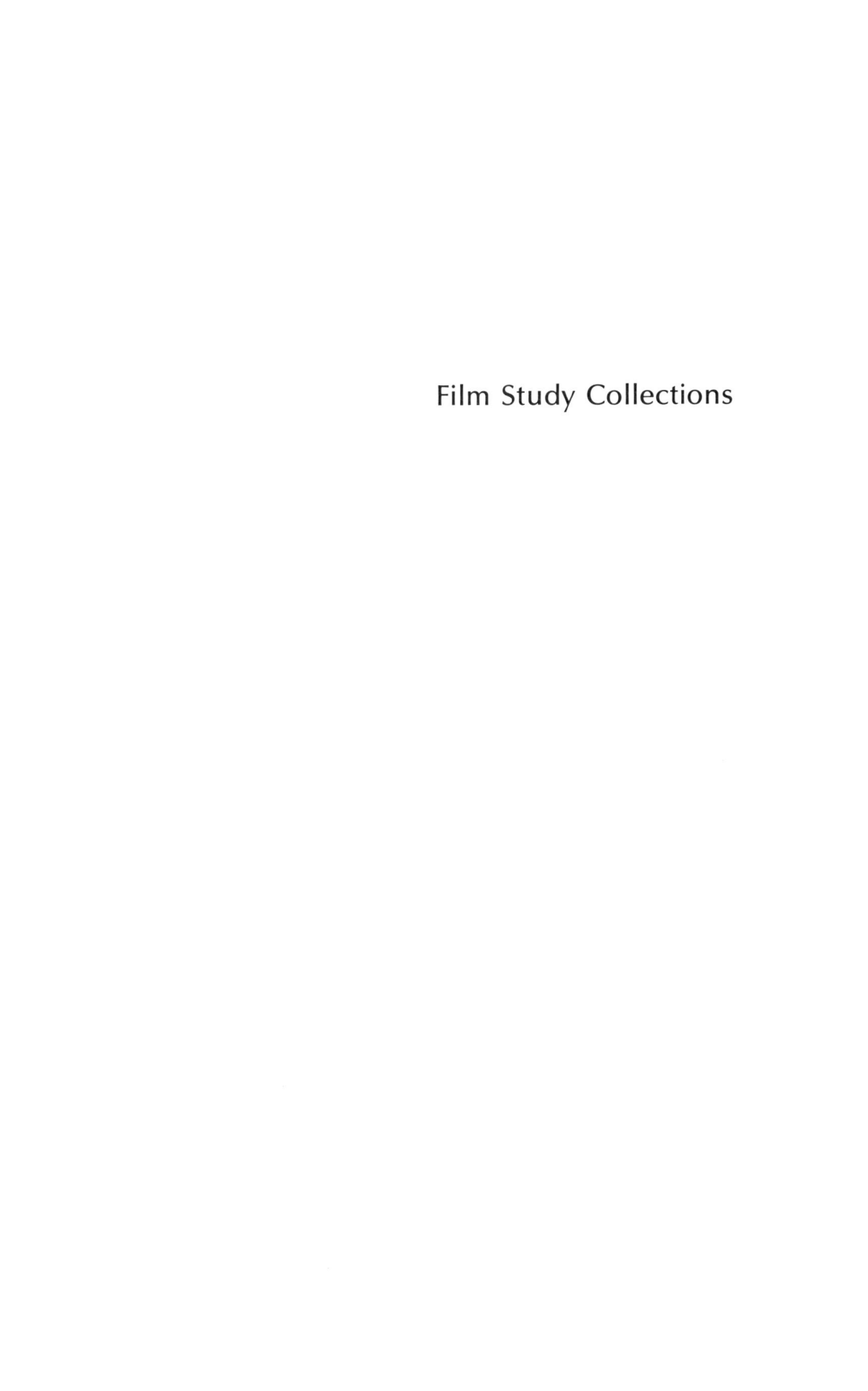

# Film Study Collections

# 1
# Film Study and Its Evolution

Film study at the university level is still at an early stage of development. The interdisciplinary nature of film study is both a problem and an asset when it comes to organizing a degree program and supporting it with library materials. Universities and colleges with film programs have been coping with this problem in broadly similar ways, but common concerns include teacher education, the standardization of the curricula, the planning of curricula, budgetary problems related to high rental and equipment costs, and coping with (or vying for) the large enrollment in film courses.[1] These problems affect the libraries which support research of film students and teachers, and, therefore, deserve the serious attention of librarians and library users.

The education of teachers of film study is probably a temporary

---

[1] Armour, Robert. "A Survey: The Teaching of Film in English Departments." *Journal of the University Film Association*, Vol. 287, No. 4 (Fall 1975), pp. 11–16.
Hodgkinson, Anthony W. "Film—A Central Discipline?" *Literature/Film Quarterly*, Vol. 3, No. 4 (Fall 1975), pp. 327–333.
Plotkin, Richard. "Approaches to Film Study at the University of Illinois." *Journal of the University Film Association*, Vol. 27, No. 4 (Fall 1975), pp. 17–21.
Schneider, Harold W. "Literature and Film: Marking Out Some Boundaries." *Literature/Film Quarterly*, Vol. 3, No. 1 (Winter 1975), pp. 30–44.

problem. As more and more graduate students develop serious research commitment to cinematic topics and themselves become teachers, we will see better staffed film departments and more knowledgeable film course instructors. Until then, however, film courses will continue to be taught by faculty who have shown interest in the subject but who may not have formal training in the discipline. Literature professors, language experts, historians, journalists, and members of many other teaching and research departments are teaching film, publishing on that subject, and learning as they go. According to Sam Grogg, head of the American Film Institute's educational program, less than one-third of the persons attending a 1975 City University of New York Conference had undertaken any formal coursework on film.[2] It is here we see the dual nature of the problem facing the library. Not only do students need basic instruction in film research technique and help with library resources, but so do their teachers.

The development and maintenance of library collections is another area in which the library is directly affected by the background of the teaching faculty. Curricula are often built around the research interests of specific teachers. Libraries are affected by this fact in two ways. First, academic library collections have a minimum requirement to support the curricula of the institutions they serve and must therefore reflect changes in emphasis in coursework. The second imperative for academic libraries is to support the research needs of the teaching faculty. Directions in curricula and research are not always the same, but together, they will always have the primary impact on the ways in which libraries maintain and develop their collections. The librarians responsible for acquisition of library material must rely on close cooperation with the teaching faculty for information on course development, student interests, and faculty research needs. Therefore, the faculty members who work with those librarians will have an important role in determining acquisition policy.

Film courses invariably attract large enrollments. These large enrollments have both positive and negative aspects. Though the college or university should offer serious coursework to the interested student, it should also strive to avoid courses which attract students with a superficial interest in the topic and a desire for entertainment rather than instruction. A balance must be found between the serious educational necessities and the obvious attractions of the topic when planning the introductory film courses. As enrollments rise, money

---

[2] Grogg, Sam L., Jr. "Where Do Film Teachers Come From?" *American Film*, Vol. 1, No. 1, p. 3.

comes into the department; this budgetary situation makes a centralized and organized approach to film coursework less attractive to departments relying on film course enrollments to improve their financial positions.

When hundreds (or in a large university, thousands) of students enroll at one time in college courses in any one discipline, the library collection is put under severe stress. Introductory courses requiring term papers, film reviews, research papers, and compilation of filmographies or biographies may send five hundred students to the library within a very short span of time. Assigned library reading lists are lengthy because the choice of textbooks for students to purchase is limited, and teachers are often unsatisfied with readings from required texts. Circulating collections are heavily used not only by students enrolled in film courses but by the entire university population, since movie books are well illustrated, attractive, and interesting to almost everybody. Unfortunately, a good many movie books are mutilated (photos, stills, and illustrations are snipped out of everything from biographies of Brigitte Bardot to works with less obvious attractions, such as published theses). Constantly circulating material soon becomes dilapidated to the point where it must be replaced. The books are seldom shelved neatly, and the circulation rate is so high that two-thirds of the titles may be charged at any one time and are therefore not available to the majority of users. Duplicate copies are necessary, and this expense puts stress on a book budget already stretched thin by the ever increasing cost of both current publications and out-of-print titles. In sum, heavy use of a library collection is gratifying because we see proof that the collection answers the patrons' needs, but the problems involved are substantial.

Budget problems go beyond the library's book funds. Purchase of films, rental of films, purchase of individual or small-group viewing facilities, and space for large-group viewing are all very expensive matters. The teaching department usually has responsibility for the accessing of films for class viewing, but other areas remain to be settled. Who should provide playback facilities for individual study? Who should purchase or prepare software packages for study of cinematic technique? Copyright issues are clearly involved, and in many cases the lines of responsibility between the department and the library are not well drawn. Since great sums of time and money are involved, the problems are not easy to settle.

It is clear that libraries in academic settings are strongly affected by trends in teaching departments, and it is, therefore, necessary to look more closely at the situation across the nation.

Information on college courses in film and television can be gained from close examination of the American Film Institute *Guide*.[3] There have been three editions of this listing: 1972–3, 1975–6, and 1978. The statistics given here are taken from the *Guide* and from the summaries provided in each edition.

The most obvious trend is that the *Guide* is larger each time it is published. The 1972–3 edition lists 163 schools offering coursework in film, television, and communications. In 1975–6, 791 schools were listed for film and television only, and 1978 shows the greatly increased figure of 1,513 responding schools. The number of courses offered at these colleges and universities has increased at a somewhat similar rate, starting at 5,889 film, television, and communications courses, growing to 8,225 film and television courses, and, most recently, totaling 9,228 film and television courses. This is an increase of 57 percent over 1972–3 and 12 percent over 1975–6. It should be noted that the number of courses is increasing far more slowly than the number of schools offering these courses. Since we are primarily interested in film study, it might be valuable to indicate film course statistics without television, broadcasting, or general communications, although the content and course titles of the listings often overlap, so determination of emphasis is not always possible. In 1972–3, 48 percent of the courses listed (2,818) were in film; in 1975–6, 47 percent (3,873) of the courses were in film, and in 1978, 45 percent (4,161) of the courses were film study courses with an additional figure of 15 percent of the total described as a combined study of film and television.

As film study becomes a more popular area for research on the graduate and postgraduate levels, changes occur in the number of courses offered at the undergraduate level preparatory to such extended study. More undergraduate degrees are shown in the 1978 *Guide* than in the previous editions. In 1972–3, 60 percent of the film courses were offered to undergraduates only, 12 percent were graduate level only, and 23 percent were combination, or upper-level undergraduate and graduate together. In 1975–6, 76 percent of the courses were for undergraduates and 24 percent for graduate students (no figures are given for combination courses). And in 1978, 83 percent of the film courses were offered to undergraduates and 28 percent to graduate students. (These numbers include the combination courses.) It is clear that the absolute number of courses offered to undergraduates is increasing (because the percentage of under-

---

[3] *The American Film Institute Guide to College Courses in Film and Television*. Edited by Sam L. Grogg. 2nd ed. Washington, D.C.: Acropolis Books, 1975.
*The American Film Institute Guide to College Courses in Film and Television*. Edited by Dennis R. Bohnenkamp and Sam L. Grogg, Jr. 3rd ed. Princeton, N.J.: Peterson's Guides Publications for the American Film Institute, 1978.

graduate courses is holding steady, or slightly increasing) and that there are therefore more students prepared to enter graduate programs in film with a solid background of coursework in the field.

Statistics for faculty teaching college-level film and television courses are also revealing. In 1973, a total of 2,460 faculty members were teaching film study and related courses (of these, 39 percent were full time, and 61 percent part time). In 1975, 2,622 faculty members were teaching some aspect of cinema. This increase of 7 percent hardly matches the increase in student enrollment or the increase in the number of courses, but there was a slight shift from part-time to full-time teaching. This must have helped ease the teaching loads (45 percent were full time, up 7 percent from 1972–3; 55 percent were part time, down 6 percent from 1972–3). In 1978, 4,200 faculty members were engaged in teaching courses in film and television. This represents a 71 percent increase over 1972–3 and a 61 percent increase over 1975–6. Moreover, in 1978, 67 percent of the faculty taught film or television courses full time, and only 33 percent taught part time. This increase of 71 percent and 61 percent is matched by an increase in the number of courses taught: 57 percent and 12 percent as compared to 1972–3 and 1975–6, respectively, demonstrating that because enrollments in the courses are up dramatically, more sections of each course title are necessary to keep the student-faculty ratios within acceptable limits. Although the number of courses is increasing, so is the enrollment in each of the courses.

As a supplementary study, a random sample of fifty schools (taken from the American Film Institute *Guide*) was studied to see if there is a relationship between school size (as measured by total enrollments) and the change in film study coursework indicated over the last five years. The data were taken from the 1972–3 and 1978 editions of the *Guide*. In the following results a small school is defined as one having less than 10,000 students and a large school as one having more.

Five of the schools in the sample offered courses in television study only and were therefore not included in the figures given below. Of the remaining 45 schools, 16 were small and 29 large.

|  | Small | Large | Total |
|---|---|---|---|
| Decreased number of courses: | 4 | 3 | 7 |
| Same number of courses: | 4 | 5 | 9 |
| Increased number of courses: | 8 | 21 | 29 |

In general, film course enrollments decreased, remained stable, or increased in line with the decrease, stability, or increase in courses, though one school (a large school) with decreased courses had an increase in course enrollment, and two schools (one large and one small) with the same number of courses had decreased film course enrollments.

In summary, 72.4 percent of the large schools increased the number of their courses as against only 50 percent of the small schools; conversely 25 percent of the small schools decreased the number of their courses whereas only 10 percent of the large schools decreased theirs. There is a clear correlation between school size and the stability and growth of film courses.

A partial study of the schools in the survey (partial because not all schools gave these details in the third edition of the *Guide*) revealed that undergraduate courses have increased at a faster rate than graduate courses.

The libraries supporting growing programs experience stress. Rapidly increasing enrollments put demands on library collections which must be met quickly. More money has to be spent on duplicate copies of heavily used material, but at the same time, a wider range of titles on a wider variety of topics at more levels becomes necessary. Changes in course offerings have to be met by changes in library service. For example, as more students enroll in basic undergraduate film courses, the library should purchase more nonprint materials in order to reach those students in a more effective manner. Librarians must become more aware of both demand and the publishing trends and developments which will meet the demand; an effort is required to increase awareness both of faculty expectations and of student needs.

These needs have been increasing in urgency for the past ten years. Evidence on teaching needs was collected in a survey[4] of film and television higher education covering 1975 to 1976 and published in 1976. Copies of this report, and the data from the report, are available from the American Film Institute offices at the John F. Kennedy Center for the Performing Arts in Washington, D.C. Statistical excerpts from this report are worthy of note. Column A shows the percentage of respondents who currently used this material. Column B shows the percentage who thought the material was needed but was not currently used. Column C shows the percentage who were not interested in using this material, and Column D shows the percentage who did not respond to the question. The last column probably demonstrates the high percentage of either ignorance of or indifference to library or instructional material.

When respondents were asked what type of books were needed, an amazing 48 percent did not respond, probably because they did

---

[4] The American Film Institute. *National Survey of Film and Television Higher Education. Report of Findings.* Washington, D.C.: The American Film Institute, 1976.

## Printed Materials for Classroom Instruction

|  | A (use now) | B (needed) | C (not interested) | D (N/R) |
|---|---|---|---|---|
| anthologies | 46% | 16% | 18% | 23% |
| biographies | 22 | 29 | 27 | 26 |
| histories | 56 | 16 | 12 | 22 |
| interviews | 39 | 18 | 5 | 31 |
| program notes | 23 | 20 | 28 | 31 |
| reference works | 58 | 8 | 5 | 23 |
| study guides | 22 | 21 | 31 | 29 |
| technical texts | 60 | 15 | 11 | 19 |
| unpublished scripts | 19 | 34 | 22 | 30 |

## Nonprint Materials for Classroom Instruction

|  | A | B | C | D |
|---|---|---|---|---|
| complete films, video tapes | 76 | 23 | 2 | 11 |
| excerpts from films | 48 | 42 | 6 | 18 |
| films on film | 49 | 36 | 8 | 19 |
| out takes | 19 | 43 | 16 | 27 |
| slides/filmstrips | 32 | 23 | 23 | 27 |
| videotapes on film | 33 | 33 | 14 | 27 |

## General Teaching Resources

|  | A | B | C | D |
|---|---|---|---|---|
| books/periodicals | 71 | 18 | 2 | 17 |
| college owned films/tapes | 61 | 37 | 1 | 15 |
| commercial film distributors | 56 | 18 | 8 | 22 |
| commercial theaters | 32 | 20 | 17 | 34 |
| film societies | 35 | 21 | 14 | 32 |
| film/video archives | 27 | 43 | 7 | 29 |
| photo/slide collections | 27 | 29 | 16 | 31 |
| privately owned film/tapes | 31 | 28 | 11 | 32 |
| public library film/tapes | 32 | 30 | 12 | 31 |
| script collections | 21 | 36 | 15 | 33 |
| television programs on the air | 48 | 17 | 12 | 27 |

not know what books were available. When asked to place library books and periodicals in priority order with other resources such as additional faculty, films for purchases, and production equipment, the response was as follows (1 = most needed, 6 = least needed):

| 1 | 2 | 3 | 4 | 5 | 6 |
|---|---|---|---|---|---|
| 4% | 9% | 12% | 15% | 16% | 14% |

When asked what resources faculty could do without, 22 percent said library books and periodicals. These statistics show a sad lack of understanding of the importance of library resources. This lack of understanding is probably based on the fact that libraries supporting most film study programs are inadequate. There are only a handful of libraries holding more than fifty film-related journals and more than five hundred to eight hundred film books. It naturally follows that when the only contact teachers have with library holdings brings frustration and dissatisfaction, those teachers will place libraries and printed resources low on a priority list. Academic libraries must improve collections, and they must consider both print and nonprint materials vital to students and faculty. Libraries are the only readily accessible source of film information for the student and scholar. If the library does not have a wide range of books, periodicals, and visual material, many students and teachers will not know such materials exist, and will not appreciate the value of these materials, both for classroom instruction and for personal research. The high rate of "no response" in the 1975 survey shows how many respondents were unfamiliar with these resources. Very few libraries have, up to now, invested in large collections of book material, scripts, or nonprint items. Those teaching film study need such material, and if they do not express that need, it is the responsibility of the progressive librarian committed to excellence in teaching and library support of research to "sell" the need for library collections, and to work toward building better library resources for the hundreds of film study courses taught today. The statistical realities of 1975 have clear effects on the library and the use of library materials purchased to support new and expanding courses for today and for the next generation of film students.

# 2

# Monograph Series

Until about 1975, many publishers produced long lists of titles in a similar format under a series title. New titles were added on a regular basis, and the easiest way for libraries to keep up with the publication of new items was to place a standing order. The standing order idea has several advantages, chief among them that the collection will "automatically" grow without the effort by the library staff of ordering each book separately, and that the library will not miss any of the elements of the series by overlooking an advertisement. Disadvantages include an inability to predict how much money the standing order will cost, and, as some publishers include a variety of types of books in a series, the possibility of receiving more than the library needs.

Currently, the number of publishers' series of monographs is much reduced. Many have been discontinued. Of the titles in discontinued series, many are out of print. If the series is still open, there are often no immediate plans for new additions. Even if there is a series title on the book and in the catalog record for a book, this does not guarantee that the publishers will accept standing orders. It may be necessary to order each title separately anyway. In this case, it is still beneficial to be aware of the existence of the series for several reasons. First, one may rely on the quality and format of the books. Second, if there is a general editor, one may rely on his or her credentials as the individual who determines which new books will appear with the series title. Third, parts of a series may be published by several publishers. The books may have the same format and the numbering of the series may continue. Being familiar with the series title can avoid confusion.

Although the number of monograph series is less than it was five years ago, there are still many active and excellent titles suitable for standing order. Information about these series titles is available from three or four sources, listed here; as new supplements appear, you may gather current information about series for yourself. For information on availability, ordering methods, cost, or other problems, write or phone the publisher for a catalog or for the answer to a specific question.

Baer, Eleanora A., comp. *Titles in Series: A Handbook for Librarians and Students*. 3rd ed., New York: Scarecrow Press, 1978, 4 vols.

*Books in Series in the United States 1966–1975*. 1st ed. New York: R. R. Bowker Co., 1977.

This lists—as stated in a lengthy subtitle—original, reprinted, in-print and out-of-print books, published or distributed in the United States in popular, scholarly, and professional series. Closed or discontinued series are not indicated as such, but out-of-print series are so marked. It is supplemented by the *Books in Series Supplement*, 1978.

Library of Congress. *Monographic Series*. Washington, D.C.: Library of Congress, 1974—.

This is a compilation of LC printed catalog cards. It represents all monographs cataloged by LC as part of a series. It is issued three times each year and cumulated annually. Each issue shows cards printed the previous quarter. The date of the issue does not represent the publication dates of the items listed. It is useful for finding out what are recent additions to series, but it is not the most convenient way to get a list of the contents of a series and gives no indication of availability.

*The Publishers' Trade List Annual*. New York: R. R. Bowker Co., 1873—.

This is a compilation of specially produced catalogs supplied by publishers. It can be very useful because it contains current booklists, and some publishers show their series and the contents of the series. However, all publishers are not listed in PTLA, and all those listed do not show their series. If a series is not shown, it probably means the publisher does not accept standing orders and one must order each book separately.

## Monograph Series 13

The list which follows is a compilation of series titles in film study which are shown in the above sources. Reminders: availability of items in these series is not guaranteed, and the publisher should be contacted for current information. In many cases, the existence of a series title does not mean much since books must be ordered separately.

Appleton Century Crofts. *Film Scripts Series.* This series contained only a few titles and has been discontinued.

Arno Press, Inc. *Dissertations on Film Series.* This series is part of the Arno Press Cinema Program. Dissertations are published in typescript, as written. There are more than 50 dissertations and research reports available at this time, and more than 100 other reprinted classic titles.

A. S. Barnes & Co., Inc. Several series have been produced, including these closed series: *Screen Series, International Film Guide Series,* and these continuing series: *The Hollywood Professionals, Screen Textbook Series; Film in Sweden.* Standing orders are accepted. A. S. Barnes publishes many series originally published in Great Britain by Tantivy.

William C. Brown Company, Publishers. *Pictorial Treasury of Film Stars Series.* This series includes fans' books on such names as Cary Grant, Bette Davis, Clark Gable, Elizabeth Taylor, and others. Items should be ordered separately.

Citadel Press. *Films of ——— Series.* This is an active series of biography/ filmography books on actors and actresses. Several pages of text and illustrations are devoted to each film, including cast, credits, and a critical commentary with plot summary.

Crown Publishers, Inc. *Cinéma d'Aujourd'hui in English.* These translations are about major directors, and include screenplay excerpts, critical articles, biographies, filmographies, bibliographies, and indexes. The series is discontinued.

DaCapo Press, Inc. *Theater, Film, and the Performing Arts Series.* Books with this series title must be ordered separately and are reprints of other publishers' work. They are all done in different formats.

Dickinson Publishing Company, Inc. *Literature and Film Series.* This series is closed. It included 3 titles called *From Fiction to Film* on different literary works transferred to the screen.

Doubleday and Company, Inc. *Cinema World.* Seven books published in association with the British Film Institute in 1968; all out of print. *Movie Makers.* Four titles (on Bogart, Brando, Chaplin, and Hitchcock) published in 1975; no plans for adding to the series.

Dover Publications, Inc. *Dover Film Series.* This series is being continued, but includes a wide variety of books ranging from serious film theory texts to an illustrated quiz book. Most of the titles are mandatory for a college collection, and none is without merit.

Gordon Press Publishers. *Gordon Press Film Series.* This is an active series of very expensive books ranging in price from $40–$175 for a two-volume set. There are 15 items currently available, on topics ranging widely from *Dickens and Film* to *Horror: Film and Literature.*

Grove Press, Inc. *Film Book Series.* Not a publisher's series. Any books with this series title must be ordered separately.

G. K. Hall & Company. *Reference Publications in Film.* A director series offering a critical survey, film synopsis and credits, writings by and about the director, and archival sources for each director.

Harper & Row, Publishers, Inc. *Masterworks Film Series.* Contains only a few titles. Each book contains cast and credits and the entire script for films representing a national cinema.

Hastings House Publishers, Inc. *Library of Film and Television Practice.* An active series of illustrated texts on various aspects of film and television production. They are well indexed and contain lists of films, individuals mentioned, and glossaries.

Hopkinson & Blake, Inc. *Cinema Studies Series.* Discontinued series. The few books published under this series title had varying formats and topics.

Indiana University Press. *Cinema One; Cinema Two; Filmguide Series. Cinema One* and *Cinema Two* are numbered series published by Secker and Warburg in London and picked up in this country primarily by Indiana University Press. Viking and the University of California Press have also published some numbers. All are in the same format and are printed in England. *Cinema One* volumes are all still available through Indiana University Press. *Cinema Two* is an active series. *Filmguide Series* is not closed by Indiana University Press, although they have no immediate plans for adding titles.

Little, Brown & Company. *American Film Institute Series.* Order any of the books with this series title individually. It is not a series for which the publisher accepts standing orders. The books are done in coordination with American Film Institute and are on a variety of theoretical topics concerning filmmaking, film and society, and scripts of major films.

Jerome S. Ozer, Publisher, Inc. *Moving Pictures—Their Impact on Society.* A reprint series including books on topics from censorship to sociology of film. The publisher has no immediate plans for adding to this series.

Praeger Publishers, Inc. *Praeger Film Books.* Titles in this series are out of print. *Praeger Film Library.* This was a series edited by Ian Cameron. Some titles have been published in London by Studio Vista in the same format. Most are out of print.

Prentice Hall, Inc. *Film Focus Series.* This series is closed. It was edited by Ronald Gottesman and Harry Geduld and consists of collections of essays on films, filmmakers, and film genres. A descriptive statement on the series says it combined criticism with history, biography, and analysis of technique.

Pyramid Publications. *Illustrated History of Movies Series.* This series was edited by Ted Sennett and is now closed. Each title chronologically examined a film personality or genre. Most of the titles were published in 1973 and 1974 and include bibliographies, filmographies, and indexes, as well as editorial criticism.

Revisionist Press. This *Cinema Series* is still active, with five titles in the series so far and new titles planned. They are primarily reference and scholarly volumes.

Simon and Schuster, Inc. *Essandess World of Film Series.* A small series which has been phased out. *Modern Film Scripts. Classic Film Scripts.* Two very good series of scripts which were phased out. Some titles have been added by Lorrimer in London, but not recently. Each book contains cast, credits, and a scenario, with footnotes describing differences between versions of the script. *Monarch Film Series.* There are new titles on filmmakers or genres appearing with this series title, but they should be ordered individually.

Southern Illinois University Press. *Screenplay Library Series.* Screenplays by well-known authors such as Anita Loos and Raymond Chandler are currently available.

Twayne Publishers. *Theatrical Arts Series.* This is a new series on filmmakers aimed at college audiences. Standing orders are accepted.

Frederick Ungar Publishing Co., Inc. *Ungar Film Library.* This is an active and rapidly expanding series. Standing orders are accepted. Topics include criticism, costume design, and screen writing. There is special emphasis on the relationship between film and both literature and history. Illustrated and indexed.

University of California Press. *Movie Editions.* This discontinued series is in the same format as the Praeger series edited by Ian Cameron.

University of Wisconsin Press. *Wisconsin/Warner Bros. Screenplay Series.* A new series of final shooting scripts from the Warner Brothers Film Library. 38 titles are currently listed as in production or forthcoming.

The Viking Press. All titles must be ordered separately.
   *Cinema One.* Same format as Indiana University Press volumes on film theory, genre, and people. *MGM Library of Film Scripts.* Six film scripts by MGM published in 1972. *Paperback Film Scripts* (Grossman). Collections of screenplays by international directors.

# 3
# Collection Development—Retrospective

When using bibliographies to compile a list of older books for purchase, decisions must be made about the scope and subject emphasis of the collection. An acquisition statement that outlines which subdivisions of film study are to be emphasized in relation to patron requests, research demands, and existing and future curricula should be prepared.

Annotated bibliographies, selective or critical bibliographies, booklists, reference collection lists, and descriptions of special collections are all helpful to the librarian building a film study collection. This bibliography of bibliographies should serve any kind of collection development project by allowing the librarian to locate citations to as much material as possible. The only works omitted here are descriptions of special or manuscript collections which do not show other holdings. These works are listed on page 60. Complete addresses of publishers are given in the Appendix.

Blum, Eleanor. *Basic Books in the Mass Media*. Urbana, Ill.: University of Illinois Press, 1972. An annotated, selected booklist covering general communications, book publishing, broadcasting, film magazines, newspapers, advertising, indexes, and scholarly and professional periodicals. A chapter on film annotates 108 books which are a mixture of reference and basic film theory and history sources. New edition forthcoming.

*Bibliographic Guide to Theatre Arts.* Boston, Mass.: G. K. Hall and Co., 1975—(annual). An author, title, subject list with a full Library of Congress entry for each item; includes books on cinema, biography, and shooting scripts in the Research Libraries of the New York Public Library with additional entries from MARC tapes for items on theatrical topics.

Bowles, Stephen E., comp. *An Approach to Film Study: A Selected Booklist.* New York: Revisionist Press, 1974. Author, title, and publication date are given for each book listed in this bibliography divided into detailed categories and subjects.

Bowles, Stephen E., comp. and ed. *Index to Critical Film Reviews in British and American Film Periodicals, Together with Index to Critical Reviews of Books About Film.* New York: Burt Franklin, 1974–5. Part III of this two-volume set contains an index to reviews of film books and a subject index to the books reviewed.

British Film Institute, London—Library. *Catalogue of the Book Library of the British Film Institute.* Boston: G. K. Hall, 1975. 3 vols. *The British Film Institute Personality and General Subject Index,* ca. 1935–1974. London: World Microfilms Publications in association with the British Film Institute, 1975. *The British Film Institute Film Title Index, 1908–1974.* 2nd completely rev. ed. London: World Microfilms Publications in association with the British Film Institute, 1975. *The British Film Institute Film Title Index, 1975–76.* Update to 2nd completely rev. ed. London: World Microfilms Publications, Ltd. in association with the British Film Institute, 1977. The book catalog includes indexes which allow access to the copies of cards shown in call number (Dewey) order. The last three items are microfilm indexes to the clipping files of the British Film Institute. They give full citations to the articles and cover a huge mass of literature.

Bukalski, Peter J., comp. *Film Research: A Critical Bibliography with Annotations and Essay.* Boston: G. K. Hall, 1972. This lists periodicals, annotates 50 essential works, and lists without annotations about 3,000 film books by category.

*Catalog of the Library of the Museum of Modern Art, New York City.* Boston: G. K. Hall, 1976. 14 vols.

Chicorel, Marietta, ed. *Chicorel Index to Film Literature.* 1st ed. New York: Chicorel Library Publishing Corporation, 1975. (Chicorel Index Series, Vol. 22). There are over 3,000 books listed in 15,000 entries by subject without annotations. Biographies are listed under both author and subject.

Dyment, Alan R. *The Literature of the Film: A Bibliographical Guide to the Film as Art and Entertainment, 1936–1970.* New York: White Lion Publishers, 1975. This provides 1,303 citations with annotations for books by subject. There are author and title indexes.

Library of Congress. Divison of Bibliography. *Moving Pictures in the United States and Foreign Countries: a Selected List of Recent Writings.* 2nd ed. Washington, D.C.: Government Printing Office, 1940. (Compiled by Anne L. Baden under the direction of Florence S. Hellman, Chief Bibliographer.) Both editions (1st ed., 1936) total about 1,400 titles, with some annotations. Author index.

Manchel, Frank. *Film Study: A Resource Guide.* Rutherford, N.J.: Fairleigh Dickinson University Press, 1973. Nearly 900 books are annotated as part of essays on subjects in film study, and about 3,000 articles are listed in footnotes.

McCarty, Clifford. *Published Screenplays: A Checklist.* 1st ed. Kent, Ohio: Kent State University Press, 1971. (Serif Series: bibliographies and checklists, No. 18.) This includes screenplays published in full or in part in monographs and periodical literature.

Monaco, James, and Schenker, Susan. *Books About Film: A Bibliographical Checklist.* 3rd ed., rev. New York: New York Zoetrope, 1976. About 500 books are listed. Some have very brief annotations or recommendations. The list is divided into familiar topical sections with brief information on series.

Perry, Ted, ed. *Performing Arts Resources.* New York: Drama Book Specialists, Vol. 1, 1975—.

Poteet, G. Howard. *Published Radio, Television, and Film Scripts: A Bibliography.* Troy, N.Y.: Whitson Publishing Co., 1975. This lists 667 film scripts which have been published in entirety or in part.

Rehrauer, George. *Cinema Booklist.* Metuchen, N.J.: Scarecrow Press, 1972. Supplement One, 1974; Supplement Two, 1977. A total of 3,999 books are annotated. The books are in title order, with subject and author indexes. Film scripts are listed and Supplement Three is forthcoming. The primary purpose of the list is to serve as a collection development aid for all types of libraries and laypeople.

Schoolcraft, Ralph N. *Performing Arts Books in Print: An Annotated Bibliography.* 1st ed. New York: Drama Book Specialists, 1973. "A thoroughly revised, rewritten, and up-dated edition of *Theatre Books in Print,* originally published in 1963 and revised in 1966." There is a long section on motion pictures, radio, and television. Quarterly supplements are found in *Annotated Bibliography of New Publications in the Performing Arts.*

Sheahan, Eileen. *Moving Pictures: A Bibliography of Selected Reference Works for the Study of Film, With Emphasis on Holdings in the Libraries of Yale University.* New Haven: Yale University Library, 1973. This annotates 320 titles in general categories and indexes them by author, title, and series. The same author's newest work is titled *Moving Pictures* and is published by A. S. Barnes, 1978.

University of California at Los Angeles Library. *Motion Pictures: A Catalog of Books, Periodicals, Screenplays, Television Scripts, and Production Stills*. Edited by Audree Malkin. 2nd ed., rev. and exp. Boston: G. K. Hall, 1976. The UCLA collection is shown in parts: books and periodicals, published and unpublished screenplays, TV scripts, and stills.

Vincent, Carl; Redi, Riccardo; and Venturini, Franco, eds. *General Bibliography of Motion Pictures*. New York: Arno Press, 1972. Lists are divided into 11 general subjects and some entries are annotated. There is a name index only. Text is in English, French, and Italian.

Whalon, Marion K. *Performing Arts Research: A Guide to Information Sources*. Detroit, Mich.: Gale Research Co., 1975. (Performing Arts Information Guide Series, Vol. 1. Gale Information Guide Library.) An extensively annotated guide to theater arts resources, this includes film, radio, and television guides; dictionaries; handbooks; and other reference sources. There is a good crosslisted index.

Writers' Program. *The Film Index: A Bibliography*. Edited by Harold Leonard. New York: The Museum of Modern Art Film Library and the H. W. Wilson Co., 1941; reprinted by Arno Press, 1966. Annotated list of books and periodical articles published up to 1935, indexed by author, title, and subject, and divided into topics.

The following are important bibliographies not in English:

*Bibliografie Internationala Cinema/Bibliographie Internationale Cinéma*, 1966—Bucharest: Archiva Nationala de Filme, 1967—(annual). International in scope. Arranged by categories/subjects. Indexes by author, title, publisher, and country. Annotated in Rumanian and French.

Centro Sperimentale de Cinematografia. Biblioteca. *Catalogo Della Biblioteca*. Vol. 1: Sez, 1ª—CINEMA e TV. Rome: Il Centro, 1973. International in scope. Arranged in ten broad categories, with author index.

Jones, Karen. *Nye Boger on Film, 1–12; New Books on Film, 1–12*. Copenhagen: Det Danske Filmmuseum, 1974. Cumulative edition of periodic new accessions lists. International in coverage. "Arranged more or less according to the classification scheme used by the Filmmuseum's library."

International Federation of Film Archives. *Catalogue Collectif des Livres et Periodiques Publiés Avant 1914 en Possession des Cin-*

ématheques Membres de la Fédération Internationale des Archives du Film: Union Catalogue of Books and Periodicals Published Before 1914 held by the Film Archives Members of the International Federation of Film Archives. Provisional edition. Brussels: Royal Film Archive of Belgium, 1967. Arrangement is chronological by year of publication with indexes by authors and titles. Not annotated.

Manz, H. P., ed. *Internationale Filmbibliographie,* 1952–62. Supplement I, 1963–4. Supplement II, 1965. Zurich: Verlag Hans Rohr, 1963–65. International in scope. Arranged by categories, with author, title, and subject index. Short annotations in German often included. Kept up-to-date by catalogs from Hans Rohr Bookstore.

Mitry, Jean. *Bibliographie Internationale du Cinéma et de la Télévision.* Paris: Institut des Hautes Etudes Cinématographiques, 1966—. Basic approach is by country. So far France (4 vols.), Italy (2 vols.), and Spanish/Portuguese-speaking countries (1 vol.) completed. Annotated in French.

Mostra Internazionale del Libro e del Periodico Cinematografico, Televisivo e Fotografico: *Catalogo.* Venice: Edizioni Mostra Cinema, 1955—(annual). Lists new publications from nearly all countries. Geographical arrangement with subject subdivisions. Author and publisher index. Annotated in Italian.

Turconi, Davide, and Bassotto, Camillo, eds. *Il Film e la Sua Storia (per una Bibliografia delle Storie del Cinema).* Bologna: Capelli, 1964. International in scope. Geographical arrangement with listings for each country subdivided by three broad categories. Author index. Annotated in Italian.

Vioculescu, Ervin. *Repertoriu Mondial al Filmografiilor Nationale: Repertoire Mondial des Filmographies Nationales.* Bucharest: Archiva Nationala de Filme, 1970. Geographical listing of filmographies from 45 countries. Not annotated.

# 4

# Collection Development— Current

For comprehensive book buying, it is obvious that the librarian needs to check all citations to new material. However, even for selective buying, it is important for the librarian to know what is available so that the choices may be the best ones possible.

It is not difficult to locate citations to most of the major work in the field. Film is a popular area, and publishers can be fairly sure of reasonable profits from sales. To locate new books published by trade publishers, standard selection tools for adult material can be used. *Library Journal, Choice, Publisher's Weekly, Booklist,* and *Weekly Record* will keep the academic librarian aware of the majority of new titles. The *Subject Guide to Books in Print* and the *Supplement to Books in Print* will help the acquisition officer to locate citations to books which may not have appeared in selection journals or which simply did not catch the eye.

Not all these tools furnish reviews or annotations, however, and unless a large book budget allows comprehensive buying, selection decisions should be made on the basis of the author's reputation, the publisher's reputation, or the sum of critical comment. Locating such reviews or critical comment can be very time-consuming, and each librarian must place limits on the efforts expended to gather selection information. A reasonably efficient way to see reviews is to examine copies of journals to which the library subscribes. The inherent problem of this approach is that only libraries large enough to fund comprehensive buying can afford journals to assist in effective selective buying. The solution is to subscribe to some and not all of the journals which offer criticism and reviews. A guide to these serials follows. If the serials budget is quite limited, it might be worthwhile to write for sample copies of some of these titles. Complete addresses are given in Appendix A.

*Action.* Hollywood, Cal.: Directors Guild of America, Inc., 1966—; bimonthly. The "Books" column by George L. George contains 25-word comments on 10 to 20 books. Author, title, and publisher are given for each.

*American Cinematographer.* Los Angeles, Cal.: American Society of Cinematographers, 1920—; monthly. International journal of motion picture photography and production techniques. The "Bookshelf" column by George L. George shows 20 to 25 titles with 25-word annotations for each.

*American Film.* Washington, D.C.: American Film Institute, 1975—; monthly. "A journal of the film and television arts." There is a regular "Books" column, with very long signed reviews. Complete publication data is not provided.

*Cineaste.* New York: Cineaste, 1967—; quarterly. The regular feature "Books" contains two to four columns of critical reviews, signed. The format of the "Books" section varies from comparative articles on more than five titles to individual reviews of two to four books. It is international in scope; non-English-language books are reviewed. The "Book Briefs" column contains paragraphs of 75–250 words by members of the editorial board or contributing reviewers. This is followed by a list called "Books Received," with a citation for each book included. The most recent titles are listed here. The publication dates on the other books reviewed range from one to three years earlier than the publication date of the quarterly.

*Cinema Journal.* Evanston, Ill.: Society for Cinema Studies, 1961—; semi-annual. There is a regular "Book Reviews" section with very long signed articles, usually by qualified academics. The articles are evaluative, addressing the merit and scholarship of each title reviewed.

*Classic Film Collector.* Indiana, Pa.: Classic Film Collector, 1962—; quarterly. This tabloid-format publication contains advertisements and citations to private printings and to unusual or small-press publications.

*Film Comment.* New York: Lorien Productions, 1962—; bimonthly.

The book section treats titles at length (more than 1,200 words) in each issue. The publication dates are recent; books are often less than one year old.

*Film Culture.* New York: Film Culture, 1955—; quarterly. In the "Books Received" section, there are about five pages of citations shown without annotations. Full bibliographic information is given, and the titles are one to five years old. The citations are not in title or subject order. There are also lengthy review articles in the body of the journal.

*Film Quarterly.* Berkeley, Cal.: University of California Press, Vol. 12, 1958—; quarterly. (Successor to QFRT.) Each issue has several book reviews which range from short evaluatory pieces to longer (more than 1,000 words) critical articles. New film magazines are also noted.

*Film Review.* London: EMI Cinemas Ltd., 1951—; monthly. Each year there is a bibliography called "Film Books of the Year." The reviewer, Ivan Butler, lists commentary on books under general topics such as history and biography. The list is long, but not comprehensive, including 80–100 titles. Each is reviewed in 200 words or more and receives a favorable or unfavorable opinion.

*Filmmaker's Newsletter.* Ward Mill, Ma.: Suncraft International Corporation, 1967—; monthly. The "New Book" column contains reviews of relatively recent books in articles of 500–600 words. The reviews are signed, and each reviewer writes critical commentary comparing many titles.

*Films and Filming.* London: Hansom Books, 1954—; monthly.

*Films Illustrated.* London: Independent Magazines Ltd., 1971—; monthly. There is a regular "Books" column with one longer review by a contributing writer and several short reviews by the editor. Complete bibliographic information is not provided.

*Films in Review.* New York: National Board of Review of Motion Pictures, 1950—; monthly. The book review column contains signed reviews 600–800 words long. The titles are usually three or less years old.

*Focus on Film.* London: Tantivy Press, 1970—; quarterly. (Distributed in the United States by A. S. Barnes.) It features an "In Print" column edited by Allen Eyles. Reviews not by the editor are signed. Each critical article is relatively short (300 words) and focuses on recent publications.

*Journal of Popular Film.* Bowling Green, Ohio: Center for the Study of Popular Culture, Bowling Green Popular Press, 1972—; quarterly. This contains a "Reviews" section where recent publications receive brief attention with reviews ranging from less than 100 words to more than 400. Reviewers take a critical stance and are usually academics.

*Journal of the University Film Association.* Philadelphia, Pa.: University Film Association, Temple University, 1949—; quarterly. (Editorial offices vary.) The "Books Received" section appears in most but not all issues and contains four or five pages of annotations. There are also very long academic articles either devoted to a single title or of a comparative nature. These are found in the regular "Reviews" section.

*Literature/Film Quarterly.* Salisbury, Md.: Salisbury State College, 1973—; quarterly. This offers reviews limited to 1,500 words which treat selected titles in an in-depth, critical, and scholarly manner. The books chosen are not necessarily recent literature.

*Mass Media Booknotes.* Philadelphia, Pa.: Department of Radio/TV/Film, Temple University, 1969—; monthly. Media-related books are reviewed each month, but one issue per year is dedicated to film books. In this issue, brief reviews are listed by topic. The reviews are primarily critical annotations concerned with format and content and are 25–75 words long.

*Quarterly Review of Film Studies.* Pleasantville, N. Y.: Redgrave Publishing Co., 1976—; quarterly. QRFS publishes articles on topics of film study rather than reviews. These articles are often comparative analyses of scholarly works, however, so the literature of cinema is often at the center of attention.

*Sight and Sound.* London: British Film Institute, 1932—; quarterly. The reviews are long (more than 1,000 words) critical articles on many foreign titles as well as on English-language literature. Most articles are signed, and publication information is not provided. "The international film quarterly."

*Take One.* Montreal: Unicorn Publishing Corp., 1966—; monthly. The "Book News" column lists new in-print titles with annotations and evaluations, as well as upcoming books. There are also long (more than 1,200 words) signed reviews of recent books. "The film magazine."

*Variety.* New York: Variety, Inc., 1905—; weekly. A column toward the end of each issue, called "Literati," focuses on literary news. Each season, new film books are listed by publisher. The reader who scans the entire issue will spot occasional items on new books and ads for more obscure titles, although ordering information is seldom given.

*Wide Angle.* Athens, Ohio: Athens International Film Festival, 1976—; quarterly. Reviews older titles (three to five years old) in long articles by film professors. There is usually one title per issue.

Over 125 publishers listed in *Books in Print* currently have books available on film study topics. The *Subject Guide to Books in Print* lists publications by topic, including such headings as Politics in Motion Pictures, Film Adaptations, Cinematography, Moving Picture Audiences, Moving Picture Actors and Actresses, Moving Picture Cartoons, and many more. The major publishers of cross-disciplinary and general books—such as Prentice-Hall, Macmillan, Ungar, Putnam, Viking, and McGraw-Hill—all offer film books, either in series or separately. Dozens of other major publishers of special or subject material have published film titles, from Abrams to Seabury to Van Nostrand Reinhold. Many university presses publish in this area, including Oxford, Tennessee, Michigan, California, Wisconsin, Temple, New York, and Kent State. To get current information on new publications, one may ask to be placed on publishers' mailing lists of advertisements and catalogs of new books. The following list is of those publishers who have produced or are now producing monograph series in the subject of cinema (asterisked), as well as of those American firms which have issued more than two film books in recent years. For addresses of these and other publishers cited, see Appendix A.

Appleton Century Crofts*
Arlington House Publishers
Arno Press*
A. S. Barnes & Company*
Barnes & Noble Books
R. R. Bowker Company
William C. Brown Company, Publishers*
Citadel Press*
Crown Publishers, Inc.*
DaCapo Press, Inc.*
Dell Publishing Company, Inc.
Dial Press
Dickinson Publishing Company, Inc.*
Doubleday and Company, Inc.*
Dover Publications, Inc.*
Drama Book Specialists Publishers
E. P. Dutton & Company, Inc.
Eastman Kodak Company
Gordon Press Publishers*
Grove Press, Inc.*
G. K. Hall & Company*
Harcourt Brace Jovanovich, Inc.
Harper & Row, Publishers, Inc.*
Hastings House Publishers, Inc.*
Hill & Wang, Inc.
Hopkinson & Blake, Inc.*
Indiana University Press*

Little, Brown & Company*
McGraw-Hill Book Company
Macmillan Publishing Company, Inc.
Morgan & Morgan, Inc.
William Morrow & Company, Inc.
New American Library, Inc.
New York Zoetrope
Oxford University Press, Inc.
Jerome S. Ozer, Publisher, Inc.*
Penguin Books, Inc.
Praeger Publishers, Inc.*
Prentice Hall, Inc.*
Pyramid Publications*
Random House, Inc.
Revisionist Press*
Scarecrow Press, Inc.
Seven Arts Press, Inc.
Simon and Schuster, Inc.*
Southern Illinois University Press*
Lyle Stuart, Inc.
TAB Books
Twayne Publishers*
Frederick Ungar Publishing Co., Inc.*
University of California Press*
Van Nostrand Reinhold Company
The Viking Press*
Watson-Guptill Publications, Inc.

# 5

# Selecting Periodicals

In academic libraries, the three most important criteria to apply to the selection of periodicals are uniqueness of coverage, research use, and whether the periodical is covered by indexing services. If the library has a stable or diminishing serial budget and can only afford a core collection, the librarian will want to pay only for titles which will be well used by both faculty and students. Research at all levels begins with the use of author, title, and subject indexes. Since the index is of small value unless the library subscribes to and holds the journals indexed, a list of the most frequently indexed film periodicals is of clear value as a core collection. Not all the periodicals listed here are currently available, but suppliers of out-of-print material, microfilm copies, and interlibrary cooperation can all be used to make out-of-print titles available. They can also be used to fill in incomplete back sets. If a currently published periodical is unfamiliar to the potential purchaser, most publishers will supply sample or review copies.

This list of periodicals was compiled by comparing the list of indexed journals in nine indexes to film literature. The indexes referred to briefly are given full citations on p. 38, and publishers' addresses are given in Appendix A.

# A Core Collection of Frequently Indexed Film Periodical Titles

*Action.* Hollywood, Cal.: Directors Guild of America, Vol. 1, 1966.
   Indexed 4 times in:  *Film Literature Index*
                               *International Index to Film Periodicals*
                               MacCann and Perry, *The New Film Index*
                               Schuster, *Motion Picture Directors*

*Afterimage.* New York: Visual Studies Workshop, Vol. 1, 1972.
   Indexed 3 times in:  *Film Literature Index*
                               MacCann and Perry, *The New Film Index*
                               Schuster, *Motion Picture Directors*

*American Cinematographer.* Hollywood, Cal.: American Society of Cinematographers, Vol. 1, 1920—.
   Indexed 6 times in:  Bowles, *Index to Critical Reviews*
                             *Film Literature Index*
                             Gerlach, *The Critical Index*
                             *International Index to Film Periodicals*
                             Schuster, *Motion Picture Directors*
                             Schuster, *Motion Picture Performers*

*Cahiers du Cinéma in English.* New York: Cahiers Publishing Co., No. 1, 1966—.
   Indexed 4 times in:  Bowles, *Index to Critical Reviews*
                             *International Index*
                             MacCann and Perry, *The New Film Index*
                             Schuster, *Motion Picture Directors*

*Cineaste.* New York: Cineaste, Vol. 1, Summer 1967—.
   Indexed 8 times in:  Batty, *Retrospective Index to Film Periodicals*
                             Bowles, *Index to Critical Reviews*
                             *Film Literature Index*
                             *Film Review Digest*
                             Gerlach, *The Critical Index*
                             *International Index to Film Periodicals*
                             MacCann and Perry, *The New Film Index*
                             Schuster, *Motion Picture Directors*

*Cinema.* Beverly Hills, Cal.: Spectator International, Vol. 1, 1963. (Frequency varies. Some issues lack date. Issues for Fall 1972 called also issue No. 31.)
   Indexed 6 times in:  Batty, *Retrospective Index to Film Periodicals*
                             Bowles, *Index to Critical Reviews*
                             Gerlach, *The Critical Index*
                             *International Index to Film Periodicals*
                             MacCann and Perry, *The New Film Index*
                             Schuster, *Motion Picture Directors*

*Cinema Journal.* Evanston, Ill.: The University of Chicago Printing Dept., Vol. 1, 1961—. (Frequency varies. Title varies: 1961–8, *Journal.* Issued by the Society for Cinema Studies [called 1961–spring, 1969, Society of Cinematologists].)
 Indexed 7 times in: Batty, *Retrospective Index to Film Periodicals*
         Bowles, *Index to Critical Reviews*
         *Film Literature Index*
         Gerlach, *The Critical Index*
         *International Index to Film Periodicals*
         MacCann and Perry, *The New Film Index*
         Schuster, *Motion Picture Directors*

*Film.* London: British Federation of Film Societies, 1954—.
 Indexed 5 times in: Bowles, *Index to Critical Reviews*
         *Film Literature Index*
         *Film Review Digest*
         MacCann and Perry, *The New Film Index*
         Schuster, *Motion Picture Directors*

*Film Comment.* New York: Lorien Productions, Vol. 1, 1962—. (Title varies: Spring–Summer 1962, *Vision; a journal of film comment.*)
 Indexed 7 times in: Batty, *Retrospective Index to Film Periodicals*
         Bowles, *Index to Critical Reviews*
         *Film Literature Index*
         Gerlach, *The Critical Index*
         *International Index to Film Periodicals*
         MacCann and Perry, *The New Film Index*
         Schuster, *Motion Picture Directors*

*Film Culture.* New York. No. 1, Jan. 1955—. (Frequency varies. Issues for Jan. 1955 to April 1958 called also Vol. 1–Vol. 3, No. 3. Includes some numbers with variant title: *Film culture—expanded arts.* Some numbers accompanied by supplementary material.)
 Indexed 7 times in: Batty, *Retrospective Index to Film Periodicals*
         Bowles, *Index to Critical Reviews*
         *Film Literature Index*
         Gerlach, *The Critical Index*
         *International Index to Film Periodicals*
         MacCann and Perry, *The New Film Index*
         Schuster, *Motion Picture Directors*

*Film Heritage.* Dayton, Ohio: Jack Behrle Printing Co., Vol. 1, Fall 1965.
 Indexed 7 times in: Batty, *Retrospective Index to Film Periodicals*
         Bowles, *Index to Critical Reviews*
         *Film Literature Index*
         Gerlach, *The Critical Index*
         *International Index to Film Periodicals*

MacCann and Perry, *The New Film Index*
Schuster, *Motion Picture Directors*

*Film Journal.* Carlton, Victoria: New Melbourne Film Group and Melbourne University Film Society, 1955–1965. Ceased.
Indexed 3 times in: Bowles, *Index to Critical Reviews*
Gerlach, *The Critical Index*
Schuster, *Motion Picture Directors*

*The Film Journal.* Hollins College, Virginia, Vol. 1, Spring 1971—.
Indexed 4 times in: *Film Literature Index*
Gerlach, *The Critical Index*
*International Index to Film Periodicals*
Schuster, *Motion Picture Directors*

*Film Library Quarterly.* Greenwich, Conn.: Film Library Information Council, Vol. 1, Winter 1967–8.
Indexed 6 times in: Batty, *Retrospective Index to Film Periodicals*
Bowles, *Index to Critical Reviews*
*Film Literature Index*
Gerlach, *The Critical Index*
MacCann and Perry, *The New Film Index*
Schuster, *Motion Picture Directors*

*Film Quarterly.* Berkeley, Cal.: University of California Press, Vol. 12, Fall 1958—. (Successor to QFRT and continuing its volume numbering through with an omission of one year in dating.)
Indexed 8 times in: Batty, *Retrospective Index to Film Periodicals*
Bowles, *Index to Critical Reviews*
*Film Literature Index*
*Film Review Digest*
Gerlach, *The Critical Index*
*International Index to Film Periodicals*
MacCann and Perry, *The New Film Index*
Schuster, *Motion Picture Directors*

*Film Society Review.* New York: American Federation of Film Societies, Vol. 1, 1965. (Title varies: Feb. 1965, *Film Society Newsletter*. Issues from 1965 to 1968 lack numbering. Some numbers accompanied by supplements with title: *Film Society Bulletin*. Superseded by *Critic*. Supersedes *For Film*.)
Indexed 6 times in: Batty, *Retrospective Index to Film Periodicals*
Bowles, *Index to Critical Review*
*International Index to Film Periodicals*
MacCann and Perry, *The New Film Index*
Schuster, *Motion Picture Directors*
Schuster, *Motion Picture Performers*

*Filmmakers' Newsletter.* New York: Suncraft International, Inc., 1967—. (Formerly *Filmmakers' Cooperative*.)

Indexed 4 times in: *Film Literature Index*
Gerlach, *The Critical Index*
*International Index to Film Periodicals*
Schuster, *Motion Picture Directors*

*Films and Filming*. London: Hansom Books, Vol. 1, October 1954—.
Indexed 9 times in: Batty, *Retrospective Index to Film Periodicals*
Bowles, *Index to Critical Reviews*
*Film Literature Index*
*Film Review Digest*
Gerlach, *The Critical Index*
*International Index to Film Periodicals*
MacCann and Perry, *The New Film Index*
Schuster, *Motion Picture Directors*
Schuster, *Motion Picture Performers*

*Films in Review:* New York: National Board of Review of Motion Pictures, Inc., Vol. 1, Feb. 1950—. (Supersedes *New Movies*.)
Indexed 7 times in: Batty, *Retrospective Index to Film Periodicals*
Bowles, *Index to Critical Reviews*
*Film Literature Index*
*Film Review Digest*
*International Index to Film Periodicals*
MacCann and Perry, *The New Film Index*
Schuster, *Motion Picture Directors*

*Focus on Film*. London: Tantivy Press, No. 1, Jan./Feb. 1970—.
Indexed 5 times in: Bowles, *Index to Critical Reviews*
*Film Literature Index*
Gerlach, *The Critical Index*
*International Index to Film Periodicals*
Schuster, *Motion Picture Directors*

*Hollywood Quarterly*. Berkeley, Cal.: University of California Press, Vol. 1, 1945–1951. (Now published as *Film Quarterly*.)
Indexed 6 times in: Batty, *Retrospective Index to Film Periodicals*
Bowles, *Index to Critical Reviews*
Gerlach, *The Critical Index*
MacCann and Perry, *The New Film Index*
Schuster, *Motion Picture Directors*
Schuster, *Motion Picture Performers*

*The Journal*. Beverly Hills, Cal.: Producers Guild of America, April 1952—. (Issued 1952–1966 as *Screen Producers Guild*. Numerous errors in numbering.)
Indexed 3 times in: *Film Literature Index*
*International Index to Film Periodicals*
MacCann and Perry, *The New Film Index*

*The Journal of Popular Film*. Bowling Green, Ohio: Bowling Green

University Popular Press, Vol. 1, Winter 1972—. (Issued by Popular Culture Association.)
    Indexed 4 times in:   *Film Literature Index*
                          Gerlach, *The Critical Index*
                          *International Index to Film Periodicals*
                          Schuster, *Motion Picture Directors*

*Movie*. London: Movie Magazine, Ltd., No. 1, June 1962—. (Publication suspended 1966–67.)
    Indexed 6 times in:   Batty, *Retrospective Index to Film Periodicals*
                          Bowles, *Index to Critical Reviews*
                          Gerlach, *The Critical Index*
                          *International Index to Film Periodicals*
                          MacCann and Perry, *The New Film Index*
                          Schuster, *Motion Picture Directors*

*Ms., The New Magazine for Women*. New York: Ms. Magazine Corp., Vol. 1, 1972.
    Indexed 3 times in:   *Film Literature Index*
                          *Film Review Digest*
                          Schuster, *Motion Picture Directors*

*New York Review of Books*. New York: A. Whitney Ellsworth, Vol. 1, February 16, 1963. (Ellsworth is current publisher.)
    Indexed 3 times in:   Bowles, *Index to Critical Reviews*
                          *Film Literature Index*
                          Schuster, *Motion Picture Directors*

*The Quarterly of Film, Radio and Television*. Berkeley, Cal.: University of California Press, 1951–7. (Superseded *Hollywood Quarterly*, 1945–1951. Now published as *Film Quarterly* 1958—.)
    Indexed 6 times in:   Batty, *Retrospective Index to Film Periodicals*
                          Bowles, *Index to Critical Reviews*
                          Gerlach, *The Critical Index*
                          MacCann and Perry, *The New Film Index*
                          Schuster, *Motion Picture Directors*
                          Schuster, *Motion Picture Performers*

*Screen*. London: Society for Education in Film and Television, Vol. 10, Jan./Feb. 1969—. (Supersedes *Screen Education* and continues its volume numbering.)
    Indexed 5 times in:   Bowles, *Index to Critical Reviews*
                          *Film Literature Index*
                          *International Index to Film Periodicals*
                          MacCann and Perry, *The New Film Index*
                          Schuster, *Motion Picture Directors*

*Sight and Sound: The International Film Quarterly*. London: British Film Institute, Vol. 1, Spring 1932—. (Spring 1932–Autumn 1933 published under auspices of British Institute of Adult Education.)

Indexed 9 times in: Batty, *Retrospective Index to Film Periodicals*
Bowles, *Index to Critical Reviews*
*Film Literature Index*
*Film Review Digest*
Gerlach, *The Critical Index*
*International Index to Film Periodicals*
MacCann and Perry, *The New Film Index*
Schuster, *Motion Picture Directors*
Schuster, *Motion Picture Performers*

*Take One*. Montreal: Unicorn Publishing Corp., Vol. 1, Sept./Oct. 1966—.
Indexed 8 times in: Batty, *Retrospective Index to Film Periodicals*
Bowles, *Index to Critical Reviews*
*Film Literature Index*
*Film Review Digest*
Gerlach, *The Critical Index*
*International Index to Film Periodicals*
MacCann and Perry, *The New Film Index*
Schuster, *Motion Picture Directors*

*Time: The Weekly Newsmagazine*. New York: Time Inc., Vol. 1, 1923—.
Indexed 3 times in: *Film Literature Index*
*Film Review Digest*
Schuster, *Motion Picture Directors*

*The Velvet Light Trap*. Madison Wis.: Arizona Jim Co-op, No. 1, June 1971—.
Indexed 3 times in: *Film Literature Index*
Gerlach, *The Critical Index*
Schuster, *Motion Picture Directors*

*Village Voice*. New York, Vol. 1, 1955.
Indexed 3 times in: Batty, *Retrospective Index to Film Periodicals*
*Film Literature Index*
*Film Review Digest*

## Trade Magazines

Any library supporting advanced research in film study must collect trade magazines. It is difficult to overestimate the importance of such materials in dealing with an area of such currency as film study. Trade magazines are published daily or weekly, and most usually in newspaper format. They seldom publish indexes or are included in general indexes. Their format makes them difficult to store in hard copy. Fortunately, some back sets of trade magazines are available in microform, and pressure for more microfilming will continue to bear results. Most large film study libraries have clipping files from trade magazines which serve as a subject approach to their contents in lieu of indexes. The clipping process is time-consuming, and the results are voluminous and difficult to store. However, a clipping file based on trade magazines is invaluable to the researcher. If a library wishes to subscribe to only one trade publication, *Variety* (weekly) is recommended, not least because past issues are available on microfilm. *Variety* contains trade information for all the entertainment arts, including films, television, theater, publishing, and nightclub entertainment. Its reviews are indexed in several standard indexes.

Major trade publications for the motion picture industry are:

*Variety* weekly, 1905
Variety, Inc.
154 W. 46th St.
New York, N.Y. 10036

*Daily Variety* 5/week, 1933—
Daily Variety Ltd.
1400 N. Cahuenga Blvd.
Hollywood, Cal. 90028

*Hollywood Reporter,* daily, 1930—
c/o Tichi Wilkerson Miles
6715 Sunset Blvd.
Hollywood, Cal. 90028

*Boxoffice,* weekly, 1920—
Associated Publications
825 Van Brunt Blvd.
Kansas City, Mo. 62124

*Screen International,* weekly, 1912—
King Publications Ltd.
142 Wardour St.
London W1V 4BR
ENGLAND

# New Periodicals

Because film is such an expanding area, new periodicals appear every year. They are rarely included in indexes immediately. Many libraries will not want to invest in titles which seem likely to cease publication after only a few issues. However, a collection can quickly become outdated unless some attempt is made to purchase periodicals on new topics in film study which give voice to new trends in critical opinion, which publish new research, and which publish work by emerging scholars. As many newly advertised titles as possible should be examined for possible purchase.

## Foreign Language Periodicals

Foreign language publications are a difficult problem in several ways. Film study is carried on throughout the world, and the film study library should provide as wide a range of information as possible. The range of information, opinion, and research available in film study is limited if a library offers English language publications only, especially if those are limited to U.S. publications. One has only to look at the importance of the French cinema and of French writings on the cinema to realize how limited an exclusively English language collection is. However, most commonly used indexes cover primarily English language journals. As a result, the use of non-English language publications is slight. If a school's film studies curricula are strong in the cinema of other countries, or if film courses are taught in foreign language departments, or if research is done by the faculty of comparative literature departments, the library's holdings should reflect these circumstances by supplying appropriate journals. In most cases, libraries can avoid the large expenditures and the time-consuming processes involved in acquiring foreign titles.

The Library of Congress has holdings of foreign journals, and the University of Southern California Library holds an outstanding and comprehensive collection of foreign titles. Many large research libraries are able to supply copies of articles from foreign journals on request.

*Austria*
   *Filmkunst: Zeitschrift für Filmkultur und Filmwissenschaft,* Österreichische Filmwissenschaftliche Gesellschaft. Druck- und Verlaganstalt Gutenberg. 2700 Wiener Neustadt, Wiener Strasse 66; Rauhensteingasse 5, 1010 Vienna.

*Belgium*
   *Ciné-Revue:* 7 Avenue Marechal Foch; 1030 Brussels.

*Czechoslovakia*
   *Czechoslovak Film:* (In French, German, Russian, and Spanish editions). Subscriptions to: Artia; Ve Smeckach 30; 111 27 Prague 1.
   *Film a Doba:* (Text in Czech, summaries in English, French, and Russian). Subscriptions to: Artia; Ve Smeckach 30; 111 27 Prague 1.

*Denmark*
> *Kosmarama:* The Danish Film Museum; Store Sondervoldstraede; Copenhagen K.

*East Germany*
> *Bild und Ton: Zeitschrift für Film und Fototechnik:* (Text in German, summaries in English, French, and Russian). VEB Fotokinoverlag Leipzig; Karl-Heine-Strasse 16; 7031 Leipzig.

*France*
> *Avant-Scène Cinéma:* Éditions de l'Avant-Scene; 27 rue Saint Andre des Arts; 75006 Paris.
>
> *Cahiers du Cinéma:* 39 rue Coquillière, Paris.
>
> *Cinétheque:* Boîte Postale 65; 75722 Paris.
>
> *Écran:* Éditions de l'Atalante; 60 Avenue Simon Bolivar; 75019 Paris.
>
> *Positif:* Éditions le Terrain Vague; 14–16 rue de Verneuil; 75007 Paris.
>
> *Premier Plan; Hommes, Oeuvres, Problèmes du Cinéma:* Société D'Études, Recherches, et Documentation Cinématographiques; c/o Editor and Publisher. Bernard Chardere; Boîte Postale 3; 69396 Lyon 3.
>
> *Revue du Cinéma/Image et Son; Revue Culturelle de Cinéma:* Ligue Française de l'Enseignement et de l'Éducation Permanente; 3 rue Recamier; 75341 Paris.

*Italy*
> *Bianco e Nero:* Edizioni dell'Ateneo; Via Ruggero Bonghi 11 B; 00184 Rome. Subscriptions to: Box 7216, 00100 Rome.
>
> *Cineforum; Rivista di Cultura Cinematografica:* Federazione Italiana dei Cineforum; Casella Postale 414; 30100 Venice.
>
> *Cinema Nuovo:* Casa Editrice G.C. Sansoni S.p.A; Via Santa Guilia 67; 10124 Turin.
>
> *Filmcritica:* Piazza del Grillo 5; Rome.

*Netherlands*
> *Skrien:* Stichting Skrien Filmschrift; Postbus 318; Amsterdam 1000.

*Norway*
> *Filmjournalen:* Parkveien 5; Oslo 3.

*Poland*
*Film:* 5 Z1. Krajowe Wydawnictwa Czasopism; Nowakowskiego 14; Warsaw.

*Ekran:* Wydawnictwa Artystyczno-Graficzne RSW "Prasa-Ksiazka-Ruch"; Ul. Smolna 10; Warsaw.

*Switzerland*
*Cinema; Unabhängige Schweizerische Filmzeitschrift/ Revue Cinematographique Indépendent Suisse:* 16 Fr. Arbeitsgemeinschaft Cinema; Postfach 1949; CH-8022 Zürich.

*U.S.S.R.*
*Iskusstvo Kino:* (Contents page in English). Soyuz Rabotnikov Kinematografii SSSR; Ul. Usievicha 9; Moscow A319.

*Soviet Film/Sovetskii Fil'm:* (Editions in Arabic, English, French, German, Russian, and Spanish). Mezhdunarodnaya Kniga; Moscow G200.

*West Germany*
*Film und Ton-Magazin:* Herring Verlag GmbH; Ortlerstrasse 8; 8000 Munich 70.

*Filmkritik:* Ainmillerstrasse 4; 8000 Munich 13.

*Yugoslavia*
*Filmska Kultura; Jugoslavenski Casopis za Filmska Pitanja:* (Text in Serbo-Croatian). Aleja Borisa Kidrica 46; 41020 Zagreb.

## Related Areas

Another factor to consider when creating or augmenting a collection of journals for film study is that of periodicals concerned with related subject areas. Even a cursory examination of film study departments in academic institutions of all kinds shows that film study is truly interdisciplinary. The collection development policy of the library has to reflect this fact. Even if the film study collection is part of a small- or medium-sized library, consideration should be given to journals in such areas as television, popular art, mass communication, radio broadcasting, literature, photography, and psychology. For example, *Film Literature Index* does selective indexing of the following titles in nonfilm areas: *American Heritage, American Scholar, The American West, Art in America, Century, Columbia Journalism Review, Communication Education, Dance Magazine, Drama Review, Economist,*

*English Journal, History Teacher, The Humanist, Journal of American Studies, Journal of Creative Behavior, Media and Methods, Modern Photography, Opera News, Progressive Architecture, Sports Illustrated,* and *Teaching Sociology.* These titles are not necessarily recommended for purchase by all libraries, but serve to illustrate the point that the scope of cinema-related literature is indeed wide. The film study librarian has to be aware of a great number of fields and of their impact on, and interrelationship with, the "core" discipline.

## Indexes Examined for Journals Frequently Covered

Batty, Linda. *Retrospective Index to Film Periodicals, 1930–1971.* New York: R. R. Bowker Co., 1975.

Bowles, Stephen E., ed. and comp. *Index to Critical Film Reviews in British and American Film Periodicals. Together with: Index to Critical Reviews of Books About Film.* New York: Burt Franklin, 1974. 3 vols.

*Film Literature Index.* Albany: Filmdex, Inc., Vol. 1, 1973—. (Vol. 1, No. 1 is preceded by an unnumbered issue dated April 1973 and called "Prototype issue.")

*Film Review Digest.* Millwood, N.Y.: Kraus-Thomson Organization, Vol. 1, Fall 1975—.

Gerlach, John C., and Gerlach, Lana, comps. *The Critical Index: A Bibliography of Articles on Film in English, 1946–1973, Arranged by Names and Topics.* New York: Teachers College Press, 1974.

*International Index to Film Periodicals.* New York: R. R. Bowker, Vol. 1, 1972—. (For the International Federation of Film Archives.)

MacCann, Richard Dyer, and Perry, Edward S. *The New Film Index: A Bibliography of Magazine Articles in English, 1930–1970.* With special editorial assistance by Mikki Moisio. New York: Dutton, 1975.

Schuster, Mel, comp. *Motion Picture Directors: A Bibliography of Magazine and Periodical Articles, 1900–1972.* Metuchen, N.J.: Scarecrow Press, 1973.

Schuster, Mel, comp. *Motion Picture Performers: A Bibliography of Magazine and Periodical Articles, 1900–1969.* Metuchen, N.J.: Scarecrow Press, 1971.

Schuster, Mel, comp. *Motion Picture Performers: A Bibliography of Magazine and Periodical Articles. Supplement No. 1, 1900–1974.* Metuchen, N.J.: Scarecrow Press, 1976.

# 6
# Evaluation of Published Material

The process of selecting material has to be organized and made consistent. In order to do this, certain fundamental criteria have to be established and applied. These criteria are set out here in the form of questions which have to be answered before a judgment on acquisition can be made. Of course, the importance of an individual criterion will vary according to the circumstances of individual libraries. Once understood, the criteria will have to be interpreted by the local librarian informed of and sensitive to local needs. The information necessary to perform this evaluation may not be available except by inspection of the material. In addition, the thoroughness of evaluation will vary depending on the size of the collection and the volume of use.

Acquisition of material is not the only reason for in-depth analysis or evaluation. Use of the books will be made much more effective with proper attention to their form, content, and purpose. Anyone who purchases film study material soon realizes that sooner or later it will be necessary to locate information "hidden" in unexpected places. And, of course, awareness of the location of any information will enable a well-spent book budget to be effectively used.

## Reference Books

The definition of a reference book is a difficult matter. If such a definition is not made, hundreds of film books which could better be used in the homes and offices of library patrons might be shelved in a reference area. Some effort must be made to distinguish between those books which should remain on the library shelves at all times and those which should circulate.

The format of the item is the most common aspect by which this is determined. The presence of a dictionary or encyclopedic entry format, the list or chart format, or the combination of text and factual information presented in a regularly repeated standard way for each topic in the book are all signs of a reference book. Index format or bibliography entries without a textual presentation are also common indications of reference material. The format is an indication of the author's intent for the book. The quick retrieval of facts or information is usually the purpose of reference material. However, a great number of books are published without such a clear indication of intent. There are numerous books on individuals which give reference (biographical, filmographical, photographic) information on several people without having a reference-type format. Perhaps as many as six or seven persons might be included in such a work. The librarian has the responsibility for deciding whether or not the information in the book needs always to be available or whether the book would more conveniently be used outside the library building. There are many books on films of other nations which contain credits, cast lists, statistics on production, and critical opinion for selected films of an individual country. The librarian must determine if the information presented is available in other reference works, whether enough films are discussed to cause the book to be in frequent demand, and if the format lends itself to the efficient location of the desired fact.

Each library situation is different. Patron inquiries are on differing levels, and the volume of film reference questions varies, as does the existence of supplementary materials elsewhere in the library system or community. The librarian must use common sense and an awareness of local needs to shape the reference collection. Nothing is permanent about the location of a book; items may be relocated and moved at any time. Moreover, the location of the book does not have to be determined before it is examined, although consideration of its possible uses is an essential selection criterion.

For each type of film study material, beginning with forms of reference material, a list of appropriate evaluative criteria is presented, with an example for discussion. The examples are selected as representative of the type of material discussed, and as being relatively well known, so readers will be able to observe the evaluative process adequately.

## Bibliographies

EXAMPLE: Nachbar, John G. *Western Films: An Annotated Critical Bibliography.* New York: Garland Pub., 1975.

| | |
|---|---|
| Is it annotated? | Yes. All entries have annotations of between 15 and 100 words. |
| What indexes are there? | An author index, and a subject index which includes film titles. |
| Is the introduction explanatory? | Yes. The organization, numbering system, reference sources, and criteria for inclusion are all clearly stated. |
| How inclusive is it? | It includes reference to "all serious criticism in English." |
| Does it have international coverage? | No. |
| Are books and magazines indexed? | Yes. |
| How long is the bibliography? | 80 pages. |
| How is it organized? | By topic, then by "books" and "articles." |

## Dictionaries and Encyclopedias

EXAMPLE: Manvell, Roger, ed. *The International Encyclopedia of Film.* New York: Crown Publishers, 1972.

| | |
|---|---|
| What is its purpose? | Personal reference, with high browsing potential. Second, library reference. |
| How well is it illustrated? | With color plates, and with many black and white photos and stills. |
| To what extent is it biographical? | Not exclusively, but with a majority of name entries. |
| Which individuals are included? | Persons important to international film: actors, directors, screenwriters, animators, cinematographers, etc. |
| What is in the entries? | Name entries have identification only, accompanied by partial filmographies. Glossary entries are very short, and topical entries are very long, with historical coverage of subjects and national cinemas. |

42　FILM STUDY COLLECTIONS

| | |
|---|---|
| How is it indexed? | Index of title changes, index of films, index of names. |
| Any other features? | An extensive bibliography. |

## Credit Indexes or Catalogs

EXAMPLE I: Gifford, Denis. *The British Film Catalogue, 1895–1970: A Reference Guide.* New York: McGraw-Hill, 1973.

EXAMPLE II: Stewart, John, comp. *Filmarama.* Metuchen, N.J.: Scarecrow Press, Vols. 1–2, 1975–7.

| | |
|---|---|
| Does it contain film or personal credits? | I. Film credits.<br>II. Personal credits. |
| Does it reflect a certain collection? | I. No.<br>II. No. |
| How is it arranged? | I. Chronologically by date of exhibition.<br>II. By personality name. |
| How is it indexed? | I. Film title index.<br>II. Film title index. |
| What is given in the entries? | I. Date, title, title change, length, censor certificate, silent or sound, screen ratio, production company, distributor, reissue dates, producer, director, story source, screenplay, narration. Major cast and characters, subject keyword, one-sentence plot summary, awards, and series.<br>II. Players' real names and *representative* record of stage, radio, and television work. |
| Is there any other information in charts or addenda? | I. No.<br>II. Lists of films in serials, names of Keystone Kops and Bathing Beauties, birth and death dates of all entries, and brief biographies of award winners with vital statistics. |
| Are there cross references? | I. No, but all versions of titles appear in the index.<br>II. Some, but not all forms of names appear in see-references. |

## Biographical Material

EXAMPLE I: Truitt, Evelyn Mack. *Who Was Who on Screen.* New York: R. R. Bowker Co., 1974.

EXAMPLE II: Eyles, Allen. *The Western*. South Brunswick, N.J.: A. S. Barnes, 1975. (1st ed. published in 1967 with title: *The Western: An Illustrated Guide*.)

| | |
|---|---|
| What are the dates of inclusion? | I. Those who died between 1920 and 1971. |
| | II. Not applicable. |
| What is the scope of inclusion? | I. Screen appearances of primarily American, British, and French players. |
| | II. 404 persons associated with westerns, including writers, actors, composers, and a few of the original people. |
| What is given in the entries? | I. Birth date; death date, place, and cause; description of career; list of appearances on screen with date and title; real name; miscellaneous information, such as significant marriages. |
| | II. Birth and death dates, a narrative paragraph on contribution to westerns, dates of first and last films, and a filmography listing film titles. |
| Are there illustrations? | I. No. |
| | II. Yes. |
| What is the format? | I. Alphabetical brief entry followed by credits. |
| | II. Alphabetical brief entry followed by credits. |
| How many entries are in the work? | I. Over 6,000. |
| | II. 404. |
| Is there any critical information or editorial comment? | I. No. |
| | II. Some entries have editorial comment. |
| Is there any reference to nonmoving picture performances? | I. Vaudeville, short films. |
| | II. Television films. |
| Is there any literature reference given? | I. No. |
| | II. No. |
| What indexes does it contain? | I. None. |
| | II. Film title index. |

## Guides to Critical Literature

EXAMPLE I: Hochman, Stanley, comp. and ed. *American Film Directors*. New York: Frederick Ungar Publishing Co., 1974. (A Library of Film Criticism.)

EXAMPLE II: MacCann, Richard Dyer, and Perry, Edward S. *The New Film Index: A Bibliography of Magazine Articles in English, 1930–1970.* New York: Dutton, 1975.

| | |
|---|---|
| Does it cover books and/or journals? | I. Both, and also newspapers.<br>II. Magazines only. |
| How many and what kind of sources are indexed? | I. 75 magazines and newspapers, and many collections of critical work in book form.<br>II. 38 film magazines, and all general magazines covered in general indexes. There are over 12,000 articles covered. |
| Are the citations annotated? | I. Excerpts from critical comments are selected rather than completely indexed.<br>II. Yes. |
| Is there international coverage? | I. Yes.<br>II. No. |
| Are reviews included? | I. Yes.<br>II. No, but extended analysis articles are included and so are articles on production of particular films. |
| What indexes are provided? | I. Index of critics and film titles.<br>II. Author index. |
| What is the subject emphasis? | I. To provide critical material on 65 directors.<br>II. To provide subject and name access to film literature. |
| What special information is given in the introduction or elsewhere? | I. Filmographies are shown for each director.<br>II. This is intended to be a personal reference source, not a library one. Name or alphabetical subject indexes would have made it easier to use. Some articles are listed under more than one topic. |

# Nonreference or Circulating Books

## Biography/Criticism of Individuals

EXAMPLE I: Deschner, Donald. *The Films of Cary Grant.* Secaucus, N.J.: Citadel Press, 1973.

EXAMPLE II: Thomas, Bob. *Thalberg: Life and Legend.* Garden City, N.Y.: Doubleday, 1969.

## Evaluation of Published Material 45

| | |
|---|---|
| Does it emphasize the life or films of the person? | I. The films.<br>II. The life and career. |
| Is there critical opinion provided on the films? Are there citations to critical opinion? | I. For each film there is a selection of reviews (without citations) reprinted.<br>II. The text is critical in nature, although there is no bibliography of criticism. |
| How well illustrated is it? | I. There are several stills from, or a poster for, each film.<br>II. There are many photographs and publicity shots. |
| Is there a complete filmography? | I. Yes.<br>II. Yes. |
| Is there complete biographical information? | I. Yes.<br>II. Yes. |
| Is there a bibliography? Index? | I. Neither.<br>II. Both |
| Is it a fan's study or a serious critical work? | I. Although the information in it can be used in different ways by different readers, it is mostly a fan's book.<br>II. It is a serious study. |
| Is it part of a series? | I. Yes.<br>II. No. |
| What is the format? | I. A 24-page biography is followed by a chronological presentation of the films. Each film chapter includes cast, credits, synopsis, and one or more reviews.<br>II. A straight text organized into chronological chapters is followed by chapters on the Thalberg award and winners. |
| If the subject is living, is there an interview? | I. No.<br>II. Not applicable. |

## Histories or Chronological Accounts

EXAMPLE: Rhode, Eric. *A History of the Cinema: From its Origins to 1970.* New York: Hill and Wang, 1976.

| | |
|---|---|
| What is the scope of the work? | It is a general history with international coverage. |
| How much critical or editorial opinion is offered? | Some, but it is not a critical history. |

| | |
|---|---|
| How is the book organized? | There are five chapters with straight text. There are footnotes, a bibliography, and indexes of film and personal names. |
| How well is it illustrated? | There are numerous illustrations, but it is not primarily an illustrated history. |
| How much detail is given to individual films? | Plot summaries are very often incorporated into the text. |
| Is there a particular theme or uniting slant to the history? | Social aspects and influences on the history of film are emphasized, but all aspects of film history are covered. |

## Theory and Criticism

EXAMPLE I: Jarvie, Ian C. *Movies and Society.* New York: Basic Books, 1970. (Published in Great Britain under the title, *Towards a Sociology of the Cinema.*)

EXAMPLE II: Kauffmann, Stanley. *Figures of Light: Film Criticism and Comment.* 1st ed. New York: Harper and Row, 1971. (Film reviews covering the period 1967–70.)

| | |
|---|---|
| Are parts of the book or the whole book reprinted? | I. No.<br>II. Yes. |
| From what standpoint does the author write? | I. That of a scholar.<br>II. That of a critic. |
| What is the format? | I. By chapters.<br>II. By film title, with the addition of several essays. |
| Is there a bibliography? Indexes? | I. There is a bibliography which is quite extensive, and a subject, name, and film index.<br>II. There is no bibliography; there is a general index with names of films and persons. |
| Is the content contemporary or historical? | I. Both.<br>II. Contemporary. |
| Is the critical comment on general theory or on specific review of films? | I. General theory.<br>II. Specific films. |

## Technical Works

EXAMPLE: Malkiewicz, J. Kris. *Cinematography: A Guide for Film Makers and Film Teachers.* New York: Van Nostrand Reinhold Co., 1973.

*Evaluation of Published Material* 47

| | |
|---|---|
| What is the audience of the book? | Cinematography teachers and amateur filmmakers. |
| What limits are placed on the scope? | Concentrates on the work of the cinematographer and on the necessary equipment. It touches on sound, editing, and production. |
| What kind of illustrations are shown? | Many photos of equipment, many diagrams and examples. |
| How technical are the scientific aspects of the text? | Most principles are explained, and diagrammed. Some basics of photography are assumed. |
| Is there a glossary of terms? | Yes. |
| What is the style of the text? | The author directly addresses the reader with advice and instruction. |

## Genre Treatments

EXAMPLE I: Johnson, William, comp. *Focus on the Science Fiction Film*. Englewood Cliffs, N.J.: Prentice-Hall, 1972.

EXAMPLE II: Kobal, John. *Romance and the Cinema*. London: Studio Vista, 1973.

| | |
|---|---|
| Are individual films covered separately in the text? | I. Yes, essays on representative major films are included.<br>II. No, not in depth. However, film stars receive quite a bit of individual attention. |
| What factual information is given, such as filmography or credits? | I. There is a short filmography and a bibliography.<br>II. None. |
| What kind of audience is the author writing for? | I. Film students or others seriously interested in the topic.<br>II. A general audience including film buffs. |
| Is it international in scope? | I. The films are English language films, but there are translations of foreign language critical opinions.<br>II. Somewhat, but with greatest emphasis on American films and film stars. |

## Books on Individual Films

There are three of these categories: screenplays, production accounts, and critical appraisals. Different questions should be asked in evaluation of each of these types of books. There are also numerous examples of books which are combinations of these categories.

## Screenplays

For discussion and vocabulary of screenplays and scripts, see p. 58. Most published screenplays are either a final version of the shooting script or a dialogue continuity with ample descriptions of the action. The major difference between these kinds of scripts is that the shooting script is used to create the film and the continuity form of script reflects the finished product.

The amount of visual support in published screenplays varies widely. Some series of scripts try to illustrate the script for the reader's interest, while others are a shot-by-shot analysis of the film. In a great many cases, unfortunately, the reader cannot ascertain what script version he or she is using. In the evaluation process, the extent of visual representation of the film and the version of the script are the two most important matters to determine.

EXAMPLE: Wake, Sandra, and Hayden, Nicola, comps. and eds. *The Bonnie and Clyde Book*. New York: Simon and Schuster, 1972.

| | |
|---|---|
| How much of the film is shown in frames or stills? | There is usually one or more picture per page. |
| What version is the script? | From the screen. |
| Are complete cast, credits, and characters given? | Yes. |
| Is any critical commentary given? | Yes, excerpts from seven reviews. |
| Are there any interviews? | Yes, and there are also essays by the director, screenwriters, and a critic. |
| Is production information on such things as camera setups or lighting given? | No. |

## Production Accounts

EXAMPLE: Hughes, Eileen Lanouette. *On the Set of Fellini Satyricon: A Behind-the-Scenes Diary*. New York: Morrow, 1971.

| | |
|---|---|
| Are facts or narration on preproduction activities included? | Not much. |
| What is the format? | A day-by-day account, including conversations and description of filming. |
| Is critical opinion included? | Some, in the afterword. |
| Are there indexes, bibliography, credits, filmography? | None. |
| Has there been serious research done, or is the account a casual, fan-oriented report? | Fans will enjoy it, but the insights into the director's working style are valuable to a wide range of readers. |

*Criticism or Analysis*
EXAMPLE: Cawelti, John G., ed. *Focus on Bonnie and Clyde.* Englewood Cliffs, N.J.: Prentice-Hall, 1973.

| | |
|---|---|
| Are cast, credits, and characters given? | Yes. |
| Are there reviews excerpted or given in whole? | Yes, in whole. |
| Is the analysis or criticism by the author, or is there a collection of essays? | Collected essays. |
| Is there shot-by-shot or scene-by-scene analysis? | No, but there is a content outline without critical comment. |
| Is there critical analysis of the director's work other than this particular film? | Yes. |
| Are there excerpts from the script? | Yes. |
| What other features are included in the analysis? | Plot summary, account of script changes, filmography, bibliography, and miscellaneous press items on the original characters. |

Other areas of literature are Hollywood gossip or personal reminiscences, novels on film or novelized screenplays, and books on such topics as censorship, violence and film, children and film, blacks in film, and many other subject areas. Books on subdivisions of the general areas listed and described above should be considered in the same way as is the general area, unless the library has a special collection of material in a particular area.

# 7
# Nonprint Material

Classroom showings of films are the basic and standard way of beginning film study, often with repeat showings at arranged times. The equipment necessary to show parts of films to individual students or to allow close examination of films is expensive. Problems involved in renting and buying films require a good deal of time and money to solve. Locating, scheduling, projecting, and repeating rental films are major administrative chores, and the funding of this process can be difficult. Should a library decide to purchase rather than rent its films, it is presented with the problems of classifying, housing, protecting, and circulating the films and determining the policy for their use. The preservation of films can cause problems: even with the best projection equipment and the most experienced projectionists, the material required to repair films and the maintenance of projection equipment can prove to be major expenses. Overall, the visual approach to film study is an expensive matter, and it becomes more so when detailed study of cinematography, or art direction, or other technical aspects requires numerous viewings.

Apart from the financial and other difficulties associated with the use of source films themselves—which may be surmounted by the use of an archive or film library—the film librarian needs to consider other visual aids. Nonprint sources for instruction and study are available for purchase and rental. There are a great number of 16mm films on film study. Their quality varies in terms of their level of presenta-

*Criticism or Analysis*
EXAMPLE: Cawelti, John G., ed. *Focus on Bonnie and Clyde.* Englewood Cliffs, N.J.: Prentice-Hall, 1973.

| | |
|---|---|
| Are cast, credits, and characters given? | Yes. |
| Are there reviews excerpted or given in whole? | Yes, in whole. |
| Is the analysis or criticism by the author, or is there a collection of essays? | Collected essays. |
| Is there shot-by-shot or scene-by-scene analysis? | No, but there is a content outline without critical comment. |
| Is there critical analysis of the director's work other than this particular film? | Yes. |
| Are there excerpts from the script? | Yes. |
| What other features are included in the analysis? | Plot summary, account of script changes, filmography, bibliography, and miscellaneous press items on the original characters. |

Other areas of literature are Hollywood gossip or personal reminiscences, novels on film or novelized screenplays, and books on such topics as censorship, violence and film, children and film, blacks in film, and many other subject areas. Books on subdivisions of the general areas listed and described above should be considered in the same way as is the general area, unless the library has a special collection of material in a particular area.

# 7

# Nonprint Material

Classroom showings of films are the basic and standard way of beginning film study, often with repeat showings at arranged times. The equipment necessary to show parts of films to individual students or to allow close examination of films is expensive. Problems involved in renting and buying films require a good deal of time and money to solve. Locating, scheduling, projecting, and repeating rental films are major administrative chores, and the funding of this process can be difficult. Should a library decide to purchase rather than rent its films, it is presented with the problems of classifying, housing, protecting, and circulating the films and determining the policy for their use. The preservation of films can cause problems: even with the best projection equipment and the most experienced projectionists, the material required to repair films and the maintenance of projection equipment can prove to be major expenses. Overall, the visual approach to film study is an expensive matter, and it becomes more so when detailed study of cinematography, or art direction, or other technical aspects requires numerous viewings.

Apart from the financial and other difficulties associated with the use of source films themselves—which may be surmounted by the use of an archive or film library—the film librarian needs to consider other visual aids. Nonprint sources for instruction and study are available for purchase and rental. There are a great number of 16mm films on film study. Their quality varies in terms of their level of presentation, production, and topics covered. The majority of such films are at the general or introductory level, suitable only for high school students or the most elementary college-level instruction. There is, however, a substantial minority of readily available 16mm films which cover the basic principles of areas such as animation technique, directing, acting, screenwriting, editing, camera work, and special effects, and which are suitable for a higher level of student. Other supplementary films to be used in the classroom for the discussion of psychological or societal aspects of films, film genres, the history of the film industry, national traditions in film, and individual filmmakers or specific film titles are available for rental or purchase. In most colleges and universities, the general book library is not responsible for supplying films to teachers or to individual students. Either teaching departments or special instructional media offices usually arrange for films to be made available. However, as more libraries make plans for library media centers to make nonprint material available to students and teachers, more librarians will need to be aware of methods for locating and selecting such instructional resources.

Access to 16mm films can be gained by consulting these sources, which cover all substantial areas of film study.

## Retrospective Selection Guides:

Limbacher, James L., comp. and ed. *Feature Films on 8mm, 16mm and Videotape: A Directory of Feature Films Available for Rental, Sale, and Lease in the United States and Canada.* 6th ed. New York: Bowker, 1979.

*Learning Directory,* 1970—. New York: Westinghouse Learning Corporation.

NICEM. *Index to 16mm Educational Films.* 6th ed. Los Angeles: National Information Center for Educational Media, University of Southern California, 1977.

## Indexes to Reviews:

*International Index to Multimedia Information.* Pasadena: Audio-Visual Associates, 1970—Title varies: *Film Review Index,* 1970–72.

*Media Review Digest.* Ann Arbor, Mich.: The Pierian Press, 1971—.

## Current Review Journals:

*Audiovisual Instruction, Booklist, EFLA Review Cards, Film News, Learning Resources, Media and Methods, Previews, Sightlines.*

These suggestions for nonprint selection aids are taken from Angie LeClercq, "Collecting Non-Print Media in Academic Libraries," *Tennessee Librarian,* Summer 1975, pp. 84–7. Another list of evaluation aids can be found in a bibliography by Humphrys[1] and a recent book-length guide was written by Mary Robinson Sive.[2]

In addition, catalogs of 16mm film rental and cooperative organizations will have subject indexes. Film distributors' catalogs often show film study series as well as feature films for rent. When selecting 16mm films on film study, the best way to evaluate the film is to preview it. Unfortunately, the distributor will not allow free previewing in many cases. If previewing is not possible, one should locate reviews of the film. In addition, one must rely on the indications given by rental or distribution catalogs. The date of the film is important, as is the level for which the film is intended. If the summary shows a survey or general approach, it is probably too general for any specific use in higher educational instruction, although it may be appropriate as a library holding to be retrieved individually by students needing extra or more elementary instruction.

There is a great deal of literature on the selection and evaluation of educational films. Two basic books on film libraries are Harrison[3] and Rehrauer.[4] A list of cooperatives and circuits is found in Weber,[5] although a complete guide to regional media centers and collections has yet to be published.

However, 16mm films are not the only other source of visual education. Film-strips with records or cassettes, slide sets, video cassettes, and stills or photographs are also available for purchase. These can all be used in group or individual instruction and are relatively inexpensive to purchase compared to the cost of building a library of films. Filmstrips and slide sets are not only valuable in communicating the story and narration of films but can be used to illustrate other points, such as camera angles, lighting, etc., unrelated to those topics. The instructor or student can use individual images in this way to study the work of a director or cinematographer.

It is essential that libraries supply materials relevant to the courses

---

[1] Humphrys, Barbara. "Information Sources: Programmers' Tools." *Film Library Quarterly,* Vol. 7, No. 3, 4, 1974, pp. 71–7.

[2] Sive, Mary Robinson. *Selecting Instructional Media; a Guide to Audiovisual and Other Instructional Lists,* 2nd ed. Littleton, Colo.: Libraries Limited, 1978.

[3] Harrison, Helen P. *Film Library Techniques: Principles of Administration.* New York: Hastings House, 1973.

[4] Rehrauer, George. *The Film User's Handbook: A Basic Manual for Managing Library Film Services.* New York: R. R. Bowker, 1975.

[5] Weber, Olga S., comp. *North American Film and Video Directory: A Guide to Media Collections and Services.* Compiled by Olga S. Weber with the assistance of Deirdre Boyle, consultant. New York: R. R. Bowker, 1976.

that are taught, and that they supply these materials at all levels in as many ways as possible. Academic libraries have suffered in the past from a dearth of good film material on an advanced level. At the present time there are enough good quality films to allow a collection of film study films at all college levels. There are filmstrips for advanced undergraduate students. Even the more basic filmstrips, if creatively used, can be of use to the film teacher. It is not necessary for an entire program to be used; selected images or segments may be illustrative of one aspect of the course. The introductory level student can learn from even basic presentations if they are made available as learning resources for individual retrieval in the library.

A substantial amount of material (aside from the film itself) is produced as a part of the film production process or in connection with the promotion of the films. These include portraits, stills, posters, lobby cards, and souvenir programs. Such by-products have value for scholars, researchers, and publishers. Although these materials are most commonly used for illustration, they can be and are used for thesis topics and other research. They are also used as the core of those illustrative texts known as pictorial histories by making clear major points on visual aspects of films and film histories. Production stills are especially important in the close examination of artistic aspects of filmmaking, such as makeup, lighting, and costume design. Repeated viewings of the same print can damage a film. A good collection of slides and stills can be an effective and inexpensive alternative for the student or the teacher.

Changes in advertising techniques and in other aspects of the industry of film production can be seen through the study of promotional material. Changes in audience and society are illustrated in posters and other advertising material. Libraries and archives usually acquire such material through donations rather than by buying them outright. The biggest market for advertising and promotional material at this time is the film buff, but more libraries and other institutions are becoming aware of the range of visual material available. Many dealers in film memorabilia hold large collections of portraits and stills as well as posters and souvenir items. Some of these dealers offer catalogs, but most welcome "want lists" by film title or individuals' names. Important definitions in considering supplementary visual material are:

Lobby cards: $8 \times 10$, $10 \times 14$, $15 \times 22$—photographs or stills mounted on heavy paper, usually with a border.
Production stills—photographs in black and white or color from the film itself or from the making of the film. All the photos may not be found in the film. Some photos are taken as a record of

sets, costumes, makeup, lighting, etc., and do not reflect the dramatic progress of the film.

Inserts (or title cards)—6 × 10, 8 × 10, 8 × 14 photographs.

Portrait stills—photographs in black and white or color, usually 8 × 10 or 11 × 14, of players or individuals related to the film.

Posters—1-sheet, 27 × 41
    2-sheet, 33 × 55
    3-sheet, 41 × 81
    6-sheet, 81 × 81

Other commonly encountered sizes of posters are 22 × 28, 30 × 40, 40 × 60. There is also the 24-sheet size (a billboard).

Pressbooks (factbooks)—booklets containing cast, credits, plot summaries, and other such information as well as advertising material for theater managers to select from.

Press-sheets—short summaries, usually with plot, characters, and credits, as well as some promotional text.

Souvenir programs (premiere booklets)—aimed at the audience and containing general production and biographical information.

(An interesting book for the collector of movie mementos is Sol Chaneler's *Collecting Movie Memorabilia*.[5])

Other types of supplemental cinema material sometimes available for purchase and found in bookstore catalogs are sheet music for film scores, realia, souvenirs, and color transparencies ranging from 35mm slides to 8 × 10 transparencies. This sort of material for projection can, of course, be valuable for instructional purposes, and may be purchased in various formats for use on differing kinds of equipment.

Firms selling visual or advertising materials are: Adrienson and Post (Box 98, Ambassador Sta., Los Angeles 90070); Bob Smith Poster Service (Box 517, Canton, OK 73724); Bond Street Bookstore; Cherokee Bookshop (Box 3427, Hollywood, CA 90028); Cinema City; Cinemabilia; Collectors Bookstore; Creative Film Society (7237 Canby, Reseda, CA 91335); Duncan Poster Service; Eddie Brandt's Saturday Matinee; H and H Bookstore (3958 W. 6th St., Los Angeles 90020); Hollywood Book Service (1654 Cherokee, Hollywood, CA 90028); Hollywood Review; Jerry Ohlinger's; Larry Edmonds; Movie Star News, The Silver Screen; and Stephen Sally. Other addresses are on p. 64.

Another kind of supplementary nonprint material which is not yet

---

[5] Chaneler, Sol. *Collecting Movie Memorabilia*. New York: Arco Publishing Co., 1977.

commonly available for purchase is the recording termed "oral history" or interview. These are sometimes on video tape but are more commonly aural, being found on reels of tape or cassettes, or in text form. The American Film Institute (AFI) oral history programs may be purchased on microfiche. Some interview films have also been made for educational purposes on 16mm film for distribution to schools or for promotional purposes for showing on television or as advertising shorts for theaters. Radio spots are also listed in several cinema catalogs, but are not usually long enough for any instructional value.

## Nonprint Material and Copyright

In the past, librarians have frequently relied on copying nonprint material to build or preserve library holdings. Films are notoriously expensive to purchase, and video cassettes, slide sets, and other nonprint formats are certainly a drain on any budget. Librarians have therefore often engaged in very liberal interpretations of the well known "fair use" phrase. In addition, a lack of published or commercially available media packages on a sufficiently advanced level has encouraged many librarians and educators to create their own instructional packages—and, in so doing, to risk violation of the law.

However, since the 1976 law on copyright, librarians and educators have been exposed to a great deal of information and opinion on the various interpretations of the law. It is no longer easy to ignore the copyright law, and the library's interpretations of the rulings pertaining to nonprint material are much more important to consider. A great deal of confusion exists, since at this early stage of new practice, court decisions have not yet tested all aspects of the law. There is no library authority to contact on this issue, and the only real authority—the law—is constantly being developed. Case-by-case guidelines, both from the government and from experts in the educational and library fields, are becoming more available and reliable, but the librarian must thoroughly examine the issues, read a great deal of literature, possibly consult with the American Library Association committees on copyright, and carefully balance the risks of liberal interpretation of fair use privileges with a strict reading of the law before setting library policy. Conflicts between the interests of the publishing industries and educational institutions make an accurate copyright policy imperative; any institution can be subject to suit.

For the film studies librarian, there are many specific circumstances where decisions must be made about copyright and media. Several of the most frequently encountered instances will be discussed here to demonstrate the issues involved.

## Case A

This commonly encountered case concerns making copies of printed material, such as stills, book illustrations, or textual material, for use in slide, fiche, or filmstrip formats. The standard library decision on this case is that copyright permission must be gained before a copy can be used in a different format. However, a more liberal interpretation of the rule may be that excerpts from text or a portion of other printed material may be used for explanatory or instructional purposes, in the way that excerpting is freely permitted for the purposes of critiquing any material. The basic question of whether or not a librarian or educator must try to apply for copyright permission is therefore in question. If it is determined that an attempt must be made to get permission, it may be that the material to be copied is in a journal which has ceased to exist. A liberal interpretation which is often used says that if one tries to gain permission and fails to receive a response, copying may be performed under the fair use clause. However, the journal may be controlled by a clearinghouse which controls copyright even after the title is ceased, so this may not be a valid interpretation in every case. In fact, the publisher simply may not answer. The publisher is not bound to answer, and a supposedly fair use copy may be in violation of the law. It is obvious that these issues are not clear.

## Case B

In order to create a media presentation on a film, it may be required to use individual frames from the film in a different format (slide, filmstrip, or photographic print). A conservative interpretation says that permission must be gained if a film segment or frames from a film are to be used in a presentation of differing format than the original. A more liberal ruling may permit frames to be used on the grounds that the frames used do not comprise a large enough portion of the entire film to justify the necessity for permission. Another argument maintains that the excerpting of a portion of a film for instructional purposes is subject to the portion of the copyright law pertaining to critique. Jerome Miller says:

> Example 3: A teacher shows a number of films in her film study class each semester. The films are rented and they are usually available for only one day. The teacher asks the media center to reproduce several key frames from each film. The frames are duplicated onto slides. The slides are then used in class to review and discuss the film.
>
> Answer: This clearly falls within the intent of the fair use section to permit copying for the purpose of criticism. The amount of the film that was copied was slight. This seems to be a fair use.

Example 4: A university film study instructor also has copies made of selected frames of the films used in his class. The copies are to be placed in the library for independent study by students enrolled in the class. The library does not have slide projectors or viewers, so the slides are reproduced on microfiche.

Answer: The fact that the film frames had to be duplicated onto slides and then onto microfiche was dictated by the limits of the available technology. It remains a duplication of a small part of the work for the purpose of criticism. It seems to be a fair use.[6]

## Case C

This case concerns the video taping of television programming off the air. The court cases concerning taping for individual pleasure or entertainment are well known, but taking programming off the air for instructional purposes is not a clear-cut case. Public television programming may in some cases be taped under the seven-day rule, where the tape can be used for the seven days following the initial presentation; but not all broadcasts are legally tapable. There are monthly lists of programs which cannot be taped, even for use within seven days. These lists are published in television literature, and the local PBS station should receive the list. Taping nonpublic television broadcasts is as of this writing still not a clear issue.

Other commonly encountered situations are fairly clear by now. One such case involves copying for purposes of preservation. If the material to be copied is available for purchase, copying for preservation is not permitted. The library must buy two copies—one for preservation and one for circulation. Another case involves changing formats of purchased material. It is fairly well known that slides last longer under heavy use than filmstrips. If a library purchases a filmstrip, cuts it up, mounts the images into slides, and presents the sequence in the same manner as it was originally intended, in its entirety, no permission is necessary. If the library changes the content or the sequence of the presentation, it will be considered to be infringing on copyright legislation.

For trustworthy information on instances such as these, the librarian and the educator should rely only on authoritative statements based on court decisions. Other policies based on unproven opinions may result in infringement. Liberal interpretations of the law may result in legal proceedings, so the librarian must be well informed and cautious.

---

[6] Miller, Jerome K. *A Copyright Guide for Educators and Librarians.* Chicago: American Library Association, in press, pp. II, 68a–69 in the manuscript copy.

# 8
## Scripts

Films are studied in many ways and from many perspectives, but one of the most important approaches is that which is known as "film as literature" but which would more accurately be described as "the screenplay as literature." The written content of other performing arts has been studied for many years, notably in the case of the live theater. Movie scripts are studied seriously and given critical attention. They are treated as an independent form of literature different from, but bearing similarities to, the dramatic play. The complete movie, unlike live theater, is preserved on film, therefore the script—though as with the theater it is only one aspect of the production, and a critical aspect—has received less attention than it deserves. The work and molding influence of the screenwriter, director, producer, and most others of the large group of people whose composite impact is shown on the screen can be studied through the screenplay and by comparing the screenplay with the movie. Film is the result of a process, and the screenplay, probably more than any other aspect of the film, can reflect and illuminate that process.

The screenplay deserves attention on its own merits, but also receives scrutiny as evidence of various aspects of film production and as part of the study of the total film. Scripts are essential in studying film as a form of communication. Though dialogue is, of course, only part of the technique of communication and of the merit of a film, it is vital to the whole. The film considered as a reflection of society can show evidence of the cultural impact of the film and of the influence of the audience on the film. Even the visual aspects of film can be studied through the screenplay, since camera direction, costume, sets, and character description can often be found in full versions of screenplays.

There are three important aspects of the study of screenplay as film documentation. Firstly it has importance as a form of literature. Secondly, it has importance as *evidence* in the study of a film. Thirdly, the screenplay has meaning as reflecting film as a *process* of creative activity, showing changes made in the various stages of the creative process during the progression from source to screen.

The vocabulary used in describing different types of film script is inconsistent; however, there are some generally accepted definitions. Apart from the varying usage of these terms, the format of scripts varies from studio to studio.

"Shooting script" means the script is one of various versions used in the actual production of the film. It may have camera instructions on it or it may have only dialogue. In addition, there may be narrative describing the action, sets, or other aspects of performance. The format of these scripts is fairly standard.

The "white draft" is either the first or last version, since changes made during the progress of the film are inserted in colored paper. Many copies of shooting drafts contain notations and other marginalia which are of great value to the serious scholar who wishes to examine in detail the process of filmmaking.

The term "continuity" means a script which displays the progression of the events in the film as they are shown on screen. A continuity script is made from the finished product, before or after editing. It is common to find various versions of the continuity script, just as one can find different versions of the shooting script.

"Cutting continuities" usually show the footage of each shot and are used for editing. Their importance lies in that they usually contain segments of the film which do not appear in the released version of the film.

"Dialogue continuities" contain only dialogue in the order of the finished version. This type of script is usually deposited in the Library of Congress for copyright reasons.

There is another type of continuity which is created for subtitling. This type of script shows two versions of the dialogue, often in the form of a chart.

Most published scripts are continuities, but there are some publications based on shooting scripts. A few even show changes between versions of the script.

Published scripts are not numerous when one considers how

many films have come out of Hollywood alone. Some of these may be located by using McCarty[1] and Poteet.[2] This absence of source documents poses a dilemma to the film scholar. Even though there are major deposits of studio archives in libraries in the United States (and other countries) and most of these collections contain scripts, the scholar's dilemma is not solved since there is no index or union catalog of script titles. Those in search of a script must locate libraries holding scripts of films from a particular studio, and then must write to those libraries with specific inquiries. There are some published guides to manuscript collections which are of importance to the searcher for film scripts. They describe the holdings of manuscript archives by listing areas of collection, names of donations, and, sometimes, specific titles. Obviously, libraries continue to acquire donations of special collections, either from studios or individuals, in large and small quantities, so the date of publication of each of these reference sources is important. The librarian should update these sources by maintaining files of current information available to him or her.

British Film Institute, London—Library. *Catalogue of the Book Library of the British Film Institute.* Boston: G. K. Hall, 1975.

*Catalogo Biblioteca de Cinematica Nacional* (Lisbon). Lisbon: Cinematica Nacional, 1959. Supp. 1, 1961; Supp. 2, 1965.

Mehr, Linda Harris, comp. and ed. *Motion Pictures, Television, and Radio: A Union Catalog of Manuscript and Special Collections in the Western United States.* Boston: G. K. Hall, 1977.

University of California at Los Angeles Library. *Motion Pictures: A Catalog of Books, Periodicals, Screenplays, Television Scripts, and Production Stills.* Edited by Audree Malkin. 2nd ed., rev. and exp. Boston: G. K. Hall, 1976.

Wheaton, Christopher D., and Jewell, Richard B., comps. *Primary Cinema Resources: An Index to Screenplays, Interviews and Special Collections at the University of Southern California.* Boston: G. K. Hall, 1975.

Young, William C. *American Theatrical Arts: A Guide to Manuscripts and Special Collections in the United States and Canada.* Chicago: American Library Association, 1971.

In addition to these guides to North American or English collections, there are book catalogs from various European libraries and un-

---

[1] McCarty, Clifford. *Published Screenplays: A Checklist.* 1st ed. Kent, Ohio: Kent State University, 1971. (Serif Series: bibliographies and checklists, No. 18.)

[2] Poteet, G. Howard. *Published Radio, Television, and Film Scripts: A Bibliography.* Troy, N.Y.: Whitson Pub. Co., 1975.

published lists of film-script holdings at major collections such as The Academy of Motion Picture Arts and Sciences' Margaret Herrick Library, the American Film Institute's Charles K. Feldman Library, the Wisconsin Center for Film and Theater Research, and the University of Iowa.

Here is a list briefly describing, by studio, archival collections containing scripts available for study:*

Walt Disney Productions:
    Disney Archives
    University of California at Los Angeles Theater Arts Library (1937–1939).
Edison Company: Museum of Modern Art, New York.
    American Film Institute, Charles K. Feldman Library
    New York Public Library at Lincoln Center (Continuities, 1929–date)
    University of California at Los Angeles Theater Arts Library (1925–date)
    University of Southern California Department of Special Collections (1919–1958).
    Dartmouth College Libraries (Thalberg Collection)
Monogram Films: Wisconsin Center for Film and Theater Research
Paramount:
    Academy of Motion Picture Arts and Sciences (1914–1970)
    University Film Study Center (about 80–100 titles)
RKO Radio Pictures:
    Glendale Public Library (1934–1941)
    RKO Corporate Archives
Republic Pictures: University of California at Los Angeles Department of Special Collections (1935–1955)
Hal Roach: Hollywood Center for the Audio Visual Arts (1930s and 1940s)
Twentieth Century-Fox:
    American Film Institute, Charles K. Feldman Library (1951–1971)
    University of Iowa
    University of California at Los Angeles Theater Arts Library (1929–1949)
    University of Southern California, Department of Special Collections (1916–1971)
United Artists: Wisconsin Center for Film and Theater Research
Universal:
    Universal Research Library

---

*Taken in part from a list prepared for the American Film Institute Workshop on Film/TV Documentation, Summer 1978.

University of Southern California, Department of Special Collections

Warner Brothers:
Academy of Motion Picture Arts and Sciences (story resumés)
Burbank Public Library (assorted scripts)
University of Southern California, Department of Special Collections
Wisconsin Center for Film and Theater Research

If a library or an individual film scholar wishes to purchase scripts, or to locate a particular title for purchase, the bookstores specializing in film scripts are the best choice. Catalogs are not invariably available, but "want lists" are always welcome. Buying scripts can be an expensive venture, since each title costs between thirty and one hundred dollars. Particularly valuable film scripts may cost even more. The cost of the script depends on its format and its rarity. Photocopies or mimeo versions are less expensive than typescripts.

Of the many bookstores responding to a survey on the nature of their stock, only a few indicated holdings of unpublished scripts. Among these are: Collectors' Bookstore, Sterling Books, Jerry Ohlingers, Black Sun Books, etc. See Chapter 9 for more complete descriptions of stock and for addresses.

# 9

# Bookstores and Film Memorabilia Dealers

Private businesses such as those listed here are very often the only sources for purchase of out-of-print books, back sets, or missing issues of periodicals, posters, stills, shooting scripts, and other unpublished material. Many shops produce catalogs and will send them on request. In addition, "want lists" are generally accepted by these dealers.

Every large city has used bookshops that stock out-of-print film books along with books on all other subjects. This list—far from complete—was compiled by writing to more than 70 shops in the United States which indicated a special interest in cinema materials. Many of the addresses given in standard sources listing out-of-print dealers were out of date. In addition, several shops asked not to be listed for various reasons. Finally, many businesses did not respond to the repeated attempts to contact them about their holdings.

The foreign dealers and shops listed are largely taken from a handout prepared by Anne G. Schlosser for the American Film Institute Film/TV Documentation Workshop, Summer 1978.

## U.S. Film Bookstores

Birns and Sawyer, Inc.
1026 North Highland Ave.
Los Angeles, Cal. 90038

The catalog shows nearly 100 pages of film books. Each entry is annotated. It is possible to purchase groups of titles on similar subjects at discounts.

Black Sun Books
667 Madison Ave.
New York, N.Y. 10021

This business deals primarily in American and English literature, but also deals in film scripts, pressbooks, and theater scripts. These are generally sold in large collections to universities or to private collectors and usually have literary interest as well.

Bond Street Book Store
1638 North Wilcox
Hollywood, Cal. 90028

Stocks stills and lobby cards from 1940 to date, posters (27x41) from 1940 to date, pressbooks and paperbacks on film.

Cinema City
P. O. Box 7406
Ann Arbor, Mich. 48107

To quote from the catalog, Cinema City is "a contemporary film service dealing with material for most films released after 1970. All merchandise is authentic movie advertising material as used by theatres." The catalog includes stills, presskits, lobby cards, standing lobby displays, production illustrations, posters of various sizes, radio ads on record and tape, cast and credit sheets, pressbooks, TV ads on 16 mm film, trailers on 16mm film, and featurettes.

Cinemabilia
10 West 13th St.
New York, N.Y. 10011

This major bookstore has not published a catalog in some years; however, there is a 125-page catalog of souvenir programs and sheet music available at $2.00 each. They plan to publish a catalog of posters, and "want lists" are welcome. All kinds of film material are held in stock.

Collectors Book Store
6763 Hollywood Blvd.
Hollywood, Cal. 90028

The main lines of business for this well-stocked bookstore are old movie material, rare comic books, original comic book art, and rare

## Bookstores and Film Memorabilia Dealers 65

science fiction magazines. There are catalogs of these materials, but of special interest are the collections of scripts and 35mm mounted slides. The stock also includes posters, lobby cards, magazines (from 1912), and TV scripts.

Corner Book Shop
102 Fourth Ave.
New York, N.Y. 10003

The "Movies" catalog shows over 400 books, including some non-English language titles.

The Drama Book shop
150 West 52nd St.
New York, N.Y. 10019

There is not a complete catalog or subject list. Instead, all new books in the performing arts are included in the quarterly, *Annotated Bibliography of New Publications in the Performing Arts,* by Ralph Newman Schoolcraft, which is available from the Drama Book Shop for $2.50 for four issues. The collection includes books on theater and drama, technical arts, motion pictures, television and radio, mass media and popular arts, and plays.

Martin Duffy and Sons
229 Coeyman Ave.
Nutley, N.J. 07110

Holds new, used, and out-of-print motion picture titles. A catalog is now being compiled.

Duncan Poster Service
2009½ Jackson St.
Dallas, Texas 75201

A specialist in motion-picture advertising, Mr. Duncan sells 8x10 stills, 11x14 photos, posters of various sizes, inserts (14x36), and other press material.

Eddie Brandt's Saturday Matinee
P. O. Box 3232
North Hollywood, Cal. 91609

There is no catalog; write with requests. The stock includes lobby cards, posters, pressbooks, magazines, programs, autographs, portraits, and stills.

Larry Edmonds
6658 Hollywood Blvd.
Hollywood, Cal. 90028

The most recent catalog was published in 1970; it is 525 pages long and includes books, magazines, posters, lobby cards, pressbooks, programs, autographs, and other cinema material. A new catalog is in progress. "Want lists" are welcome. There is a very large stills collection which can be accessed by

66  FILM STUDY COLLECTIONS

|  |  |
|---|---|
|  | the name of an individual or by film title. One may ask to receive announcements of new stock. |
| Gotham Book Mart<br>41 West 47th St.<br>New York, N.Y. 10036 | Out-of-print and current items are shown in the monthly *GBM Film Bulletin*. |
| Jack Hamilton<br>37 West 8th St.<br>New York, N.Y. 10011 | Holds many books, periodicals, and reference sources which are listed on several stock lists. |
| Hampton Books<br>Route 1, Box 76<br>Newberry, S.C. 29108 | The most recent catalog shows nearly 1,300 items, all of which are described and briefly annotated. The stock contains quite a bit of material in European languages, many pressbooks, programs, lobby cards, stills, and portraits. |
| The Hollywood Review<br>1680 N. Vine St., Suite 918<br>Hollywood, Cal. 90028 | Anyone wishing to view material must make an appointment in advance. Orders are handled by mail, and the address listed is a mail address only. The stock consists of negatives to produce photos of major film stars and stills, as well as posters, lobby cards, souvenir books, and film magazines. There is no printed catalog. |
| Limelight Bookstore<br>1803 Market St.<br>San Francisco, Cal. 94103 | This bookstore publishes a large, partly annotated catalog reflecting its holdings in film books. Further catalogs are planned for dance and theater material. One may be placed on the mailing list for new title announcements. |
| M. M. Einhorn Maxwell<br>At the Sign of the Dancing Bear<br>80 East 11th St.<br>New York, N.Y. 10003 | This firm handles books in many areas and occasionally issues catalogs. They hold about 2,000 film books, mostly out of print, and most in English. It is a mail order business only. |
| Movie Poster Service<br>P. O. Box 517<br>Canton, Okla. 73724 | Stock holds over 200,000 posters on over 20,000 titles, not counting short subjects and foreign material. There are also stills, lobby cards, title cards, inserts, and other visual material in stock. |

Movie Star News
212 East 14th St.
New York, N.Y. 10003

The most recent catalog supplement shows black and white 8x10 photos and stills, 27x40 posters, and some books, mostly from series.

New York Zoetrope
31 East 12th St.
New York, N.Y. 10003

Stocks current print and nonprint film material.

Jerry Ohlinger's Movie Material Store
120 West 3rd St.
New York, N.Y. 10012

Lists are available for film memorabilia and collectables such as pressbooks, lobby cards, stills, posters, 16mm theatrical trailers, program books, slides, scripts from television and film, as well as more unusual items such as banners and models.

Stephen Sally
Times Square Station
P. O. Box 646
New York, N.Y. 10036

The stock list includes about 150 books and black and white portraits and stills.

The Scriptorium
927 North Canon Drive
Beverly Hills, Cal. 90210

Appraisers of cinema material and dealers in autographed material (letters, documents, contracts, manuscripts) and antiquarian manuscripts. Catalogs are available.

The Silver Screen
1193 Lexington Ave.
New York, N.Y. 10028

There is no catalog, but a recent price list shows color and black and white photos and stills, autographs, lobby cards, posters, clippings, magazines, and books.

Sterling Books
Box 22
Woodmere, N.Y. 11598

They report an extensive inventory of unpublished scripts and performing arts books.

Richard Stoddard
Performing Arts Books
1697 Broadway, Room 203
New York, N.Y. 10019

The handlist contains books in cinema, popular entertainment, theater, and technical arts. There are some non-English language materials.

Donald L. Velde, Inc.
311 West 43rd Street
New York, N.Y. 10036

There is no catalog; request lists by film title are welcome. With the exception of new Universal productions, only independent producers are handled.

# International Film Bookstores

**Australia**

Anchor Bookshop
Crystal Palace Arcade
George St., Sydney 2000

One of the best collections of film books in Australia. Posters and rare stills available.

The Film Library
7/38 Oceanview Rd., Harbord
P. O. Box 49, NSW 2096

A new direct-mail business specializing in quality film books, both general and technical.

Space Age Books
305–307 Swanston St.
Melbourne, 3000 Victoria

Full range of current film and TV titles. Also soundtracks, records, posters, and stills.

**Britain**

A. E. Cox
21 Cecil Rd., Itchen
Southampton S02 7HX

A postal business; current copy of list can be purchased cheaply. Collection includes new and second-hand items, old and rare periodicals, posters, stills, and souvenir programs.

Book City
8–12 Broadwick St.
London W1

Began as specialist in technical film literature. Collection is now comprehensive and includes TV and photographic items.

The Cinema Bookshop
13–14 Great Russell St.
London WC1

An important source of new or rare film books, and also of posters, pressbooks, memorabilia, magazines, and stills.

The Motion Picture Bookshop at the National Film Theatre
South Bank
London, SE1 8XT

Wide selection of imported books and magazines as well as the full range of British publications.

Motley Books
Mottisfont Abbey, Romsey
Hampshire SO5 OLP

A postal business. Selection of scholarly material in different languages. No "fan" material.

Peter Wood
20 Stonehill Rd.
Great Shelford, Cambridge
CB2 5JL

Specializes in books and ephemera on all the performing arts. Handles scarce items.

Treasures & Pleasures
18 Newport Court
London WC2H 7JS

A huge stock of movie memorabilia.

Zwemmer, Ltd.
78 Charing Cross Rd.
London WC2

Comprehensive selection of film books and periodicals from various countries.

## Canada

Cine Books
642 Yonge St.
Toronto, Ontario
Canada M4Y 1Z8

The Canadian center for new and used film books. Also available are magazines, stills, posters, memorabilia, and soundtracks. Efficient mail order service, and a published catalog.

## France

Les Feux de la Rampe
2 Rue de Luynes
75007 Paris

Interesting collection of movie and theater books and periodicals in various languages.

Librairie Contacts
24 Rue de Colisée
75008 Paris

Large selection of film periodicals and books predominantly in French; English and Italian titles also available.

Librairie de la Fontaine
13 Rue de Médicis
75006 Paris

Good selection of books, film stills, posters, etc.

Le Minotaure
2 Rue des Beaux-Arts
75006 Paris

Vast array of new film books, as well as long runs of out-of-print magazines, comics, models, optical toys, and other memorabilia.

Le Zinzin d'Hollywood
7 Rue des Ursulines
75005 Paris

Big selection of French and foreign film books and magazines. Over 5,000 stills, posters, sound track albums, as well as rare portraits of stars.

## Germany

Autoren Buchhandlung
Wilhelmstrasse 41
8 Munich 40

Books and periodicals on film and mass media.

Buchhandlung Walther Konig
Breite Strasse 93
5 Cologne 1

Invaluable source for current as well as out-of-print books and periodicals.

Marga Schoeller
Knesebeckstrasse 33
1000 Berlin 12

Stocks all film titles by German publishers and leading titles by British and American publishers. No out-of-print books.

Sautter & Lackmann
Klosterstern 8
2 Hamburg 13

German and foreign books and magazines on the cinema as well as related arts.

Wolfgang Gielow
Theaterinerstrasse 35
8 Munich 2

Very big stock of new and old film books. Also has sound track recordings. Write with specific wants.

## Italy

"Il Leuto"
Via Di Monte Brianzo 86
00186 Rome

Specializes not only in film but also in dance and drama. Write with specific wants.

Libreria Editrice Bonacci
Via Paolo Mercuri 23
00193 Rome

Specializes in exporting books from all Italian publishers.

## Sweden

A. B. Sandbergs Bokhandel
Humlegardsgatan 12, Box 4418
S-114, 85 Stockholm

Excellent selection of current Swedish and foreign film books. Offers lists of new titles.

## Switzerland

Filmbuchhandlung Hans Rohr
Oberdorfstrasse 5
8024 Zurich

Virtually all books on film, magazines, many rare items; also film classics on 8mm. Publishes the "Quarterly Film-Bibliographic Bulletin."

# 10

# Major U.S. Archives

Descriptions of major archives of film study documentation have been published in various locations over the last few years; however, an up-to-date description of all large holdings of documentation has not been easy to locate. The following list is alphabetical by state.

Collections of films are not included if there is not a significant library of documentation to accompany the films. An exception is the Eastman House, an important archive of films with a collection of documentation and almost no unpublished scripts.

Most of these collections are not available on interlibrary loan. The collections are for reference only, and may usually be used on the premises by scholars. It would be preferable to contact the libraries concerning both loan policies and visiting-scholar arrangements. Most of the collections, however, will copy articles and portions of books (with permission granted) for a fee. The exception to this is film scripts, which are almost never copied.

MARGARET HERRICK LIBRARY
Academy of Motion Picture Arts and Sciences
8949 Wilshire Blvd.
Beverly Hills, Cal. 90211

The library of the academy is well situated in the new AMPAS building and contains a full collection of books and periodicals, clipping files and photographs. There is an especially complete collection of trade journals. Files are maintained on well over 40,000 films and many individuals.

Studio archival collections held in the Margaret Herrick Library include the Jules White Collection of Shorts for Columbia, and 68 volumes of scrapbooks covering 23 of Samuel Goldwyn's films by United Artists and RKO. Stillbooks from Thomas H. Ince, pressbooks from Paramount (1926–1965) may be used by special arrangement.

The Paramount production facts file (1914–1970), story department material from Paramount (1912–1962) including source material, and scripts on 2,200 films, Paramount stillbooks of scene stills from 1914–1930 and scene stills, publicity, and on-set photos from 1930–1970 are all part of the large Paramount collection. This collection is described in Gill, *Paramount Collection Inventory*.[1]

The library also holds Pathé business records, RKO stillbooks 1929–1958; the Selig Collection of stills, scripts, correspondence, etc., of films produced by William Selig; the Sennett Collection, including production files, biography files, stories files, subject files, scrapbooks, and finance records; and the Universal still negatives collection of about 100,000 photographs.

Other special collections include posters, glass slides, and old film equipment. Helpful files include Academy files, award files, directors' files, film festivals, independent producers, an index to *Photoplay*, producers, television files, and writers' files. More information on smaller archival holdings is available in Linda Mehr's *Motion Pictures, Television, and Radio: A Union Catalogue of Manuscript and Special Collections in the Western United States* (G. K. Hall, 1977).

CHARLES K. FELDMAN LIBRARY
American Film Institute Center for Advanced Film Studies
501 Doheny Rd.
Beverly Hills, Cal. 90210

The Charles K. Feldman Library is an important research center and archive primarily devoted to motion pictures and television. It was designed for the use of the American Film Institute faculty, fellows, and staff, but is also available on a noncirculating basis to visiting researchers and members of the film and television industries.

The library has over 4,000 books on film, television, and related areas, and receives 175 journals. Clipping files are maintained which contain selected articles, pamphlets, reviews and ephemera on films, individuals, and other aspects of the entertainment industry. There is a subject file for television and a file for TV programs, movies, series,

---

[1] Gill, Samuel. *Paramount Collection Inventory.* Beverly Hills: Academy of Motion Picture Arts and Sciences, 1977. 2 vols.

and specials which includes reviews, casts, and credits for the past several years.

Special holdings of the library include unpublished scripts for over 2,000 American films (especially MGM and Twentieth Century-Fox), over 500 scripts from current television shows, 350 transcripts of weekly seminars of the Center for Advanced Film Studies, and over 40 oral history transcripts of interviews with film industry pioneers. Some of these interviews contain information on and from George Cukor, Allan Dwan, Howard Koch, Abraham Polonsky, George Seaton, and Harry Warren. There are about 100,000 stills available in the Columbia Pictures Stills Collection from the early 1930s to the 1950s. Special collections of manuscripts, personal papers, scrapbooks, etc., are held on George Chandler, Max Fleischer, Henry Hathaway, Harry Horner, Mitchell Leisen, Leo McCarey, Jack Mintz, Sam Peckinpah, George B. Seitz (including material on the Andy Hardy series), Erich von Stroheim, and others.

The collections are described in detail in *Motion Pictures, Television, and Radio: A Union Catalogue. . . .*[2]

UNIVERSITY OF CALIFORNIA—LOS ANGELES
Los Angeles, Cal. 90024

UCLA has three main locations for archival material on film which are described in detail in Mehr.[3] In addition, the UCLA Film/Television Archive has approximately 7,000 film titles, mostly 35mm, with special concentrations of 20th Century-Fox, Paramount, and Republic Studios films. Other special film collections include Preston Sturges and Joseph von Sternberg. Catalogs of the archives collections are available for purchase.

The Department of Special Collections has over 100 collections from and by writers, producers, directors, and individuals involved in other aspects of film production. Among these are: Hugo Ballin, Lionel Barrymore, Jack Benny, Eddie Cantor, Raymond Chandler, Tony Curtis, Benjamin Glazer, John Houseman, Thomas Ince, Ernie Kovacs, Stanley Kramer, Charles Laughton, Dudley Nichols, James Poe, Paul Rotha, Rod Serling, Preston Sturges, and King Vidor. Other special holdings are on early animated pictures, the George P. Johnson Negro Film Collection, the Hollywood Studio Strike, the *Los Angeles Daily News* Morgue File on Films from 1923–1954, Mirisch Productions production files, NBC Matinee Theater scripts and scripts from several other NBC series, the UCLA Oral History Program and tapes, and Republic Pictures Corporation Scripts.

---

[2] Mehr, *op. cit.*
[3] *Ibid.*

The Music Library holds music manuscripts from many films and television series and has collections of scores by several composers, including Henry Mancini and Alex North, as well as 2,500 folders of scores from the General Music Corporation and Sunset Music Corporation.

The Theater Arts Library has a stills and photographs collection of nearly 198,000 items; 5,700 unpublished scripts, many from Fox Film Corporation, Twentieth Century-Fox, and MGM; nearly 800 posters; 1,700 radio scripts; a large oral history collection; 2,800 television scripts; an extensive file of film subjects from 1920 to the present; and 200 serial titles, 51 of which include runs of back issues. Many of these special collections are contained in donations from individuals or studios such as Tony Barret, Walt Disney, Preston Sturges, and Haskell Wexler. Other holdings are an art direction collection, a film festival program collection, a collection of early lobby cards, MGM synopses, and music cue sheets for early silent films.

DOHENY LIBRARY
University of Southern California
Department of Special Collections

The USC Doheny Library, Department of Special Collections, holds the Farmington Plan deposit items on cinema from European countries, as well as considerable material on Asian cinema. The USC Department of Special Collections holds the largest collection of foreign films on the west coast. There is a major collection of screenplays containing scripts for over 7,000 Hollywood films, including some unproduced titles. There is a large collection of serial titles, especially short-lived and foreign titles. The publications *Primary Cinema Resources*, edited by Christopher D. Wheaton,[1] and *Motion Pictures, Television and Radio*, edited by Linda Mehr[2] (G. K. Hall, 1977) both index materials in this library and describe the many special collections of scripts, papers, and memorabilia donated to or purchased by the library. Some of these include materials from and/or on Edward Anhalt, Gladys Cooper, Joseph Cotton, William Dieterle, Philip Dunne, Dan Duryea, Roger Edens, Nelson Eddy, Richard Fleischer, Arthur Freed, Clark Gable, Ernest Laszlo, Sol Lesser, Jerry Lewis, Albert Lewin, Abby Mann, Alfred Newman, the Paramount Research Department, Joe Pasternak, Edward G. Robinson, Edward Small, Robert Sisk, John Stahl, Dimitri Tiomkin, the Twentieth Century-Fox set stills, King Vidor, Robert Wise, and Fay Wray. In addition to these collections, the library holds a large collection of taped interviews, approximately 1,400 posters, 1,400 pressbooks, 1,500 slides, and 465

---

[1] Wheaton, Christopher D. *Primary Cinema Resources*, Boston: G. K. Hall, 1975.
[2] Mehr, *op. cit.*

video cassettes of Wolper documentaries. There are 110,000 stills which are cataloged, and a large amount of uncataloged stills. The library holds 7,000 books on films and film study and a clipping file. Other large collections are the Universal Studios collections, principally from 1930 to the 1950s, which is uncataloged, and the files (to 1968) of the Burbank office of Warner Brothers Studios.

LIBRARY OF CONGRESS
Motion Picture, Broadcasting and
  Recorded Sound Division
Washington, D.C. 20540

This unit of the Library of Congress administers both the large collection of copyright deposit films and the documentation pertaining to these films. Titles are selected; the collection is not comprehensive. The paper print collection of films produced before 1915 is a well-known collection of historic value, and other such collections are numerous. Most major studios have deposited pre-print film material, but viewing copies are available for only a few of these. All films acquired by the American Film Institute are held by the Library of Congress.

The Motion Picture, Broadcasting and Recorded Sound Division also maintains a reference collection, has access to the Library's general collections, and makes available its large holding of descriptive materials (continuity scripts, pressbooks, stills, posters, etc.) deposited for copyright purposes.

UNIVERSITY OF IOWA LIBRARY
Iowa City, Iowa

The department of Special Collections holds several film-related collections of scripts, correspondence, photographs, etc. These include material from Robert Blees Productions (screenwriter and producer). Of special interest are scripts for *The Magnificent Obsession, Psycho,* and the original *A Star is Born.* From David Swift Productions are scripts for *Pollyanna, The Parent Trap, How to Succeed in Business Without Really Trying,* and others, as well as production information, set designs, models, etc. The Albert J. Cohen Production collection contains scripts from TV and film productions, budgets, correspondence, a complete story film, and shooting schedules. From Arthur A. Ross is a collection of writings including screenplays, TV scripts, and fiction. There are various scripts and designs from *The Great Race.* There are 17 boxes of material from the Victor Animatograph Company, including company records, photographs, and advertising. The Albert Zugsmith collection holds two boxes of scripts and other material which includes screenplays such as *The Lady Eve* and *Doctor Zhivago,* not by Zugsmith. The Ralph M. Junkin collections consist of film stills, lobby cards, posters, pressbooks, and drawings, mostly from silent films.

In addition to these special collections, the Twentieth Century-Fox Legal Department offices donated nearly 2,000 scripts along with records on the Roxy Theater.

WILLIAM B. MEREDITH LIBRARY
Dartmouth College Library
Hanover, N.H. 03755

The Thalberg collection contains approximately 2,500 scripts donated by Walter Wanger, Norma Shearer, and others. The scripts are primarily from MGM, Warner Brothers, and Twentieth Century-Fox, and primarily represent films for the 1930s and 1940s. In addition, Dartmouth College Library has holdings from Warner Brothers and Twentieth Century-Fox totaling approximately 700 scripts.

MUSEUM OF MODERN ART
Film Study Center
21 West 53rd St.
New York, N.Y. 10020

The Museum of Modern Art provides several major services to qualified scholars and teachers. First, there is a film archive of 8,000 titles which can be viewed at the Film Study Center. The collection covers the history of film on an international basis with areas of strength in the French avant-garde of the 1920s, Biograph films (1909–1916), British and American documentaries of the 1930s and 1940s, war-related materials (newsreels, propaganda, and war-information films), and Fox Studio films.

There is an expanding circulating collection of films available to film teachers. The intention is to include important films not currently available elsewhere in the United States.

The center houses an extensive collection of documentation. There are more than 2,000 screenplays and dialogue continuities available to qualified scholars by appointment. They are mostly American, with many Allied Artist and Republic films represented. There are also vertical files which include clippings, reviews, articles, and memorabilia on individuals, films, organizations, and film topics. This is supported by a reference and periodical collection which includes the *International Index to Film Periodicals* cards from 1972. The special collections at the center include materials from and on the Edison Company, Robert Flaherty, Thomas Ince; and correspondence and papers from D. W. Griffith, Billy Bitzer, Carol Dempster, Barnet Braverman, and the Biograph Company. The Merritt Crawford Collection contains Mr. Crawford's correspondence with many film pioneers and inventors, and supplemental documentation.

In addition, the stills collection is monumental, with over three million stills and photographs. The Stills Archive will sell reproductions of these stills for educational purposes.

GEORGE EASTMAN HOUSE
900 East Ave.
Rochester, N.Y. 14607

The several thousand films held by the archive are available by appointment for screening and study on the museum premises. The collection represents U.S. and foreign films, newsreels, animation, war films, experimental films, and many other forms of the motion picture throughout its history and development. Special collections include rare American silent films, silent German expressionist films, and films produced under the Third Reich.

Eastman House also maintains a research library of approximately 5,000 books, clipping files, many periodicals—current and those that have ceased publication and over 3,000,000 stills for the use of qualified scholars. The books are being entered into the OCLC data base so that access to these items will be possible through interlibrary loan. There is also a special collection of literature on motion picture equipment which includes a large number of manufacturers' catalogs.

Finally, there is an equipment collection of motion picture cameras, projectors, and related apparatus. Eastman House maintains some very rare items in its museum, including Reynaud's Projecting Praxinoscope, Bowly's Cinematographe, the inventor's model of the Armat Vitascope, the Lumière Cinematographe, and others.

WISCONSIN CENTER FOR FILM AND THEATER RESEARCH
University of Wisconsin—Madison
6039 Vilas Communication Hall
Madison, Wis. 53706

This collection is an archive of the University of Wisconsin—Madison and the State Historical Society of Wisconsin. The Film and Manuscripts Archive is located at the State Historical Society of Wisconsin, 816 State St., Madison, Wis. 53706.

The holdings contain several types of photographic and illustrative material. The stills and graphics collection holds more than 1,000,000 items consisting of stills, lobby cards, pressbooks, and posters on more than 20,000 films from many studios, but especially MGM, Warner Brothers, Universal, Republic, and United Artists. The performing artists section contains clippings and photos of performers in film, TV, theater, radio, vaudeville, ballet, and opera. Photocopies of photos are available for 20¢ each, and copy photographs for $3.50 if a negative is on file, $7.00 if there is no negative.

The center holds approximately 7,000 films including features, shorts, cartoons, and television programs, with particular emphasis on Warner Brothers and RKO features from the 1930s and 1940s. Only qualified researchers may view these films by appointment.

There are more than 180 special collections from individuals and companies. These collections hold approximately 3,500 scripts; correspondence; financial, business, and legal records; scrapbooks; tape recordings; journals; and other special material. Some of these collections are from Robert Altman, Paddy Chayefsky, Kirk Douglas, Melvin Douglas, John Frankenheimer, Edith Head, Hal Holbrook, papers and records of various persons and committees relating to the Hollywood Ten, Norman Jewison, Hal Kantor, Walter and Jean Kerr, Fredric March, Walter Mirisch, Dore Schary, Alan Schneider, Rod Serling, David Susskind, Dalton Trumbo, United Artist Corporation papers, Gore Vidal, and MTM Enterprises.

# II
# Reference Services

Film questions are of interest to many librarians, and this interest certainly serves as a hidden advantage to the library patron with a film query. However, it is rare for a librarian to have subject expertise in the field of cinema study. The librarian must therefore take special care to be familiar with the reference tools in film study available for purchase; and once they are purchased, the librarian should examine them carefully. This is normal practice for any librarian dealing with a subject area not part of his or her own educational background.

The unusual aspect of cinema resources is that only in recent years have most film publications appeared on the market and on library shelves. These materials do not typically form part of library school reference courses because library schools are traditionally conservative in their approach to teaching reference courses. There are several reasons for this, one of the most important being that the typical teacher of reference courses teaches rather than practices and has little exposure to new developments in the field. Reference courses generally do not contain popular topics until they become well documented areas of scholarship. Minority studies, women's studies, and popular culture are other examples of areas of new literature which are not taught in depth or not taught at all. The standard texts on reference materials contain only cursory listings in these newly emerging fields of study.

Many bibliographies of film reference material are available for the

# 80 FILM STUDY COLLECTIONS

librarian who conscientiously undertakes a search of the literature, but such a search requires a certain amount of effort. At present, the general reference librarian is not likely to happen upon guides to film reference material. In the future, as film study becomes a more established area of research and publication, it is likely that film reference sources will begin to appear more regularly in library science literature and in reference courses in library schools. Until such time, a special effort will continue to be necessary to learn about the growing number of excellent tools to answer film reference questions.

Reference questions in film studies come in all forms and from all sorts of people. Because movies are such a pervasive part of American culture, questions may be inspired by motives ranging from simple curiosity to academic research. Many questions seem almost too trivial to the librarian and may therefore not receive their due amount of time and attention. The movie trivia buff can be found at public libraries, high school libraries, and in college and university libraries. In the academic environment, such a person may be enrolled in English 104 (Introduction to Film as Literature) or even be a teacher of English 104. It is important that the librarian understand that the seemingly trivial question is often a manifestation of serious interest and therefore deserves to be taken seriously. The librarian cannot distinguish between the question requiring verification of fact which is inspired by research, and the question inspired by a five-dollar bet between friends who met in the corner bar for the Monday Night Movie on television. Making this distinction is not the librarian's function. One must remember that if the library user does not receive a serious answer to a trivial question, she or he will probably not expect any other question to receive better treatment.

Moreover, movie questions are readily answerable today. In fact, the field offers more reference sources than many other much older subjects of research and popular interest. Librarians must adjust to the wealth of film materials now available to them, must learn the details of those materials, and must be aware of the strengths and weaknesses of each source. It is also necessary for a good reference librarian to keep up with changes in publishing and in public interest.

If the librarian or scholar wishes to examine short lists of reference books, he or she may consult such indexes as *Library Literature, Bibliographic Index,* or *Film Literature Index* to locate bibliographies. Other published lists are Bohler,[1] Monaco,[2] or Samples.[3] Following is

---

[1] Bohler, Betty, Emmett, Robert, and Roberts, Sally. *Seen Through the Dark: A Guide to Film Reference Sources.* Rev. ed. Evanston, Ill: Northwestern University Library, 1976. 18 p.

[2] Monaco, James. *Film: How and Where to Find out What You Want to Know.* Montreal (Box 1778, Station B, Montreal, Quebec, H3B 3L3): Take One, 1975. 8 p.

[3] Samples, Gordon. *How to Locate Criticism and Reviews of Plays and Films.* San Diego, Cal: San Diego State Library, 1971. 23 p.

Reference Services    81

a list of reference sources compiled from many such bibliographies. The main general bibliographies of film books are not included here, but are an important part of any reference collection and are listed beginning on page 17.

The user's guide to these materials should be helpful to the librarian and the independent library user. The classifications are based on the types of film questions most frequently received.

## A Reference Collection—109 Sources

AWARDS 3, 39, *51, 60, 79*, 94, *95*

BIOGRAPHY, INDIVIDUALS' CREDITS 2, 3, 5, 6, 11, 12, 13, 15, 16, *18, 19, 21, 23, 32, 37*, 40, *46*, 51, 54, 56, 66, 69, 72, 75, 76, 79, *84, 85, 87, 91, 94, 97*, 98, *100, 101*, 102, *103*, 105

CREDITS FOR FILMS *2, 4, 25, 28, 31*, 34, 38, 43, 57, 58, 62, *72*, 77, 78, 80, 88, *94*, 106, *107*

FOREIGN FILMS 5, 12, 15, 16, 21, 37, 38, 45, 53, 66, 75, 98, 107

GENERAL DICTIONARIES AND ENCYCLOPEDIAS *11*, 39, 40, *42, 48*

GENRES 22, 25, 26, 55, 58, 71, 78, 83, 106

GLOSSARIES, VOCABULARY 11, 33, *35*, 52, 59, 70

INDUSTRY ADDRESSES 1, *15, 20*, 49, *51*, 53

LIBRARY COLLECTIONS *67*, 86, 109

LITERATURE SOURCES, SCREENWRITERS *3, 4, 6*, 19, *23, 27*, 38, 43, 58, *65, 99*

MUSIC AND FILM 17, 63, 81, 102

PHOTOS, AGENTS, AND ADDRESSES 1, 15, 105

PLOT SUMMARIES *4, 31*, 74, 78, *80, 88*

PROGRAMMING INFORMATION, DISTRIBUTORS 7, 8, 47, *62*

REMAKES *24, 27, 61*, 99

REVIEWS AND INDEXES TO CRITICISM *10, 14, 29, 30*, 31, *36*, 44, 46, 49, *50*, 58, *64*, 71, 72, 77, 88, *89*, 92, *93*, 106, *108*

SCREENPLAYS *65, 82, 90*

TECHNIQUE *33, 59*, 70

1. Academy of Motion Picture Arts and Sciences. *Academy Players Directory*. Los Angeles: Academy of Motion Picture Arts and Sciences, 1937—(annual). Contains an alphabetical list of actors and actresses with photos and agents, under various categories such as leading women, children, black actors, etc. There are also names and addresses of studio casting personnel and agents.
2. Academy of Motion Picture Arts and Sciences. *Screen Achievements Records Bulletin*. Los Angeles: Academy of Motion Picture Arts and Sciences. "Published three times per year with a cumulative annual volume to provide the industry with compiled credits." Section One contains full credits for each film. Section

Two lists each individual's films under actor, art director, film editor, music director, producer, sound, and writer. Section Three lists films by releasing company, and Section Four is an alphabetical index of individuals' credits.
3. Academy of Motion Picture Arts and Sciences. *Who Wrote the Movie, and What Else Did He Write? An Index of Screen Writers and Their Film Works, 1936–1969.* Los Angeles: Academy of Motion Picture Arts and Sciences and the Writers Guild of America, West, 1970. Indexes information by writer, film title, and award.
4. American Film Institute. *Catalog of Motion Pictures Produced in the United States. Feature Films, 1921–1930. Feature Films 1961–1970.* New York: Bowker, 1971—. All American films released in each decade with full credits, synopses, and, if known, source.
5. Armes, Roy. *French Cinema Since 1946. Vol. 1: The Great Tradition, Vol. 2: The Personal Style.* New York: A. S. Barnes, 1970. Discussion, filmographies, and film credits on selected French directors.
6. Aros, Andrew A. *An Actor Guide to the Talkies, 1965–1974.* Metuchen, N.J.: Scarecrow Press, 1977. (As Conceived by Richard B. Dimmitt.)

———. *A Title Guide to the Talkies, 1964–1974.* Metuchen, N.J.: Scarecrow Press, 1977. (As Conceived by Richard B. Dimmitt.)
7. Artel, Linda, and Weaver, Kathleen, comps. and eds. *Film Programmers' Guide to 16mm Rentals.* San Francisco: San Francisco Community Press, 1972.

Weaver, Kathleen, comp. and ed. *Film Programmer's Guide to 16mm Rentals.* 2nd ed. Berkeley, Cal.: Reel Research, 1975. The listings provide distributor and cost of features and short films. Director index.
8. Baer, D. Richard, ed. *The Film Buff's Bible of Motion Pictures, 1915–1972.* Hollywood, Cal.: Hollywood Film Archive, 1972. Gives year, length, distributor, miscellaneous comment, and a critical rating in chart form. Includes silents, shorts, and some TV movies.
9. Baer, D. Richard, ed. *The Film Buff's Checklist of Motion Pictures, 1912–1979.* Hollywood, Cal.: Hollywood Film Archive, 1978. Includes basically the same information as the "Bible" without the critical ratings or award notations. Also shows color or black and white. Columnar rather than chart format.
10. Batty, Linda *Retrospective Index to Film Periodicals, 1930–1970.* New York: Bowker, 1975. Indexes a small list of journals, but has a list of book and film reviews as well as a topic list.
11. Bawden, Liz-Anne, ed. *The Oxford Companion to Film.* New

*Reference Services* 83

York: Oxford University Press, 1976. Wide coverage of film topics including titles, personalities, companies, genres, and technical or production terms. International in scope.
12. Beattie, Eleanor. *Handbook of Canadian Film.* Ontario: Peter Martin Associates in association with *Take One* Magazine, 1973. Biographies, filmographies, and bibliographies for each individual discussed, plus sections on other topics such as music, animation, courses, archives, catalogs, and emerging artists.
13. Billings, Pat, and Eyles, Allen. *Hollywood Today.* London: Zwemmer, 1971. Brief biographies and credits for 370 persons working on recent U.S. films.
14. Bowles, Stephen E., comp. and ed. *Index to Critical Film Reviews in British and American Film Periodicals, together with Index to Critical Reviews of Books About Film.* New York: Burt Franklin, 1974–5. Three volumes in two makes a confusing format. Contains a list of reviews, a list of reviews of books, and indexes by director, film reviewer, author, book reviewer, and a subject list of the books.
15. *British Film and Television Yearbook.* London: British and American Film Holdings, 1946—(annual). Includes biographies, agents, photos, and addresses of firms in the industry in Britain.
16. Bucher, Felix. *Germany.* New York: A. S. Barnes, 1970. An alphabetical list of entries on over 400 people prominent in German film.
17. Burton, Jack. *The Blue Book of Hollywood Musicals: Songs From the Sound Tracks and the Stars Who Sang Them Since the Birth of the Talkies a Quarter Century Ago.* Watkins Glen, N.Y.: Century House, 1953. Articles typify each year's musicals from 1927 to 1952. Cast, songs, and writers are given, along with a title index and a list of albums. Features, westerns, and feature cartoons are listed. Birth date, place of birth, and real name are given for each person listed.
18. Cawkwell, Tim, and Smith, John M., eds. *The World Encyclopedia of the Film.* New York: T. Crowell, 1972. A biographical encyclopedia which offers separate lists of film titles for each individual under each role the person played (i.e., director, actor, cinematographer, etc.).
19. Corliss, Richard, ed. *The Hollywood Screenwriters.* New York: Avon, 1972. Essays and interviews on each screenwriter accompanied by filmographies.
20. Costner, Tom, ed. *Motion Picture Market Place, 1976–1977.* 1st ed. Boston: Little, Brown, 1976 (annual). Lists addresses for films and organizations in all areas of the industry.
21. Cowie, Peter. *Sweden.* New York: A. S. Barnes, 1970. 2 vols. Vol.

1 lists full or partial filmographies for Swedish directors, actors, writers, etc.; Vol. 2 provides discussion on topics.
22. Dawson, Bonnie. *Women's Films in Print; An Annotated Guide to 800 Films by Women.* San Francisco: Booklegger Press, 1975.
23. Dimmitt, Richard B. *An Actor Guide to the Talkies: A Comprehensive Listing of 8,000 Feature-length Films From January 1949 until December, 1964.* Metuchen, N.J.: Scarecrow Press, 1967–8.

 ———. *A Title Guide to the Talkies: A Comprehensive Listing of 16,000 Feature-Length Films from October 1926 until December 1963.* Metuchen, N.J.: Scarecrow Press, 1965. The actor guide refers to page numbers in the title volume (organized by film) which is primarily intended to supply sources for films, but also lists dates and production companies. Supplemented by Andrew A. Aros.
24. Druxman, Michael B. *Make It Again, Sam; a Survey of Movie Remakes.* New York: A. S. Barnes, 1975. A combination of discussion on 33 remade films and a "compendium of remakes."
25. Edera, Bruno. *Full Length Animated Feature Films.* Edited by John Halas. New York: Hastings House, 1977. An international text on the history and technique of animated film combined with a catalog of full-length animated features with credits and description, a bibliography, and index.
26. Emmons, Carol A. *Famous People on Film.* Metuchen, N.J.: Scarecrow, 1977. A list of nontheatrical biographical films.
27. Enser, A. G. S. *Filmed Books and Plays: A List of Books and Plays From Which Films Have Been Made, 1928–1974.* Rev. ed. London: Deutsch, 1975. Indexed by film title, author, and title change.
28. *Film Daily Yearbook.* New York: Film Daily, 1919–1970. Published as "Wid's Year Book," 1918–1919: "Film Daily Year Book of Motion Pictures," 1920–1969: "Film Daily Year Book of Motion Pictures and Television," 1970. Distributed by Arno Press. Gives many names, lists, and addresses. Sections on features list review dates for films from 1915, and the last year's film credits.
29. *Film Literature Index: a Quarterly Author-Subject Periodical Index to the International Literature of Film.* Albany, N.Y.: Filmdex, 1973—Indexes 225 journals, including over 100 film journals. Easy format, with author-title-subject access.
30. *Film Review Digest.* Millwood, N.Y.: Kraus-Thomson Organization, 1975–7. Gave review excerpts on U.S. and foreign films; ceased publication.
31. *Filmfacts.* Los Angeles: Division of Cinema, University of Southern California, 1958—(semi-monthly). Each entry lists complete credits, cast and characters, a synopsis, a summary of criticism,

and long excerpts from reviews. Currently received issues are dated two or three years ago.
32. *Filmlexicon Degli Autori e Delli Opere.* Rome: Edizioni di Bianco de Nero, 1958–1967. 7 vols. This set contains extensive biographical information on film people and is very comprehensive in its inclusion.
33. *Focal Encyclopedia of Film and TV Techniques.* New York: Hastings House, 1969. Basic and technical information in the areas of production.
34. Garbicz, Adam, and Klinowski, Jacek. *Cinema, the Magic Vehicle: a Guide to its Achievement. Journey One: The Cinema Through 1949.* Metuchen, N.J.: Scarecrow Press, 1975. A discussion (with partial credits) of each of almost 500 films selected internationally as being important.
35. Geduld, Harry, and Gottesman, Ronald. *An Illustrated Glossary of Film Terms.* New York: Holt, Rinehart & Winston, 1973.
36. Gerlach, John C., and Gerlach, Lana. *Critical Index: a Bibliography of Articles on Film in English, 1946–1973 Arranged by Names and Topics.* New York: Teachers College Press, 1974. Articles are categorized under 175 topics as well as by names of personalities. Not a source of film reviews, but includes critical articles. Computer produced.
37. Gifford, Denis. *British Cinema.* New York: A. S. Barnes, 1968. A list of English actors and directors with bio-filmographies and a film title index.
38. Gifford, Denis. *British Film Catalogue, 1895–1970; a Reference Guide.* New York: McGraw-Hill, 1973. 14,000 films with cast, director and writer listed for each.
39. Gottesman, Ronald, and Geduld, Harry. *Guidebook to Film: an Eleven-In-One Reference.* New York: Holt, Rinehart, & Winston, 1972. Out of date but still useful with sections on bibliography, museums and archives, distributors, bookstores, awards, and five other areas.
40. Graham, Peter John. *A Dictionary of the Cinema.* New York: A. S. Barnes, 1968. Primarily a source of individuals' filmographies, although there are also entries on types of films and very short biographies. Film title index.
41. Halliwell, Leslie. *Filmgoer's Book of Quotes.* London: Hart-Davis, McGibbon, 1973. An unpredictable collection of quotes by actors and other film people and on topics such as TV, Insults, and Cinemascope. Not very well indexed and haphazardly selected, but the only movie quote book.
42. Halliwell, Leslie. *The Filmgoer's Companion.* 6th ed. New York:

Hill & Wang, 1977. Entries on film issues, people, terms, and themes. Many of the latter are unusual, such as staircases and wheelchairs. The personal tone of the book makes it annoying to some users and fascinating to others.

43. Halliwell, Leslie. *Halliwell's Film Guide: a Survey of 8,000 English Language Movies.* New York: Granada Publishing, Ltd., 1977. Information given for each title includes alternative title, country of origin, release date, production company, color, brief synopsis and appraisal, writer, director, photographer, composer, principal cast with comments, and some critical excerpts.

44. Heinzkill, Richard. *Film Criticism: An Index to Critics' Anthologies* Metuchen, N.J.: Scarecrow, 1975. Re-indexes 40 major anthologies primarily by names of films and individuals with some topical access.

45. Hibbin, Nina. *Eastern Europe.* New York: A. S. Barnes, 1969. A section on each of the following countries has a brief text, directors, actors and others predominant in film production: Albania, Bulgaria, Czechoslovakia, East Germany, Hungary, Poland, Romania, USSR, and Yugoslavia.

46. Hochman, Stanley, comp. and ed. *American Film Directors.* New York: Frederick Ungar, 1974. Excerpts from articles on 65 directors from books, newspapers, and journals, including some foreign publications. Filmographies are listed for each director, and there is an index by film and critic.

47. Hurst, Walter (writes under pseudonyms Johnny Minus and William Storm Hale). *Film Superlist: 20,000 Motion Pictures in the U.S. Public Domain.* Hollywood, Cal.: 7 Arts Press, 1973. Copyright-free films from 1894–1939. Updated by Bruce Webster.

48. *International Encyclopedia of Film.* Edited by Roger Manvell and Lewis Jacobs. New York: Crown, 1972. Entries on biographical, historical, and general topics, some definitions of terms, and 15 long articles on special subjects such as animation, color, and documentary.

49. *International Film Guide.* New York: A. S. Barnes, 1964—(annual). State-of-the-art essays, entries on individual films, and addresses of industry firms.

50. *International Index to Film Periodicals.* New York: Bowker, 1972—(annual). The bound annual volumes are cumulations of the information provided to subscribers of a card service which indexes 60 journals. The annuals have sections on biography and individual films as well as topical coverage.

51. *International Motion Picture Almanac.* New York: Quigley Publications, 1956—. Addresses, awards, statistical, biographical, and other information are given in this annual volume.

52. Jordan, Thurston C., ed. *Glossary of Motion Picture Terminology*. Menlo Park, Cal.: Pacific Coast Publishers, 1968.
53. *Kemp's Film and Television Yearbook (International)*. London: Kemp's Group Ltd., 1956—(annual).
54. Koszarski, Richard. *The Men with the Movie Cameras: Seventy-five Filmographies*. New York: Film Comment, 1972. A list of credits of major cameramen. Most of this work appeared in the Summer 1972 *Film Comment*.
55. Kowalski, Rosemary Ribich. *Women and Film: a Bibliography*. Metuchen, N.J.: Scarecrow Press, 1976. Short annotations on most items. Includes books and journal articles.
56. Lamparski, Richard. *Whatever Became Of. . . .* New York: Crown, 1st series, 1966; 2nd series, 1968; 3rd series, 1970; 4th series, 1973; 5th series, 1979. Intended for trivia buffs, this series answers with photographs and short biographical entries the frequent question in the title.
57. Lauritzen, Einar, and Lundquist, Gunnar. *American Film-Index, 1908-1915*. Stockholm: Film-Index, 1976. Distributed by Akademibokhandeln, University of Stockholm, Sweden. 23,000 titles with brief credits.
58. Lee, Walter. *Reference Guide to Fantastic Films: Science Fiction, Fantasy, and Horror*. Los Angeles: Chelsea-Lee Books, 1972–4. This three-volume set includes references to sequels, and the following information is given for each film: date, language and country, minutes, color, animation, length, director, writer, music, classification, references to literature, source, brief description, and cast.
59. Levitan, Eli L. *An Alphabetical Guide to Motion Pictures, Television, and Videotape Production*. New York: McGraw-Hill, 1970. An encyclopedia with glossary-type definitions along with long essays explaining principles and method of production. Illustrations, photos, drawings, charts, and a subject list of entries.
60. Likeness, George. *The Oscar People: From* Wings *to* My Fair Lady. Mendota, Ill.: Wayside Press, 1965. General information on the awards; a list of best films with credits and comment, including losers; a list of Oscar stars; and capsule biographies.
61. Limbacher, James L., comp. *Remakes, Series, and Sequels on Film and Television*. 2nd ed. Dearborn, Mich.: Audio-visual Div., Dearborn Public Library, 1969 (new edition forthcoming).
62. Limbacher, James L., comp. and ed. *Feature Films on 8mm, 16mm and Videotape: A Directory of Feature Films Available for Rental, Sale, and Lease in the United States and Canada*. 6th ed. New York: Bowker, 1979. Gives year, length, description, director, major actors, and distribution information for more than 10,000 features.

88  FILM STUDY COLLECTIONS

63. Limbacher, James L., comp. and ed. *Film Music: From Violins to Video.* Metuchen, N.J.: Scarecrow Press, 1974. Historical, technical, and theoretical comment on scoring for films, along with a title index giving the date of a film so that one can find the title, company, composer, or musical director in the chronological listing. Also, a filmography of composers and a listing of recordings.

64. MacCann, Richard Dyer, and Perry, Edward. *The New Film Index: a Bibliography of Magazine Periodicals in English, 1930–1970.* New York: Dutton, 1975. Indexes general periodicals as well as 35 film journals. Critical articles are included but not reviews. The user must be familiar with the topic list because there is no index by subject, only by author. Annotated entries.

65. McCarty, Clifford. *Published Screenplays: a Checklist.* 1st ed. Kent, Ohio: Kent State University Press, 1971. (Serif Series: bibliographies and checklists, No. 18.) Screenplays published in magazines and books, in entirety or in excerpt. Director, production company, screenwriters, and source are listed for each film.

66. Martin, Marcel. *France.* New York: A. S. Barnes, 1969. A list of 400 individuals with partial filmographies.

67. Mehr, Linda Harris, ed. *Motion Pictures, Television and Radio: a Union Catalogue of Manuscript and Special Collections in the Western United States.* Boston: G. K. Hall, 1977. Detailed description of holdings for eleven western states.

68. Meyer, William R. *The Film Buff's Catalog.* New Rochelle, N.Y.: Arlington House, 1978. Information on stills, books, magazines, fan clubs, and other issues of interest to the film buff and collector.

69. Michael, Paul. *The American Movies Reference Book: the Sound Era.* Englewood Cliffs, N.J.: Prentice-Hall, 1969. Brief biographies of 600 players and a list of their English language films. Cast lists and brief credits for about 100 films, and American sound credits for 50 producers and 50 directors.

70. Miller, Tony, and Miller, Patricia George. *Cut! Print!* Los Angeles: O'Hara Press, 1972. The bulk of this book is a glossary of film terms, mainly pertaining to production. There are also charts representing preproduction, production, and post-production activities and budget breakdowns.

71. Nachbar, John G. *Western Films: An Annotated Critical Bibliography,.* New York: Garland, 1975. Includes sections on film titles, performers, directors, history, and theory. Author and subject indexes.

72. *New York Times Film Reviews.* New York: Arno Press. 1913–1968, vols. 1–6, with index volume. Additional volumes for 1969–70,

71-2, 73-4, and 75-6. Chronologically arranged copies of NYT reviews with indexes.
73. *Newsbank. Review of the Arts: Film and Television.* Greenwich, Conn.: NewsBank, Inc., 1975—. "Newspaper reviews of films, books, plays, art exhibits, concerts, television and other cultural endeavors are compiled from 190 newspapers in 130 major cities and reproduced in their entirety on microfilm and grouped by Subject matter in printed indexes." Published every other month and cumulated annually. One of the four subject indexes is "Film and Television" and it even provides access by major actors in films.
74. Niver, Kemp R. *Motion Pictures from the Library of Congress: Paper Print Collection, 1884–1912.* Berkeley, Cal.: University of California Press, 1967. Producer, copyright number, and footage is followed by a short plot summary or scene description.
75. Parish, James Robert. *Film Actors Guide: Western Europe.* Metuchen, N.J.: Scarecrow Press, 1977. Provides "a single compendium of motion picture actors—in this instance, those based in Western Europe exclusive of Scandinavia—who have performed in feature-length films," with credits for each entry.
76. Parish, James Robert, and Pitts, Michael R. *Film Directors: A Guide to Their American Films.* Metuchen, N.J.: Scarecrow Press, 1974. List of credits for each director.
77. Parish, James Robert, and Pitts, Michael R. *Great Spy Pictures.* Metuchen, N.J.: Scarecrow Press, 1974. Credits, actor-character lists, critical annotations, and excerpts from reviews.
78. Parish, James Robert, and Pitts, Michael R. *The Great Western Pictures.* Metuchen, N.J.: Scarecrow Press, 1976. Cast and characters, credits, a plot summary, and commentary for each of the "Great Western Pictures;" a list of westerns on radio, and TV; and a bibliography of 1,000 western novels.
79. Parish, James Robert. *The MGM Stock Company: The Golden Era.* New Rochelle, N.Y.: Arlington House, 1973. Biographical and credit information on MGM players and capsule biographies on MGM executives. MGM awards and nominations are also listed. For information on contract players for other studios, see the same author's *Paramount Pretties* (Arlington House, 1972), *The RKO Gals* (Arlington House, 1974), and *The Fox Girls* (Arlington House, 1972).
80. Pickard, R. A. E. *Dictionary of 1000 Best Films.* New York: Association Press, 1971. Basic credits and brief plots. Emphasis on American films.
81. Pitts, Michael, and Harrison, Louis H. *Hollywood on Record: The*

*Film Stars' Discography*. Metuchen, N.J.: Scarecrow Press, 1968. Lists recordings made since 1948 by motion picture performers, including recordings such as original cast recordings, L.P.s, compilation L.P.s and 45s.
82. Poteet, G. Howard. *Published Radio, Television, and Film Scripts: A Bibliography*. Troy, N.Y.: Whitston Publishing Co., 1975. Lists 667 scripts of motion pictures.
83. Powers, Anne, comp. and ed. *Blacks in American Movies: a Selected Bibliography*. Metuchen, N.J.: Scarecrow Press, 1974. Books, reference sources, dissertations, and bibliographies; an alphabetical and subject list of periodical articles; and a filmography of features by and about blacks from 1904–1930. Author and subject indexes.
84. Ragan, David. *Who's Who in Hollywood, 1900–1976*. New Rochelle, N.Y.: Arlington House, 1976. Brief bio-filmographies given for over 20,000 people, both living and deceased.
85. Rigdon, Walter. *Biographical Encyclopedia and Who's Who of the American Theater*. New York: J. H. Heineman, 1965. Many film people who also have theatrical experience are listed here.
86. Rose, Ernest D. *World Film and Television Study Resources: a Reference Guide to Major Training Centers and Archives*. Bonn-Bad Godesberg: Friedrich-Ebert-Stiftung, 1977. Guide to U.S. and foreign film study centers, with descriptions of some U.S. university and special film study archives.
87. Sadoul, Georges. *Dictionary of Film Makers*. Berkeley, Cal.: University of California Press, 1972. Bio-filmographies and excerpts from critical articles. Includes directors, screenwriters, composers, and many others but not actors.
88. Sadoul, Georges. *Dictionary of Films*. Berkeley, Cal.: University of California Press, 1972. Brief credits, plots, characters and actors, and excerpts of critical articles for about 1,200 films selected internationally.
89. Salem, James M. *A Guide to Critical Reviews. Part IV: The Screenplay, From* The Jazz Singer *to* Dr. Strangelove. Metuchen, N.J.: Scarecrow Press, 1971. Indexes general magazines for film reviews in two volumes.
90. Samples, Gordon. *The Drama Scholars Index to Plays and Filmscripts: A Guide to Plays and Filmscripts in Selected Anthologies, Series, and Periodicals*. Metuchen, N.J.: Scarecrow Press, 1974. Locates various versions and translations of scripts. Emphasis is on plays rather than scripts.
91. Sarris, Andrew. *The American Cinema: Directors and Directions, 1929–1968*. New York: Dutton, 1968. A critique and a filmography

are offered for each director. There is a film index and a list by year of directorial activity.

92. Schuster, Mel. *Motion Picture Directors: a Bibliography of Magazine and Periodical Articles, 1900–1972.* Metuchen, N.J.: Scarecrow Press, 1971. A list of articles from 340 magazines on more than 2,300 directors.

93. Schuster, Mel. *Motion Picture Performers: A Bibliography of Magazine and Periodical Articles, 1900–1969.* Metuchen, N.J.: Scarecrow Press, 1971. A list for selected performers.

94. *Screen World.* Edited by John Willis. New York: Crown, 1949— (annual). Lists production and cast/character credits for domestic and foreign films released in the United States for each year. Other selections give awards, obituaries, and selected biographies.

95. Shale, Richard, comp. *Academy Awards: An Ungar Reference Index.* New York: Frederick Ungar Publishing Co., 1978 (Ungar Film Library). The text is organized by Academy Award categories, 1927–1977, as well as by year. All nominations are listed with the name of the film and production company. It is indexed by every name occurring in the book, including film titles, song titles, and special awards. Also, bibliography, history, and procedures of the Awards.

96. Shipman, David. *The Great Movie Stars: The Golden Years.* New York: Bonanza Books, 1970.

    ———. *The Great Movie Stars: The International Years.* New York: St. Martin's Press, 1973. The film careers of about 150 stars are outlined in paragraph form in each volume.

97. Stewart, John, comp. *Filmarama.* Metuchen, N.J.: Scarecrow Press, Vol. 1: *The Formidable Years, 1893–1919,* 1975; Vol. 2: *The Flaming Years, 1920–1929,* 1977. Lists credits for major and minor actors and actresses. The credits are "a representative record of stage, radio, and television work" as well as screen credits.

98. Svensson, Arne. *Japan.* New York: A. S. Barnes, 1971. People and issues of Japanese film. Also, production statistics for features from 1946 to 1968.

99. Thiery, Herman (writes under pseudonym Johan Daisne). *Dictionnaire Filmographique de la Littérature Mondiale.* Gand: E. Story-Scientia, Vol. 1 (A-K), 1971; Vol. 2 (L-Z), 1975; Supplement (A-Z), 1977. Indexed by book and film title. The explanatory material is in English, French, German, and Dutch.

100. Thomson, David. *A Biographical Dictionary of Film.* New York: William Morrow, 1976. (Published in 1975 with the title: *A Biographical Dictionary of the Cinema.*) A selective presentation of

essays and facts for individuals important to film internationally.
101. Truitt, Evelyn Mack. *Who Was Who on Screen*. 2nd ed. New York: R. R. Bowker, 1977. Brief biographies on famous and not-so-famous people who have appeared on screen.
102. Vallance, Tom. *The American Musical*. New York: A. S. Barnes, 1970. A dictionary of people and theses important to the genre with filmographies of musical work.
103. Weaver, John T., comp. *Forty Years of Screen Credits 1929–1969*. Metuchen, N.J.: Scarecrow Press, 1970. 2 vols.
———. *Twenty Years of Silents, 1908–1928*. Metuchen, N.J.: Scarecrow Press, 1971. Primarily screen credits, with interesting lists included, such as the Keystone Kops, and the Our Gang Kids. The volume of silent credits includes credits for directors and producers, a list of corporations and distributors, and a section showing vital statistics for directors and producers.
*Weaver, Kathleen. See Artel, Linda.*
104. Webster, Bruce. *Film Copyright Reference Book: Films in the Public Domain, from June 1940–June 1946*. Published by the author. See also Hurst, Walter.
105. *Who's Who in Show Business: The International Directory of the Entertainment World*. Edited by Ken Hecht. New York: Who's Who in Show Business, Inc., (annual). Often lists brief credits, but always the agent or address of the entertainer. A classified talent list allows one to locate jugglers, M.C.'s, singers, etc.
106. Willis, Donald. *Horror and Science Fiction Films: A Checklist*. Metuchen, N.J.: Scarecrow Press, 1972. Credits and literature references with brief but amusing description of plot category.
107. *World Filmography, 1967*. General Editor, Peter Cowie. New York: A. S. Barnes, *World Filmography, 1968*. General Editor, Peter Cowie. New York: A. S. Barnes, 1977. "Lists credits and a brief categorisation of feature releases in 45 (49 in the 1968 volume) countries with indexes by director and film title." No films less than 1,000 meters are included. Future volumes will go backward in time.
108. Writers' Program. *The Film Index: A Bibliography*. Edited by Harold Leonard. New York: The Museum of Modern Art Film Library and the H. W. Wilson Co., 1941; reprinted by Arno Press, 1966. Annotated list of books and articles published up to 1935, indexed by author, title, and subject, and organized by topic.
109. Young, William C. *American Theatrical Arts: A Guide to Manuscripts and Special Collections in the United States and Canada*. Chicago: American Library Association, 1971. Although the emphasis is on theater, many collections from film companies and individuals active in moving pictures are listed.

# Reference Referral

In the automated society of today, business, education, and communications are all strongly influenced by computer technology. Libraries are concerned with and affected by all these fields, and the common conception of libraries as quiet book depositories is therefore very far from reality. Many large libraries are deeply involved in computerization. The world of libraries has to take advantage not only of the obvious benefits of speed and efficiency that the computer has to offer but also of the new structures and networks of the emerging technology.

## State and Regional Networks

Interlibrary loan networks function nationally in some cases and within states or regions in others. State and regional networks are often based on teletype communications, sending requests for books and other library holdings from library to library. If a small public library does not have a specific item required by a library user, the request will go to a county or regional library. The book is then mailed (or the journal article copied) to the small public library and delivered to the user with only a short time delay. In this way, library resources within a state or region are shared, and access to all material is improved. If, for some reason, the requested item cannot be loaned to the small public library, at least the requester is made aware of its location and where it can be used.

Other bibliographic networks such as NELINET, SOLINET, and AMIGOS, cross state lines. These networks contain many records in computer files and are replacing the union catalogs of the past by furnishing descriptions of library holdings on-line so that those holdings may be located and shared. Most libraries today, regardless of their size or location, can gain access to these networks and the holdings they describe. Interlibrary loan requests do not come only from small libraries. Large bibliographic networks are increasing the frequency of loans between million-volume libraries such as those of the University of Illinois and Yale University.

Many of the interlibrary loan (ILL) systems which function on a statewide basis refer and process requests for information as well as requests for books, journals, or microfilmed theses. In general, these information requests are handled in the same way as a request for a particular author-title citation. Request forms are filled out by the librarian, who records and formalizes the user's question. The request form is forwarded to the next largest resource center (a county or regional library system, or a large academic library), where that center's staff search for the information and either answer the question or refer it onward. It is obvious that the processes of accurately interpreting the user's query, setting limits on the extent and form of the answer, and recording the query are crucial steps in the reference referral procedure; and standards for these processes have yet to be established.

Awareness of these networks is especially important to the cinema librarian and the film student. Small public libraries and academic libraries—and larger libraries belonging to colleges and universities without film studies curricula—are unlikely to have even the basic reference material in film study. High school libraries, which generally have restricted book budgets, cannot afford to acquire or house holdings sufficient to support the term papers of students in film classes. Librarians in such libraries are unlikely to be film study specialists. If a difficult film reference question is asked in any of these libraries, it is very likely that the local librarian will not be able to answer it from the material available to her or him. If the librarian is aware of information networks and knows how to use them, there will be a much more positive result. The process of getting information from a network may take time, but if the question is serious and the answer important, such a time delay may be considered tolerable.

Reference questions sent through ILL networks belong to five categories. These five categories are derived from an analysis by C. E. Hieber.[1]

1. Exact reproduction. A particular piece of text or an illustration is required, such as a quotation or a photograph.
2. Fill in the blank, or factual. A statistic, a name, a list, or other specific information is required.
3. Descriptive. Descriptive or explanatory text is necessary, but one of several approaches or sources will satisfy the inquiry.
4. Information about. A subject area is stated and the inquirer needs one more document on the topic. These questions are more general than the third category.
5. List of references. A list of references or citations rather than actual documents is required.

In the first, third, and fourth cases, the patron with the inquiry receives a book, photocopy, or some other form of document as an answer or containing the answer. This involves the complexities of document delivery, and it is therefore obvious why interlibrary loan networks work well in combination with reference referral systems.

---

[1] Hieber, C. E. *An Analysis of Questions and Answers in Libraries.* Bethlehem, Pa: Center for the Information Sciences, Lehigh University, 1966.

In the second case, no document is necessary, although a citation indicating the source of the information may be supplied. This does not involve document delivery, though many ILL networks do this kind of reference referral as well, frequently by using the telephone and large reference collections to locate facts. In the last case, a literature search is necessary—as it may be in the third and fourth cases—but the documents are not delivered. The literature search may be done in the card catalog of a specific library, in the data base of a regional network which would include holdings information, or in the data bank of an indexing service such as MEDLINE or *Social Sciences Citation Index*.

The structure of ILL systems varies widely from state to state, and it is important to understand the structure of the system as well as the strengths of the resources available in the state. Some states have highly developed systems of regional libraries within the state. Illinois (ILLINET) and Wisconsin (WILS) are two examples. In these states, the ILL requests for documents or for information to be found in documents, as well as factual questions, are referred from the source library through the regional centers to the major library resource centers of the state. In many states there are several such major centers, including state libraries, large public libraries, and university libraries.

In Wisconsin, academic libraries are not among the state's resource centers. This means requests are referred to the Milwaukee Public Library rather than to the University of Wisconsin at Madison, the home of the Wisconsin Center for Film and Theatre Research (WCFTR). The film question could be sent directly to the WCFTR, but if it is routed through the ILL network, it may end up at the public library instead. Depending on the question, this may be perfectly satisfactory. It is likely that in the future, WILS will include the University of Wisconsin libraries in order to improve their already well developed interlibrary loan services. It is clear that differences in population distribution and in library funding both have major impacts on planning for state ILL networks, but in a majority of states, referral of questions and requests for information on any subject is possible. In order for the librarian to know whether to send a film reference question through the state ILL network, it is necessary to know which of the state's resource centers are a part of the ILL system.

Many large libraries have access to computer-based information holdings or indexes through vendors such as Bibliographic Retrieval System (BRS), Systems Development Corporation (SDC), or Lockheed. Data bases serviced in this way contain indexes to and citations from large areas of subject literature and may be searched to produce lists of citations (in some cases with abstracts) on the subject of interest. Some states, such as South Dakota, do this kind of data base searching as a matter of procedure if the question demands a list of citations. The cost of the search may be borne by the state or it might be passed on to the patron. For more information on data bases of interest to the film student, see page 97.

The reference question or subject request which has been sent through a state interlibrary loan network will probably be answered adequately, especially if data base searching is performed. It is even possible that a list of additional sources or resource centers for the inquirer to contact may be supplied. Some states (for example, Colorado) do not refer subject requests or reference questions outside the state, but only requests for specific documents. Other states (for example, Oklahoma or South Dakota) will try to get an answer even if the request involves long-distance phone calls or out-of-state contact. In general, if a library can locate a document with the use of a national bibliographic network, the library will try to borrow it no matter where it is held.

Up to this point in the development of library networks, emphasis has been placed by the constructors of those systems on document delivery and bibliographic information-sharing. Structured systems of reference question referral do not yet exist, though the bases for those systems have been developed in at least embryonic form. Many state systems fill subject requests without really advertising this service because the ILL systems are not, as yet, constructed in such a way that numerous questions can be efficiently and accurately processed. Both transmitting questions and answering them when the person asking the question is not present pose obvious problems. The librarian at the Denver Public Library cannot ask the sophomore at home in Boulder what she really meant by the question, how much information is necessary, or why she wanted to know. If the question is properly recorded on the best possible form, the battle is half won; but even so, remote reference service can be difficult to control and evaluate. For this reason, some states do not include reference referral in their interlibrary loan systems. In such a state it should be possible for an individual or a library to gain access to data bases or other information services independently.

Some information brokers or other institutions will only accept questions when they have been processed by an intermediary (a librarian or a library). Some will accept telephone or mail requests and some will not. Some charge a fee to certain classes of clientele; some are completely free. In this confused situation, potential users of these systems are well advised to study the advantages, disadvantages, and policies of the system they intend to use.

## Data Base Searching

There is no complete directory of organizations and institutions which do data base searching for clients. Although most large universities have offices responsible for providing access to data bases, or have libraries which subscribe to the services of one or more of the information vendors such as BRS, Lockheed, or SDC, not all universities will do searches for individuals outside the university community. One can ask the library where to have searching done (in some instances, large public libraries will do searching), or one can contact the information vendor for a list of its customers in the state or region. One might also locate an information broker in this way. Such brokers charge a fee for doing computer searching, but will almost certainly accept all customers, unlike many state-supported universities.

Once the agency which will formulate and perform data base searching has been located, it is often appropriate to inquire about Selective Dissemination of Information (SDI) services. These provide a continuing flow of up-to-date citations in one's area of interest. They may be available through a library, a data base producer or vendor, an information broker, or a university information office. Once the search is formulated, it is stored and then run periodically against the updated data base to retrieve a printout of new citations relating to the most recent literature in the field of interest.

Here follow descriptions of data bases of interest to the cinema scholar who is working in a film-related area of study. Information systems and services specifically devoted to film literature do not exist. Guides to information services such as Anthony T. Kruzas' *Encyclopedia of Information Systems and Services*[2] do not list any services under film, cinema, motion or moving pictures, performing arts, or theater, and have listings only for educational media and audiovisual services. Relevant available data bases cover areas in the social sciences, humanities, and business.

\* AHL (American History and Life). 1/1954—
> Full indexing of 150 journals, selective indexing of 1,750 journals, with abstracts on U.S. and Canadian history and culture from prehistoric times to the present. Lockheed.

---

[2] Kruzas, Anthony Thomas. ed. *Encyclopedia of Information Systems and Services.* 1st ed. Orange, N.J.: Academic Media, 1972.

\* Information on these data bases was taken from Martha Williams and Sandra H. Rouse. *Computer-Readable Bibliographic Data Bases: A Directory and Data Sourcebook.* Washington, D.C.: American Society for Information Science, 1976—(updated every 6 months).

Artbibliographies Modern. 1973—
: Covers publications in the fields of modern art and design from 1800 to the present. Lockheed.

*CDI (Comprehensive Dissertation Index). 1861—
: Contains citations of doctoral dissertations for degrees granted from 1801 to the present in the U.S. and Canada, including those in multidisciplinary and social sciences categories. Lockheed.

*CNI (Canadian Newspaper Index). 1/1977—
: Covers information on Canadian affairs as well as indexing the following dailies: *Montreal Star, Toronto Star, Toronto Globe and Mail, Vancouver Sun,* and *Winnepeg Free Press.* SDC.

*ERIC (Educational Resources Information Center).
: Composed of citations and abstracts from *Current Index to Journals in Education* (CIJE) from 1969 and *Research in Education* (RIE) 1966—. Subject categories of interest are information resources, language and linguistics, career education, and educational media and technology. BRS, Lockheed, SDI.

CIJE
: Indexing of 317 journals, selective indexing of 415 journals.

RIE
: Contains reports filed by contractors and grantees on the results of funded educational research, curriculum materials, and other education-related materials. There are 32 percent government reports or documents, 14 percent monographs, 19 percent preprints or conference papers, and 35 percent other material such as legislation, UN documents, bibliographies, annual reports, and directories.

*Federal Index. 10/1976—
: Covers proposed rules, regulations, bill introductions, speeches, hearings, roll calls, reports, vetoes, court decisions, executive orders, and contract awards as covered in *Congressional Record, The Federal Register, Presidential Documents, Commerce Business Daily, The Washington Post,* and citations to the *Code of Federal Regulations, The U.S. Code,* House and Senate bills, and other federal documents. Includes all subject categories in social sciences and interdisciplinary topics. Lockheed.

Foreign Language Index. 1972—
: Non-English language coverage of social sciences, economics, and public affairs literature. Lockheed.

*HA (Historical Abstracts). 1/1965—
: Abstracts of articles on world history, excluding the United States and Canada, from 1450 to the present. Full indexing of 10 journals, selective indexing of 1,890 journals. Lockheed.

The Information Bank (a subsidiary of The New York Times Company).

Includes all news and editorial matter from *The New York Times* (at this time, 1969 to the present), other general circulation newspapers such as the *Atlanta Constitution, Chicago Tribune, Los Angeles Times, San Francisco Chronicle,* and *Washington Post;* business publications such as *Advertising Age, Business Week, Forbes,* and *Wall Street Journal;* international affairs publications such as *Atlas, Foreign Affairs, Manchester Guardian,* and *Times of London;* science publications; and many other newsweeklies, monthlies, and quarterlies, including *Atlantic, Commonweal, Current Biography, National Review, The New Yorker, Saturday Review, Variety,* and *Village Voice.*

\* International Statistics. 1/1960—

Published forecasts with historical data exclusive of the United States covering general economics, all industries, detailed products, and end-use data. Covers approximately 1,000 journals for information. Lockheed.

\* Language. 1/1965—

Language and language behavior abstracts; contains abstracts in communications and social sciences. Lockheed.

\* LIBCON

Subject categories include architecture and design, arts, business, communications, education, history, multidisciplinary, psychology, social sciences, and many hard and natural sciences. SDC.

\* MARC (Machine Readable Cataloging).

Books: records for books in all subjects cataloged by the Library of Congress in English 1/1968; German 1975—, French 1973—.

Films: 1/1972—records for all film material (films, filmstrips, slides, transparencies, and videorecordings) released in the United States or Canada which have educational or institutional value. L.C.

\* NICEM (National Information Center for Educational Media), 1913—

Covers information on nonbook educational media: 16mm films, 35mm filmstrips, transparencies, videotapes, audiotapes, phono records, 8mm motion picture cartridges, slides and slide sets; will include video discs.

\* NTIS (National Technical Information Service Bibliographic Data File).

"Reports for this data base are registered by the following four sectors: NASA, DDC, ERDA, and many departments and independent agencies . . .; STAR, DDC, NSA, and the EPA Reports System are parts of NTIS Bibliographic Data File and can be accessed as separate systems." 7/1964—

Multidisciplinary coverage of technical reports generated by U.S. Government-sponsored research. Lockheed, BRS, SDC.
* PAIS Bulletin (Public Affairs Information Service Bulletin). 1/1976—
Public affairs literature in English as well as literature on economics and social sciences. Selective indexing from 800 journals; 1,200 titles are reviewed; 17 percent of data base is government reports and documents. Lockheed.
* PAIS FLI (Public Affairs Information Service Foreign Language Index). 1/1972—
Literature in French, German, Italian, Portuguese, and Spanish: 10 percent government reports and documents, 25 percent monographs, 65 percent journal literature, with 600 titles reviewed.
* PATELL (Psychological Abstracts Tape Editions Lease Licence). 1/1967. Nonevaluative summaries of the world's literature in psychology and other behavioral sciences. Full indexing of 140 journals; selective indexing of 650 journals. The data include 25 percent monographs. ERIC/IR, Lockheed, BRS.
* Sociological Abstracts. 1/1963—
Covers international literature of sociology, including such fields as social work, ethnology, psychology, etc. The data are 80 percent journal articles, 55–65 percent of which are in English; 50 percent monographs; and 15 percent preprints or conference papers. Full indexing of 150 journals; 1,100 are selectively indexed. Lockheed.
* SSCI (Social Sciences Citation Index). 1/1971.
Worldwide coverage of the prime journals of the social sciences in addition to the related journals of the natural, physical, and biomedical sciences. Full indexing for 1,000 journals. Lockheed.
* UCUCS-1 (University of California Union Catalog—Supplement 1). 1/1963—12/1967. Catalog records of all monographs processed by catalog departments of all UC campuses 1963 to 1967 in all subjects.

The following newspaper data bases cover selected articles with emphasis on socio-political events:
* *Chicago Tribune* Newspaper Index 1/1972—
* *Detroit News* Newspaper Index 1/1976—
* *Houston Post* Newspaper Index 1/1976—
* *Los Angeles Times* Newspaper Index 1/1972—
* *Milwaukee Journal* Newspaper Index 1/1976—
* *National Observer* Newspaper Index 1/1962—12/1968. SDC.
* *New Orleans Times Picayune* Newspaper Index 1/1972.
* *San Francisco Chronicle* Newspaper Index 1/1976—. SEC.
* *Wall Street Journal* Newspaper Index 1955–1957.
Further retrospective coverage is planned at three-year intervals.

*Washington Post* 1/1972—
Access to data bases is made by special arrangement with the offices of each paper unless otherwise indicated.

Data base searching is essentially a fee-based information service, although in different situations, the fees are paid by different people, from the taxpayer to the client. Some other fee-based services are listed annually in *The Directory of Fee-based Information Services* compiled by Kelly Warnken and published by Information Alternative, P.O. Box 657, Woodstock, N.Y. 12498. This includes listings for information brokers, free-lance librarians with subject specialties, independent information specialists, and libraries which offer services for a fee, and also includes those organizations which do data base searching. The 1977 directory lists several free-lance librarians with subject specialties of film study.

## National and Regional Film Information Sources

In addition to data bases, fee-based information services, and state networks, there are several information services which accept film reference questions by phone or by mail. They represent major resource collections in film study material but are not necessarily the places to begin your subject search. It is best to consult local resources first. In several cases, reference and research work is not one of the primary responsibilities of the organizations which follow, but an auxiliary service. This usually means that staff size is more of a problem than the availability of the resource material, and it may mean that there might be delay or that the question might be referred to a more likely source.

AMERICAN FILM INSTITUTE
Center for Advanced Film Study
Charles K. Feldman Library
501 Doheny Rd.
Beverly Hills, Cal. 90210

This library uses its impressive collection to answer phone and mail inquiries. The staff will provide brief answers to factual reference questions and will assist researchers in finding the information required. The staff will make copies for a standard charge and sets a reasonable page limit for the number of pages to be copied.

AMERICAN FILM INSTITUTE
Library and Information Services
National Educational Services
John F. Kennedy Center for the Performing Arts
Washington, D.C. 20566

This office answers phone and mail inquiries and reference questions, or it refers such inquiries to appropriate resources. There is a reference library and collection of current periodicals at the center and a professional staff to service it. This office works closely with the Charles K. Feldman Library in California (above) to make all AFI library resources available to scholars and researchers.

EDUCATIONAL FILM LIBRARY ASSOCIATION
43 West 61st St.
New York, N.Y. 10023

The EFLA office holds a library of over 1,200 books and 150 periodicals. There are also subject files, distributor catalogs, and reference materials. This information center provides reference and advisory services by mail or phone on nontheatrical film. The staff aids those who wish to locate sources of films, or who require information on film library administration, film distribution, and other aspects of nontheatrical and education film use.

LIBRARY OF CONGRESS
Motion Picture, Broadcasting and Recorded Sound Division
Library of Congress Annex Building, Room 1046
Washington, D.C. 20540

The Motion Picture, Broadcasting and Recorded Sound Division maintains the library's film collections for scholarly research and study. The staff answers mail and phone inquiries about LC holdings and makes appointments for the use of the section's reference and viewing facilities. Subject and catalog searches are not performed, but the staff uses an office reference collection and extensive files to answer reference questions, and also makes referrals to other sources of information.

NATIONAL FILM INFORMATION SERVICE
Academy of Motion Picture Arts and Sciences
8949 Wilshire Blvd.
Beverly Hills, Cal. 90211

NFIS offers a valuable collection to researchers in cinema who are not able to visit the Academy of Motion Picture Arts and Sciences' Margaret Herrick Library in person. Students, scholars, teachers, and film programmers are welcome to use NFIS services by mail or by phone. The staff will provide answers to specific reference and research questions by using the resources of the Margaret Herrick Library and will send photocopies of reviews and articles at a charge of

25¢ per page. Copies of the stills held by the library are available at $5 per 8x10 photograph. The service will also provide copies of the library's clipping files if the researcher's needs are serious and he or she has no other source of such information nearby.

The NFIS offers especially detailed services to film programmers by finding information on rental sources and print sources, and by making stills, program notes, and programming advice available. In some cases, the NFIS will provide complete program cycles on a filmmaker or film genre. Those interested in research guides on filmmakers and film topics may write for a list of research guide subjects. Current topics include British Cinema, Frank Capra, King Vidor, and Women Directors. The NFIS also offers touring exhibits of photographic enlargements on some subjects for a fee.

PACIFIC FILM ARCHIVE
University Art Museum
2625 Durant Ave.
Berkeley, Cal. 94720

This is a regional film center which has as its primary service area Northern California. If reference inquiries fall outside the Pacific Film Archives' area of special expertise, the staff will refer questions to other regional film study centers. The archive does, however, welcome nationwide inquiries by phone or mail in the areas of Avant-garde and Independent film, Russian and Japanese Cinema, Women and Film, Children's Films, and very current European films. If a large amount of photocopying is requested, there will be a fee for such copying. Questions from the Northern California area are answered on all film topics, including information on locating films, stills, screenplays, addresses, books, articles, and subject information. The volume of inquiries is quite high, and most of the questions are by phone.

UCLA THEATER ARTS LIBRARY
University of California-Los Angeles
Los Angeles, Cal. 90024

UNIVERSITY OF SOUTHERN CALIFORNIA
Doheny Library
Department of Special Collections
Los Angeles, Cal. 90007

Both these libraries offer reference services primarily to their university communities, but will try to answer queries from outside the Los Angeles area if staff time permits.

UNIVERSITY FILM STUDY CENTER
Film Information Office
Box 275, Cambridge, Mass. 02138
18 Vassar St., 20-B-120
MIT, Cambridge, Mass. 02139

The University Film Study Center is a major media and resource center serving the New England region. It was founded by a group of New England colleges and universities which now include Boston University, Brandeis University, Brown University, Dartmouth College, Hampshire College, Harvard, Massachusetts Institute of Technology, University of Bridgeport, University of Massachusetts at Amherst, University of Massachusetts at Boston, Wellesley College, Wesleyan University, and Yale. It receives funding from ten of these schools plus grants and private contributions. The center provides many services, several publications, and a mail and on-site reference service to assist with film research and curriculum planning. The staff maintains an extensive library of books, journals, and research files to provide access to information on festivals, distributors, and film programming, as well as to critical and theoretical materials. Although the primary emphasis of service is to the northeastern United States, the center will assist persons throughout the country with film-related questions.

## Regional Film Study Centers

Other regional film study centers offer reference services in addition to other programs. Abigail Nelson of the American Film Institute has provided a list of major media centers as defined by funding support from the National Endowment for the Arts. The NEA defines these centers as tax-exempt, nonprofit organizations with a yearly operating budget of $100,000 or more which carries out regional development of film, video, and radio in at least four of the following areas:

1. Exhibition of film and/or video work and publication of associated commentary
2. In-residence workshop programs
3. Provision of production and post-production facilities
4. Provision of such services as teaching, dissemination of information, and access to study and research resources
5. Maintenance of film and video collections
6. Coordination of regional media resources and services
7. Distribution of quality film and/or video work

## East

Boston Film/Video Foundation
39 Brighton Ave.
Allston, Mass. 02134
617-547-9607

Global Village
454 Broome St.
New York, N.Y. 10013
212-966-7526

The Kitchen
59 Wooster St.
New York, N.Y. 10012
212-925-3615

Media Study, Inc.
207 Delaware Ave.
Buffalo, N.Y. 14202
716-847-2555

Museum of Modern Art Film Department
11 West 53rd St.
New York, N.Y. 10019
212-956-6100

Pittsburgh Film-Makers, Inc.
P.O. Box 7200
Pittsburgh, Pa. 15213
412-681-5499

University Film Study Center, Inc.
18 Vassar St., Room 120
Massachusetts Institute of Technology
Cambridge, Mass. 02139
617-253-7612

## Midwest

Art Institute of Chicago Film Center
Columbus Drive at Jackson Blvd.
Chicago, Ill. 60603
312-443-3733

Film in the Cities, Inc.
2388 University Ave.
St. Paul, Minn. 55114
612-646-6104

Walker Art Center
Vineland Pl.
Minneapolis, Minn. 55403
612-377-7500

## South-Southwest

South Carolina Arts Commission
829 Richland St.
Columbia, S.C. 29201
803-758-3442

Southwest Alternate Media Project
(SWAMP)
1506½ Branard St.
Houston, Tex. 77006
713-522-8592

## West

Northwest Film Study Center
Portland Art Museum
1219 S. W. Park
Portland, Ore. 97205
503-226-2811

Pacific Film Archive
University Art Museum
Berkeley, Cal. 94720
415-642-1437

Rocky Mountain Film Center
University of Colorado
102 Hunter Building
Boulder, Col. 80309
303-492-7903

# 12
# Instruction to Library Users

Modern librarians believe that instruction in the use of the library is as important as more conventional forms of reference service. Library instruction is especially important in the area of film study for several reasons. First, many of the reference tools are not well known to librarians, and even less known to students and scholars. Second, at this early point in the history of film study, most people who teach film have no special training in the area or in its documents. This situation will change in the next few years, but for now, faculty members who have engaged in course work or extensive research in film practice or theory are in a minority. Most instructors in cinema studies are professors with training in language, comparative literature, English or American literature, speech communications, or fine and applied arts. This can be looked at as a strength of the field, because an interdisciplinary approach to film study can provide both an effective structure for a film department and a good theoretical base for scholarship. On the other hand, when one considers library research, it is evident that the specific literature of cinema is not the specialty of most teachers. The librarian should therefore engage in the active education of both students and teachers in the use of tools and in the methods of access to the literature they need.

## Basic Library Instruction

For those readers unfamiliar with the basic ideas behind the relatively new field of library instruction, a brief theoretical summary is necessary. Library instruction is undertaken on two levels. The first type of instruction is an extension of conventional service. It consists of the thorough explanation of the process of locating information and is aimed at the library user approaching the librarian with an inquiry. A lengthy lecture on locating subject headings may not always be appropriate, but the librarian should do more than simply give out answers. He or she should introduce the patron to the resources of the library and to the methods used in finding answers. By this process the user is made more independent, and the use of materials essential to his or her work can be made more effective. If a literature search is at hand, the indexes and journals should be discussed, at least briefly. The librarian must determine how much the patron wants to hear, of course, but in most cases if the question is of sufficient interest the process by which it is answered is also of interest.

The second type of library instruction is done with presentations to groups. The groups might consist of teaching faculty, teaching assistants, or students. The presentations should vary according to the level of the students and the subject of the course, but the material covered could be basically the same. A well-rounded presentation at a basic level should include the following:

1. An explanation of library subject headings and catalog use, especially filing problems
2. An introduction to indexes to periodical literature
3. An explanation of how, physically, to locate books and journals on film studies and related disciplines in the library
4. If scripts are held in the library, some attention should be given to problems of location, description, and entry for various types of scripts
5. Some explanation about locating and using both nonprint material and reading equipment if nonprint material on film study is held in the library
6. An introduction to the basic reference books if the group is doing any substantial research

This presentation can be given in less than an hour or can be expanded to become a series of lessons, including assignments or work sheets if the group members are going to undertake substantial research and are unfamiliar with the library or with library systems in general. Several benefits result from such talks. The recipients of the lecture meet a librarian and can subsequently contact him or her for assistance. If the lecture occurs in the library, the students (or lecturees) can be shown the location of the resources. This matter of orientation is often quite important, since indexes may be shelved some distance from dictionaries, and both may be considerably removed from card catalogs and the circulating collection. Finally, it is hoped that such instruction will result in independent library researchers—students who can locate basic information on their own and thus allow librarians to provide thorough service on difficult questions rather than to spend time with the same basic inquiries over and over.

## A Specific Presentation for Library Users

Library instruction techniques and policy are matters of current concern in librarianship. If no program for classroom presentations is offered in your library, it is reasonable for any teacher or library user group to request a presentation. Classroom lectures or discussions are commonly planned as part of an assignment in order to have retention at its highest. (If students use what they hear soon enough, they will remember it longer.) If such a presentation is not possible, the next section may be helpful. A library lecture is presented here in very general terms, and while it may not apply completely to every library, it will generally reflect most library situations. Library instruction should cover all basic research techniques, but one part should certainly cover the card catalog. The rest of this chapter is addressed to the library user.

### Understanding and Using the Card Catalog

The most commonly encountered and most frequently misunderstood tool in libraries is the card catalog. It is essential that any serious researcher understand the use of this rich resource. The most usual type of card catalog is the alphabetical or dictionary catalog, where all cards are filed together in alphabetical sequence. Each item in the library is described on one or more cards. The cards can include those to be filed under an author, editor, or compiler; title; or subject heading. In a dictionary catalog, these are all filed in one alphabetical sequence. In some catalogs, the subject entries are filed alphabetically in a separate sequence; this is known as a divided catalog.

*Subject Headings*
In either case, there are two problems which cause confusion. One is the vocabulary used for subject headings and the other is the

filing system. Most big libraries, and many smaller ones, use a standard vocabulary for subject headings. This means that cards for the catalog are ordered or prepared using subject descriptions determined by *The Library of Congress Subject Headings*.[1] The vocabulary of Library of Congress (LC) headings in the field of cinema has not been kept consistent with current usage. Also, when changes *are* made, problems result because old books are found under the old subject headings and new ones under the new terminology. The patron must therefore look in both places, since most libraries cannot afford to change all the cards whenever the vocabulary changes. The catalog should contain cards giving directions which say "See———" or "See also———," but in a drawer full of 1,000 cards, the patron may well miss these "See" cards. For these reasons, library patrons doing a search of a card catalog by subject descriptors should look at the current list of LC subject headings to discover what words to use in the search. This list will tell the user which words are correct entries, which are general and which more specific, and which will lead to related topics.

This vocabulary problem for film books has been severe. The catalog user who looks under "film" or "cinema" or "motion pictures" in a dictionary catalog will find only books with titles beginning with these words. The books on film are located under "moving pictures" or related phrases such as "moving picture actors and actresses" along with subdivisions which are separated from the major term with some kind of punctuation—dashes, commas, or parentheses. The catalog user will find entries such as these:

animation (cinematography)
cinematography, trick
experimental films
film adaptation
moving picture authorship
moving picture cartoons
moving picture film—preservation and storage
moving picture plays
moving pictures—United States*
moving pictures—moral and religious aspects
moving pictures—plots, themes, etc.
moving pictures—production and direction

---

[1] *Library of Congress Subject Headings.* 8th ed. Washington, D.C.: Library of Congress, Subject Cataloging Division, 1975.

* In some libraries, geographical subdivisions following dashes are filed before or after other subdivisions, whereas in other libraries, they are interfiled alphabetically after the dashes.

moving pictures—social aspects
moving pictures, American
moving pictures, musical
moving pictures, talking
moving pictures and children
moving pictures and literature
screen writers

Without using the master list of LC subject headings, the catalog user would not know there are similar books filed under both "film adaptation" and "moving pictures and literature," or that the correct entry for special effects is "cinematography, trick." The Library of Congress is aware of this terminology problem, both for film books and in other areas. A revised list of subject headings is being prepared.

*Filing Rules*

This situation is made much more difficult by the filing rules under which libraries arrange the hundreds, thousands, or millions of cards in their catalogs. There are rules for library filing published by the American Library Association, but each library must decide how closely to follow these rules, if at all. The rules vary, from catalog to catalog, but the basics are usually the same. The cards are filed by the top line on the card. Subject entries are filed word by word, so that "moving picture plays" comes before "moving pictures". (The blank between "pictures" and "plays" precedes the "s" at the end of "pictures.") Punctuation matters. Dashes come before commas and commas come before parentheses, so "moving pictures—plots, themes, etc." precedes "moving pictures, American," even though the words after the punctuation are not in alphabetical order. There are many more such rules. The reader should note the following points:

1. If you do not find any books under the term you tried first, either try another term, ask for help, or ask for the LC subject heading list.
2. If you cannot find something immediately, browse in the drawer. It may be filed nearby. If not, ask for help.

In an alphabetical card catalog where author, title, and subject cards are all filed together, there are rules for determining which cards come first when the initial words are the same. The basic rule for order is 1) author, 2) subject, 3) title. An example is:

London, Jack, 1876–1916.
London—Antiquities
The London spy

There are many complex variations on this rule, especially in regard to literature about and by the same person or organization, but again, if you encounter difficulty, ask for help.

Without training or experience in catalog searching, the library user is at a major disadvantage. It is not easy to be efficient or thorough. There are tips a librarian can provide for faster subject searching and ways to get a quick list of terms. For example, if your library uses sets of cards based on Library of Congress information, you have access to a list of terms used to describe each book. It is usually located at the bottom of each card and is called the "tracings." If this list is not on every card, it is probably on the author card. The list is necessary for librarians and card catalog filers, but is also useful for catalog users—if you know one appropriate book by its author or title and look at the card, you will see the list of subjects describing that book so you can find other books on the same topic.

*Special Catalogs*

It is often the case that all library holdings are not listed in the card catalog. Special formats, special collections, or other unusual material may either not be listed at all or listed in smaller catalogs. Dissertations, nonprint forms, serials, microforms, and government documents are some examples of library material which might be accessed through their own separate listings. You can find out easily enough about the situation in your library catalog by asking a librarian.

*Scripts*

Looking for published and unpublished scripts in the library catalog can be difficult. First of all, the script could be located under several entries: title, director, or screenwriter. If the library does not file enough cards for each script or screenplay, the catalog user may not be able to locate it. If the screenplay is a shooting script, the author entry may be found under the name of the screenwriter, because at the shooting-script stage of film production, the work is the major responsibility of the writer. If the screenplay is taken from the screen and represents the finished film, the director may be considered the author. Secondly, many screenplays are published in collections. When this is true, the catalog user may not find any cards filed under the name of the film at all. If only a few screenplays are published together, the user may find cards under the film title giving the name

112    FILM STUDY COLLECTIONS

of the collection—but, on the other hand, there may only be cards showing the editor and title of the collection. The answer to this situation is found in the reference collection of the library. There are indexes to screenplays, such as McCarty[2] and Poteet[3], where screenplays that are published separately, in collections, in magazines, in entirety, and excerpted are listed. Both these reference books are outdated, and nothing has yet been published on a continuing basis to locate screenplays.

---
[2] McCarty, Clifford. *Published Screenplays: A Checklist.* 1st ed. Kent, Ohio: Kent State University, 1971. (Serif Series: bibliographies and checklists, No. 18.)
[3] Poteet, G. Howard. *Published Radio, Television, and Film Scripts: A Bibliography.* Troy, N.Y.: Whitson Pub. Co., 1975.

# 13

# Cataloging and Classification of Film Study Material

(by Michael Gorman)

Cataloging and classification are the main tools used by the librarian in organizing the materials that the library holds. Traditionally, both activities have focused upon books and other printed materials. The so-called nonbook materials, both of the established kind such as manuscripts and maps and of the "new" kind typified by audiovisual materials, have been fitted into the book-based systems. This traditional approach is changing. *The Anglo-American Cataloguing Rules* (second edition[1]) is the first expression in English of a truly integrated approach to the descriptive cataloging of all library materials. The movement, pioneered in the United States and Canada, to shelve all library materials in one classified sequence has brought the advantages of systematic arrangement to all the items that a library holds, book and nonbook alike.

The film study librarian has to be concerned with the organization of all kinds of library material. Both the eclectic nature of film study and the various types of documents which contain the information

---
[1] Anglo-American Cataloguing Rules. Edited by Michael Gorman and Paul W. Winkler. 2nd ed. Chicago: American Library Association, 1978.

the film study student or researcher needs dictate that the film study library should give equal treatment to all the items that it holds and that it should make those items equally available. The first question that faces a librarian with a mixed media collection is whether to have a single integrated catalog or a separate catalog for each medium. Except in special circumstances (such as a heavily used special single medium collection with little interaction with other collections), the answer is certainly that a single integrated catalog is preferable. Most students and researchers are indifferent to the *form* in which information is to be found. What concerns the film student (and serious researchers in every subject) is the *nature* of the information. This change in attitude has resulted from the growing acceptance of microfilms, filmstrips, sound recordings, etc. and from the improved technical quality of such media.

Before examining the solutions to the problems involved in cataloging and classifying film study materials, it is necessary to state those problems. The problems center on nonbook materials and the integration of those materials with books. Enough has been written about the organization of books and of records of books to make any further description unnecessary. This chapter will, therefore, concentrate on nonbooks.

## Manuscripts

Manuscripts—and in this term one includes single-copy typescripts and manuscript collections—are uniquely valuable because they are unique. The manuscripts or original typescripts of screenplays are essential source documents for the film student. Because of their uniqueness and value, it is important that the catalog records relating to them should be full and precise. All the special characteristics of a manuscript item should be recorded so that the researcher is spared unnecessary examination of the item itself. In describing a manuscript, the most commonly encountered problem is that the manuscript may lack authoritative sources of information about itself. It may be undated or lack a statement of authorship or even a title. The cataloger must therefore go beyond the normal cataloging functions involved in recording data and may have to deduce and supply the information given in the catalog entry. When one adds to this the need to be more detailed than usual when cataloging manuscripts, it is evident that such cataloging demands both skill and time.

A particular problem faced by the film study librarian lies in the necessity of reconciling the information about a film given on a manuscript (or a unique typescript) and the information about that film given in the credits of the film itself. Essential information such as the names of the persons responsible for the screenplay and the film, or even the title of the film, may vary as between the manuscript and the final print of the film. Since the information appearing on the film is likely to be regarded as authoritative, it is essential that the cataloger of screenplays crosscheck with records about the finished film in order to provide all necessary points of access to the screenplay. The classification and arrangement of manuscripts present no special difficulty.

## Audiovisual Materials

An essential problem in dealing with audiovisual materials (filmstrips, slide/tape sets, etc.) is due to the fact that their use requires the use of a machine. In cataloging such materials, it is necessary not only to describe the item or items but also to give an indication (whether implicit or explicit) of how the item is to be used. Another problem centers on the source of information to be used in cataloging audiovisual items. Differing information can commonly be found on the item itself, on accompanying printed materials, and in the credits found at the beginning of the piece. The question of "authorship" also becomes complicated when one is dealing with audiovisual materials.

In classifying and arranging audiovisual materials, one is presented with both a physical and an intellectual problem. Physically it is not easy to integrate these materials with other materials held in the library, though some libraries have shown that it can be done and that, once done, such integration can increase the use of the collection. The intellectual problem resides in the difficulty of assigning a subject, because many of these materials can be seen as falling into a number of subject areas. This may partially be overcome by assigning a number of subject headings, though this does not solve the problem of assigning a single classification number.

## Stills, Photographs, and Printed Ephemera

These materials are, of course, of great importance to the film student and researcher. Their bibliographic control does not present any major intellectual difficulty to the librarian. Such difficulties as there are in dealing with these materials concern their possible rarity (which implies detailed cataloging) and the physical problems of housing and arranging them. An important matter which needs to be considered by the cataloger of stills, photographs, and printed ephemera is that of approach. It consists of deciding whether one should catalog each item individually or adopt the strategy of recording information relating to groups of related materials. The latter approach is that favored, mostly for practical resaons, by archives. Access to individual items is indirect in that the user of the collection has to locate a group of materials and then either consult a brief listing of the contents of that group or simply look through the group for the desired item. Such archival recording has the advantages of being inexpensive and speedy. It does not, however, provide the precise recall of individual library cataloging.

## Some Solutions

### Descriptive Cataloging

The second edition of the *Anglo-American Cataloguing Rules* (AACR2) contains, as has been stated, a truly integrated approach to all library materials. It contains complete instructions on the entry and description of all those materials. This is of particular importance to those, like the film study librarian, who wish to maintain a single coherent catalog of items belonging to a number of types of materials.

The headings (access points) provided for by AACR2 are based upon the principles of personal authorship and upon a consideration of corporate responsibility. The principle of personal authorship calls for an entry for each item under the person chiefly responsible for the intellectual or artistic content of a work, and for added entries under other people with some responsibility for that intellectual or artistic content. The consideration of corporate responsibility calls for an entry under a corporate body if that corporate body has played a part in the production of an item which goes beyond that of issuing the item or of underwriting it financially. These detailed rules boil down to the idea that a catalog should contain an entry under each name (of a person or a body) that provides useful access to the work cataloged. For film study materials, such names might include those of the producers, directors, screenwriters, principal photographers, and principal actors of the films, or their related materials. AACR2 also calls for entries to be made under the titles by which a work is identified. These include not only the title found on a piece (film, screenplay, etc.) but also other titles by which a work has been identified (for example, the original title of a film).

The rules for the description of library materials in AACR2 apply equally to all materials. That is, the descriptions resulting from these rules resemble each other closely whether they deal with printed texts, manuscripts, or audiovisual materials. (For examples of these descriptions see the end of this section.) Within this generalized approach the problems of each major type of material are dealt with separately.

The AACR2, in its description of manuscripts and manuscript collections (in which are included single-copy typescripts), covers all the major problems encountered in dealing with these materials. The sources of information for cataloging data are listed—the primary source is, of course, the manuscript itself; and, within the manuscript, title pages are preferred. The rules instruct the cataloger to supply a title when the manuscript lacks one, and specify that the title should be, where possible, the title by which a subsequently published work (in this instance, the film) is known. The rules on the physical description of manuscripts deal separately with individual manuscripts and with manuscript collections. In the latter case, the physical description contains either the number of items in the collection described, or, in the case of more extensive collections, the number of linear feet of shelf space occupied. The various notes required in cataloging manuscripts are also described and exemplified in these rules.

The rules on the description of audiovisual materials are to be found in the chapters dealing with motion pictures, sound recordings, and graphics. The *Rules* also contains instructions about the description of materials which are made up of two or more different types of material ("multimedia items"). As with other materials, the descriptions resulting from these chapters all follow the same formula and only differ one from another in the bibliographic content appropriate to each type of material. The *Rules* contains instructions on the addition of "general material designations"—words immediately following the main title which indicate the general class of material to which the item belongs. Examples of these are:

The making of Citizen Kane [filmstrip]
Man of Aran [motion picture]
Movie music of the '40s [sound recording]
Studying the movies [kit]

These general material designations act as an "early warning" to the catalog user in that they are an early-encountered indication of the type of material with which that user has to deal. The *Rules* deals comprehensively with the publication and distribution details relating to audiovisual materials and allows the cataloger to include the names of persons or bodies responsible for publication, distribution, or production of the item in the body of the catalog description. Further, the cataloger can, where necessary, add a word or phrase indicating the responsibility of the person or body named, as in:

London : Wheeler Films [production company], 1978
New York : Carroll [producer] : Simpson Inc. [distributor], 1978

The physical description of each item indicates the number of parts of which an item is made; other physical details special to the type of material described; the dimensions of the item; and a specification of any accompanying materials, as in:

1 filmstrip (70 fr.): b.&w.; 35 mm.
1 sound disc (20 min.) : 33⅓ rpm, stereo.; 12 in. + 20 slides : col.

A different approach to the description of unpublished script materials is that taken by the Documentation Commission of the Federation Internationale des Archives du Film (FIAF). The main emphasis of the FIAF is on the cataloging of films themselves. In attempting to achieve international agreement on the cataloging of films, they have become interested in the cataloging of film-related materials. The description of scripts, in particular, emphasizes the necessity of integrating the records of the films with the records of their scripts. The FIAF rules for cataloging scripts,[2] described by Bowser,[3] begin with instruction on formulating the name of the film in terms of its original title, the name of the country of origin, the name of the director, and the year of first showing, as in:

*Regles du jeu, Les* (France, Renoir, 1939)
*Sting, The* (U.S., Hill, 1973)

This name of the film is followed by the word "Script" and one of four Roman numbers indicating the type of script, so that, for example, "Script IV" indicates that a script contains only the dialogue and does not describe the action. The cataloger then adds the title of the script (only if it differs from the title of the film) and the names of the screenwriters, etc. who are named on the script. The date given on the script is added and the number of pages in the script. Any notes on other matters of importance (such as the language of the script if it is different from the language of the film) are given last in the description. (Examples of FIAF entries for scripts may be found at the end of this section.)

The differences between the AACR2 and FIAF approaches to the description of scripts are partly trivial; such differences could be relatively easily resolved. Other differences result from the different intentions of the two sets of rules. AACR2 is a detailed set of rules intended to provide standardized cataloging for a wide range of materials resulting in a single integrated catalog. The FIAF *Guidelines*

---

[2] Fédération Internationale des Archives du Film. Guidelines for Describing Unpublished Script Materials. 1st ed. Commission de documentation: Brussels, 1974.
[3] Bowser, Eileen. "Guidelines for Describing Unpublished Script Materials." *Performing Arts Resources*, Vol. 2 (New York: New York Drama Book Specialists, 1975), pp. 1–7.

are intended for catalogs of script collections which are in harmony with the catalogs of the films themselves. The choice of which rules to follow depends entirely upon the nature of the library (general or specialized) and the intentions of the catalog being considered.

---

EXAMPLES OF SCRIPTS CATALOGED BY BOTH *AACR2* AND FIAF *GUIDELINES*

1. *AACR2*
   Clifford, William H.
      The bottomless pit [manuscript] / scenario by William H. Clifford and Thomas H. Ince. — [1915?].
      [25] p. ; 26 cm.
      Typescript with handwritten notations throughout. — Describes the action of "The bottomless pit" in separate shots. — Contains shooting schedule and list of locations. — Edges burned.
      I. Title II. Ince, Thomas H.

   FIAF *Guidelines*
   BOTTOMLESS PIT, THE (US, Scott Sidney, 1915)
   *Script II*. Scenario by William H. Clifford and Thomas H. Ince. ca. 25 p. Handwritten notations throughout. Contains shooting schedules and list of locations. Edges burned by fire.

2. *AACR2*
   Lawson, John Howard
      The river is blue [manuscript] / by John Howard Lawson. — 1938 Feb. 28.
      126 p. ; 27 cm.
      Typescript. — "Final continuity" script describing the action in separate shots of the film "Blockade" (US, 1938)
      I. Title II. Blockade (motion picture)

   FIAF *Guidelines*
   BLOCKADE (US, William Dieterle, 1938)
   *Script II*, "final continuity." The river is blue, by John Howard Lawson. 28 Feb. 1938. 126 p.

---

# Subject Headings

The complexities and intricacies of the subject element of the dictionary catalog are well known to librarians but probably not widely understood by library users. The two essential problems of any verbal subject system are, first, the terminology, and, second, the reference structure which relates one subject to another. It is in both of these areas that the systematic assignment of subject headings from a list claims superiority over indexing by means of keywords in titles. When one provides access by keywords the vocabulary is uncontrolled and the headings are not related. One should, therefore, judge a list of subject headings (in particular, *the* list of subject headings, The Library of Congress *List of Subject Headings*[4] (LCSH) by how superior its terminology and reference structure are. LCSH is the most widely used list of subject headings in the world and its problems affect librarians and the users of all kinds of libraries both general and special.

The problem with the terminology found in LCSH relating to film study is a familiar one in considering any "new" or changing subject. Subject heading lists tend to be hard to change. In dealing with a subject which has grown immensely both in volume of publications and in its ramifications, this inflexibility imposes a serious burden on the library user. Ordinary people speak of the "movies" or the "film" and may be presumed to think of those terms when approaching a library catalog. It is unlikely that they would instinctively think of the term "moving pictures" to designate the general topic of film. Yet this is the term used in the most up-to-date edition of LCSH. Other examples such as "Cinematography—Trick" (for special effects) and "Moving Picture Authorship" (for screenwriting) show the difficulties experienced in adapting to a changing world. These difficulties, however genuine, are small consolation to the baffled user of the catalog. There is a crying need for the subject catalog to match the terminology of the average informed user. This need is greatest in "new" subjects such as film study. Probably only in a computer environment can speedy adaptation leading to current terminology be guaranteed.

Related to the subject of terminology is the problem of the order of terms in complex subject heading lists. The LCSH headings "Animation (Cinematography)" and "Moving Pictures, Musical" illustrate two approaches—the first, of the direct heading which scatters related subjects; the second, of the inverted heading which groups related topics. Examples of the two approaches abound in LCSH, often seeming to support a charge of inconsistency and certainly leading to uncertainty in the mind of the catalog user as she or he seeks these complex subjects.

---

[4] Library of Congress. *List of Subject Headings.* 8th ed. Washington, D.C.: Library of Congress, 1975.

The reference structure embodied in LCSH is complex. It attempts to relate chains of subjects (usually in the order general subject to special subject). Often these chains of subjects extend to many hundreds of relationships. Catalog use studies (e.g., the 1958 ALA study[5]) show that this complex apparatus of "see also" references is little understood and less used by the catalog user. Some lack of use is undoubtedly due to the most common physical form of catalog (the card catalog), in which many references are never even seen by the user; but the main reason for economizing in the application of references is that few people have the time or motivation required to trace complex chains of subjects. In other words, the average user is interested in a specific subject and uninterested in the kind of comprehensive subject search which the reference structure is intended to help accomplish.

Given the problems of LCSH and the fact that no general subject list can hope to deal adequately with a special subject collection of some depth, the inevitable question of a special subject list arises. There is no doubt that such lists have been compiled in many subject areas with varying degrees of success. Two factors seem to be crucial here. First, that the special list should be compiled by an authoritative national, or preferably international, body. Second, that the process should involve as many people and institutions as possible in compiling the list and in maintaining it. Another desirable feature (for the United States, at least) is that the special list should be an extension and refinement of LCSH, using the same conventions. These criteria being met, there is no reason why a separate, specialized film study subject-heading list should not be drawn up by such bodies as the American Film Institute, in cooperation with like institutions in Canada, Australia, Great Britain, and other English-speaking nations.

## Classification

Classification schemes are used by librarians in all kinds of libraries to arrange their materials and to compile shelflists and classed catalogs. As with subject headings, the choice for the film study librarian lies between general widely used schemes and specialized film-study schemes. Unlike subject headings, however, there are two widely used and often diametrically opposed general classification schemes and some specialized film study classifications which exist now or are in a late stage of development.

---

[5] American Library Association. *Catalog Use Study*. Edited by V. Mostecky. Chicago: ALA, 1958.

122   FILM STUDY COLLECTIONS

The most widely used classification scheme in the world is the Decimal Classification of Melvil Dewey (DC) now in its 18th edition.[6] It is securely based on a division of knowledge into ten main areas which, by and large, represent disciplines rather than things. So, for example, the subject "Houses" is scattered between the disciplines of "Building" (in the applied science class) and "Architecture" (in the fine arts class). This approach affects the film study collection greatly. The important topic of "Educational films" is to be found, as a subdivision of Education, at 371.355; many topics germane to film study can be found in Photography (778), and these are separated by a mass of irrelevant (to the film student) topics from the topic of the film as a recreation/art form which is given the number 791.43; some works relevant to "the film as literature" can be found in the Literature (811) class, but screenplays and works on screenplays appear at 791.437 (a subdivision of film). DC allows two alternative practices in dealing with bibliographic and biographical material. They can either be gathered together with subject subdivisions in 016 (bibliography) and 920 (biography) or can be classed with the subject with the appropriate subdivision. Thus, a bibliography of photography can appear at either 016.778 or 778.016, and a biography of a movie star can appear at either 927.9143 or 791.43092. Specialized collections are strongly advised to group bibliographical and biographical materials with the subject (i.e., in the examples given above, at the second number), as this is a more effective grouping for retrieval and for the browser. Whatever the problems caused for the film study librarian by the discipline approach of DC, it still has a number of advantages. These are: relative up-to-dateness caused by regular revision of the schedules; great specificity in numbering a subject, which is effective at least to the level of monographic materials; and a general rationality of organization which by and large groups books in an acceptably useful manner.

The Library of Congress classification scheme[7] deals with film topics in the P (Literature) class at PN 1993–1999 (subdivisions of "special types of drama") and in the T (Technology) class at TR 845–899 (subdivisions of "Photography"). This imperfect placing of the subject—there is no number for film topics in the N (fine arts) class—is compounded by the obsolescence of the LC schedules which are erratically and only partially revised. The American Film Institute (AFI) has made an expanded schedule[8] of the LC "PN" and "TR" classes

---

[6]*Dewey Decimal Classification and Relative Index* 18th ed. Lake Placid, N.Y.: Forest Press, 1971.

[7]Library of Congress. *Classification*. Catalog Division: Washington, D.C., 1902— .

[8]American Film Institute. Center for Advanced Film Studies. Charles K. Feldman Library. 501 Doheny Rd., Beverly Hills, Cal. 90210.

which preserves the basic numbers, adds other numbers, and adds definitions to the existing numbers. The AFI application of LC also allows for general groupings of Periodical and Reference material. This reworking is highly recommended to film study libraries in a general LC environment and for special film study libraries which already use the "unexpanded" LC.

The Museum of Modern Art has a special classification for film books[9] based on neither LC nor DC. It is used in their published catalog. A detailed scheme devised by Michael Moulds for FIAF is similarly unrelated to the two major general schemes.[10] The Moulds scheme is recommended by FIAF and is already used in the Danish Film Museum and the Netherlands Film Museum. It divides the topic of film and TV into "Reference materials" (FTO) "Institutions, etc," "Film and Television industry," "Distribution, etc.," "Society and cinema," "Education," "Aesthetics and theory," "History, genres, and specific films," "Biography," and "Miscellaneous and special collections." This scheme employs an ingenious notation in which numbers relating to both film and television start with FT, numbers relating to film start with F, and numbers relating to television with T. The scheme is comprehensive, detailed, and rational in the order which it gives to a special film study collection.

A classification-connected topic of great importance to the film study library is the physical integration of the collection. I have already stated that catalog records relating to different types of material should be interfiled. It has proven to be of great advantage to extend this policy to the materials themselves. To be truly effective a classification scheme should display to the user all the materials which the library currently has available in a given subject area. For some materials this interfiling is not possible. Others, such as microforms, filmstrips, and tape/slide sets, can be put in boxes which are specially manufactured to be shelved with books on bookshelves. When possible, these boxes should be used to enable the library to display all its resources equally. Even when items cannot be interfiled, those relating to the same subject area can be kept in proximity so that a user going to the shelves for works on photography, for example, will find all the books and nonprint materials on that topic either interfiled or grouped together.

---

[9] Museum of Modern Art. Library. 21 W. 53rd St. New York, N.Y. 10019.

[10] Moulds, Michael. *Classification Scheme for Literature, Film and Television*. Abridged version. London (27 Mildmay Grove, London, N.1.): Moulds, 1978. 10 duplicated pages.

# 14
# Survey of Film Study Libraries

Despite the importance of script collections and other special materials on film study, there is no general and comprehensive survey of the locations of these materials. Up to now there have been only two works which attempt this task, and both of these are of limited value to the film student. The two works are William C. Young's *American Theatrical Arts*,[1] which is concerned with theater collections but includes a description of some collections of film-related material, and Linda Mehr's *Motion Pictures, Television and Radio*,[2] an excellent and timely work which is limited to eleven western states. There is, therefore, a clear need for an up-to-date and comprehensive survey locating collections of value, which also gives useful information about the libraries that hold those collections. My aim was to provide film scholars with a detailed picture of the working collections of film study materials in the United States.

In January 1978, questionnaires were sent to a random sample of

---
[1] Young, William C. *American Theatrical Arts: A Guide to Manuscripts and Special Collections in the United States and Canada.* Chicago: American Library Association, 1971.
[2] Mehr, Linda Harris, comp. and ed. *Motion Pictures, Television, and Radio: A Union Catalogue of Manuscript and Special Collections in the Western United States.* Boston: G. K. Hall, 1977.

libraries affiliated with colleges and universities offering a degree in film studies or in a related area with emphasis on film. This pretest showed only minor difficulties with the form of the questionnaire, which was designed with the help of the Survey Research Laboratory of the University of Illinois. The limitations on the scope of the survey represented a deliberate attempt to pinpoint working collections with some internal rationale and consistency dependent on their practical use. The list of schools was taken from the second edition of the American Film Institute's *Guide to College Courses in Film and Television*.[3] The survey covered several areas of library operations. First, there were several questions pertaining to the location, size, and strengths of the book and periodical holdings in the area of film study. The next group of questions centered on the existence of script and other special collections, especially those collections containing unpublished scripts. The following group of questions concerned stills, films, and other nonprint or promotional materials of use in film study held by the library. The last group of questions dealt with the responsibilities within the library for supplying and selecting films and books for individual and classroom use. A supplementary form was appended to the survey for details of the library's interlibrary loan policy.

Shortly after the initial mailing of questionnaires, the third edition of the AFI *Guide* was published. This edition was used for the second mailing of questionnaires. This resulted in a revised mailing list based on the new listing of schools offering film study degrees. There was some lack of overlap in the two mailings because some schools on the first mailing list did not appear on the second. Any library responding to either mailing is shown in the survey results unless the library requested that they not be listed. The usual reason for this request was that the library felt the holdings were not substantial enough to warrant inclusion. In both mailings, only schools offering degrees were contacted—those with coursework only were not included in the study. The total number of libraries surveyed was 194. Of these, 93 responded fully, and 16 responded with partial information.

Some of the latter were so incomplete they warranted noninclusion. It took until September 1978 to gather the total of 103 listings. After summary statements of the results were prepared, copies were sent to all respondents with a letter requesting updating or revision of the information supplied. It is important to note that the results given here are not verified. I did not visit each library to check the statistics they supplied or the existence of special collections. It is therefore

---

[3] See citation, p. 6.

possible that special holdings, papers, correspondence, and documents on individuals connected to the motion picture industry do exist in libraries surveyed even if they are not indicated here. Especially in large libraries, the individual filling out the survey form may not be aware of all the library's holdings. Moreover, the questionnaire emphasized collections of unpublished scripts rather than collections of papers and correspondence.

I see this survey as a contribution toward the eventual establishment of a comprehensive and detailed union catalog of special collections and unpublished scripts. There are many such holdings in libraries not supporting film study degree programs, so with only a few exceptions the findings shown here represent only the working collections and not the equally important collections in other libraries.

The statistics given here concern only those library holdings on the subject of film study. This excludes the use of film in education or other allied areas such as television or radio broadcasting. The figures have been rounded. One important problem in interpreting these results lies in the fact that definitions of "serial" vary from library to library. For this reason, results centering on serials should be read as indicating the general nature and size of serial holdings rather than as precise and accurate results.

## Summary Results of the Survey

Taken question by question, results are as follows:

Q. Is there a librarian specifically responsible for the subject area of film studies? If so, has this individual received any special training?

A. 43.7 percent said there was no special film studies librarian; 50 percent said there was such a person; 6.3 percent did not respond to this question. Of those who said they had a film studies librarian, 33 percent said this person had had some kind of training, and 66 percent said he or she had no special training in film studies.

Q. Who selects library materials in film studies?

A. 7 percent said only librarians select library material, 8.8 percent said only teaching faculty select library material, and 70 percent said both librarians and teachers select library material. The minor responses included 3.5 percent who indicated that both faculty, librarian, and a third party such as a media center or students selected material. There was an 8.8 percent rate of no response.

Q. How are films made available and who is responsible for making them available?

A. 30 percent said they both rented and purchased films for classroom showing; 22.5 percent of the responding libraries only rent; and 3.7 percent only purchase. 14.3 percent rent as well as borrow films from some kind of cooperative, and 9.2 percent indicated other responses. Of these, 6 percent said they used films from the local public library. 20.3 percent did not respond to this question. This high no-response rate is probably a result of the fact that many libraries have little or nothing to do with showing films. 13.8 percent of the responding libraries indicated that the library arranges the film showings for classes and also makes films available to individuals. 18.3 percent said the teaching department arranges individual and classroom film showings. 11 percent said both the library and the department take some role in classroom and individual film viewings, and 16.5 percent said a media center took care of the arrangements. 18.3 percent did not respond to this question, and 21.1 percent indicated that a different arrangement exists for classroom viewings than for individual viewings. Nine percent said that no arrangements were made for individuals to view films.

Q. How much money did the library spend on film study material in 1976–7?

A.

| Amount spent | Percentage of libraries responding |
|---|---|
| Less than $100 | 2.7% |
| $101–$299 | 4.5 |
| $300–$499 | 5.4 |
| $500–$999 | 14.5 |
| $1,000–$1,999 | 9.0 |
| $2,000–$2,999 | 4.5 |
| $3,000–$4,999 | 2.7 |
| $5,000 and up | 2.7* |

*Although one library indicated a $15,000 expenditure which included the purchase of films.

20 percent gave no figure and said there was no separate budget for this subject, and 26.7 percent did not respond to this question. Although some libraries said that there was no separate accounting for film study expenditure, they gave an estimated expenditure. These figures are included in the table above.

AMERICAN UNIVERSITY LIBRARY
Massachusetts and Nebraska Aves.
Washington, D.C. 20016
Other locations: Some books, periodicals, and films are housed at the Cinema Studies Department, Ward Circle Building 310.

| | |
|---|---|
| Size of film studies collection: | 1,300 books, with strength in cinematography and filmmaking technique; 32 serial titles, 29 currently received. |
| Special collections, unpublished scripts: | None. |
| Nonprint and other library material: | None. |
| Interlibrary loan policy summary: | Books are lent for three weeks. Journal articles, including those on microfilm, are copied for a fee. Dissertations prior to 1958 are lent for three weeks. |

AUBURN UNIVERSITY
Ralph Brown Draughon Library
Ashburn, Ala. 36830

| | |
|---|---|
| Other locations: | Approximately 300 books are housed in the Speech Department. |
| Size of film studies collection: | 1,140 books, with strengths in theory and history; 27 serial titles, 20 currently received. |
| Special collections, unpublished scripts: | None. |
| Nonprint and other library material: | None. |
| Interlibrary loan policy summary: | Books, microfilm, and dissertations are lent for two weeks. Articles are copied for a fee. |

BARD COLLEGE
Kellogg-Hoffman Library
Annandale-on-Hudson
New York, N.Y. 12504

| | |
|---|---|
| Size of film studies collection: | 220 books; 8 serial titles, all currently received. |
| Special collections, unpublished scripts: | Approximately 50 scripts by Alvin Sapinsley for a network TV series. |
| Nonprint and other library material: | None. |
| Interlibrary loan policy summary: | Books are lent on approval. Articles are copied. |

BOB JONES UNIVERSITY
Mack Library
Greenville, S.C. 29614

| | |
|---|---|
| Other locations: | Various materials are housed in the Cinema Department. |
| Size of film studies collection: | 400 monographs; a few periodicals. |
| Special collections, unpublished scripts: | None. |
| Nonprint and other library material: | None. |
| Interlibrary loan policy summary: | Monographs are lent. |

BOSTON UNIVERSITY
Mugar Memorial Library
771 Commonwealth Ave.
Boston, Mass. 02215

Special collections, unpublished scripts: Among others, papers of Mary Astor, Nathaniel Benchley, Bette Davis, Evan Hunter, Gene Kelly, Roddy McDowall, Anthony Newley, Frank Nugent, Claude Rains, Max Shulman, Leonard Spigelgass, and Sam Wanamaker. See Young[1] for further information.

BRIGHAM YOUNG UNIVERSITY LIBRARIES
Provo, Utah 84602

Size of film studies collection: 2,265 monographs; 35 serial titles, 19 of which are currently received, 21 of which are substantially complete.

Special collections, unpublished scripts: 500 unpublished scripts, including 275 Cecil B. DeMille scripts, 80 television scripts from *Streets of San Francisco,* 79 scripts, stories, and synopses of Howard Hawks films, 65 other scripts, the Dean Jagger Collection (4 boxes), National Association of Theatre Owners (30 cartons), Republic Pictures Music Archives (600 cartons, 6,000 discs), Mark Evans Collection (5 cartons of tapes of interviews with show business personalities in the 1970s), the Andy Devine Collection (8 cartons), and approximately 20 smaller collections.

Nonprint and other library holdings: 700 stills, 200 posters, 3 16mm films, 1 videotape.

Interlibrary loan policy summary: Books and theses are lent for two weeks. Copies of articles, including those on microfilm, and copies of stills and photos are made for a fee.

BROOKLYN COLLEGE LIBRARY
Bedford Ave. and Ave. H
Brooklyn, N.Y. 11210

Size of film studies collection: 925 monographs, with emphasis on theory and history. Number of serials not given.

Special collections, unpublished scripts: None.

| | |
|---|---|
| Nonprint and other library material: | None. |
| Interlibrary loan policy summary: | Books are lent. Photocopies are made for a fee. Microfilm is not lent. |

## CALIFORNIA COLLEGE OF ARTS AND CRAFTS
Meyer Library
5212 Broadway
Oakland, Cal. 94618

| | |
|---|---|
| Other locations: | Film and slides are housed at the Media Center. |
| Size of film studies collection: | 200 monographs; 26 serials, 19 currently received, with 6 substantially complete sets. |
| Special collections, unpublished scripts: | None. |
| Nonprint and other library material: | 1,000 slides; 50 16mm films. |
| Interlibrary loan policy summary: | Books are lent for from two to four weeks. Back issues of unbound periodicals are lent for four weeks. Articles in bound periodicals, and theses are copied. |

## CALIFORNIA INSTITUTE OF THE ARTS LIBRARY
24700 McBean Parkway
Vallencia, Cal. 91355

| | |
|---|---|
| Size of film studies collection: | 1,900 monographs, with strength in theory and history; 60 currently received periodicals, 83 serial back sets. |
| Special collections, unpublished scripts: | 60 scripts. |
| Nonprint and other library material: | 130 slides and 550 films for film study. |
| Interlibrary loan policy summary: | Only books are lent. |

## CALIFORNIA LUTHERAN COLLEGE
Thousand Oaks, Cal. 91360

| | |
|---|---|
| Size of film studies collection: | 200 monographs; 1 periodical. |
| Special collections, unpublished scripts: | A few screenplays. For titles, see Mehr, Linda, *A Union Catalogue* [2] |
| Nonprint and other library material: | None. |
| Interlibrary loan policy summary: | Not given. |

## CALIFORNIA STATE UNIVERSITY LIBRARY AT FRESNO
Fresno, Cal. 93740

| | |
|---|---|
| Other locations: | Films are housed in the English Department, and films, research reports, and texts are housed at the Instructional Media Center. |
| Size of film studies collection: | 1,520 monographs, with strengths in |

| | theory and history; 14 serial titles, 10 currently received, 9 substantially complete back sets. |
|---|---|
| Nonprint and other library material: | None. |
| Interlibrary loan policy summary: | Books are lent for two weeks. Periodicals, microfilm, and theses are not lent. |

CALIFORNIA STATE UNIVERSITY LIBRARY AT FULLERTON
P. O. Box 4150
Fullerton, Cal. 92634

| | |
|---|---|
| Size of film studies collection: | 1,070 monographs; 36 serial titles, 24 currently received, 6 substantially complete back sets. |
| Special collections, unpublished scripts: | Approximately 50 scripts, including *Star Trek* scripts, Hal Roach (*Our Gang*) scripts, *Adventure Tomorrow* TV scripts. |
| Nonprint and other library material: | 1,300 stills; 378 posters. |
| Interlibrary loan policy summary: | Books are lent for two weeks with possible renewal. Articles in periodicals are copied for a fee. Microfilm may be copied or lent for one week with possible renewal. Unpublished scripts are lent for one week with possible renewal. Theses are lent for two weeks with possible renewal. |

CARLETON COLLEGE LIBRARY
Northfield, Minn. 55057

| | |
|---|---|
| Size of film studies collection: | 33 monographs; 10 serial titles. |
| Special collections, unpublished scripts: | 22 scripts. |
| Nonprint and other library material: | None. |
| Interlibrary loan policy summary: | Books are lent. |

CALIFORNIA STATE UNIVERSITY AT LOS ANGELES
John F. Kennedy Memorial Library
5151 State University Dr.
Los Angeles, Cal. 91330

| | |
|---|---|
| Special collections, unpublished scripts: | Anthony Quinn Collection. See Mehr[2] for details. |

CALIFORNIA STATE UNIVERSITY AT NORTHRIDGE
Delmar T. Oviatt and South Libraries
18111 Nordhoff St.
Northridge, Cal. 91330

| | |
|---|---|
| Special collections, unpublished scripts: | Ray Martin Collection of film scores. See Mehr[2] for details. |

**CASE WESTERN RESERVE UNIVERSITY**
University Libraries
11161 East Blvd.
Cleveland, Ohio 44106

Size of film studies collection: A recently acquired collection. It contains about 70 feet of books and serials. There are many film annuals from 1936 to the present, and some stills.

Special collections, unpublished scripts: None.
Nonprint and other library material: A few posters, stills, and slides.
Interlibrary loan policy summary: Not given.

**CENTRAL MICHIGAN UNIVERSITY**
Park Library
Mt. Pleasant, Mich. 48859

Size of film studies collection: 140 monographs; 40 serial titles, 25 currently received.

Special collections, unpublished scripts: None.
Nonprint and other library material: None.
Interlibrary loan policy summary: Books and photocopies are lent. Some microfilm and theses are lent.

**CENTRAL MISSOURI STATE UNIVERSITY**
Ward Edwards Library
Warrensburg, Mo. 64093

Other locations: Some films are housed in the Wood Building.

Size of film studies collection: 330 monographs, with emphasis in cinematography and filmmaking; 16 serial titles, all currently received.

Special collections, unpublished scripts: None.
Nonprint and other library material: 32 feature films on 8mm and 16mm.
Interlibrary loan policy summary: Books are lent for two weeks. Periodicals, theses, microfilm, are not circulated.

**CITY COLLEGE, CITY UNIVERSITY OF NEW YORK**
Cohen Library
Convent Avenue at 135th Street
New York, N.Y. 10031

Other locations: Films are housed at the Theatre Arts Department, Shepard Hall, 138th

*Survey of Film Study Libraries* 133

| | |
|---|---|
| | St. and Convent Ave., and books on music and film are housed in the Music Library, Room 318A, Shepard Hall. |
| Size of film studies collection: | 1,000 monographs; 12 serial titles, all currently received. |
| Special collections, unpublished scripts: | Ira Marion Collection (ABC scriptwriter) includes about 50 scripts from the MGM series *Crime Does Not Pay* (1937–1945). |
| Nonprint and other library material: | 35 16mm films. |
| Interlibrary loan policy summary: | Books are lent for two weeks. Theses are lent for four weeks. Microfilm is sometimes lent, and photocopies are made. |

CLEVELAND INSTITUTE OF ART
Jessica Gund Memorial Library
11141 East Blvd.
Cleveland, Ohio 44106

| | |
|---|---|
| Size of film studies collection: | 140 monographs; a few serials. |
| Special collections, unpublished scripts: | None. |
| Nonprint and other library material: | Approximately 50 slides. |
| Interlibrary loan policy summary: | Not given. |

COLLEGE OF STATEN ISLAND—SUNNYSIDE CAMPUS
City University of New York
715 Ocean Terrace
Staten Island, N.Y. 10301

COLLEGE OF STATEN ISLAND—ST. GEORGE CAMPUS
130 Stuyvesant Place
Staten Island, N.Y. 10301

| | |
|---|---|
| Other locations: | 16mm films and video cassettes are housed at the Media Center Library. |
| Size of film studies collection: | Sunnyside Campus has 215 monographs. St. George Campus has 425 monographs. Both campuses have emphasis on theory and criticism. The total number of serial titles is 14, all currently received, with 13 back runs. |
| Special collections, unpublished scripts: | None. |
| Nonprint and other library material: | 76 feature films on 16mm. |
| Interlibrary loan policy summary: | Books are lent for 3 weeks. |

## COLUMBIA COLLEGE LIBRARY
P. O. Box 1849
Columbia, Cal. 95310

| | |
|---|---|
| Size of film studies collection: | 125 monographs; 4 serials. |
| Special collections, unpublished scripts: | None. |
| Nonprint and other library material: | None. |
| Interlibrary loan policy summary: | Books are lent for two weeks. Bound periodicals are lent for one week. |

## COLUMBIA UNIVERSITY
Butler Library
535 West 114th Street
New York, N.Y. 10027

| | |
|---|---|
| Other locations: | Some books and periodicals are housed in the Library Service Library and the Rare Book and Manuscript Library. The Oral History Research Office contains oral history transcripts. |
| Size of film studies collection: | Approximately 3,000 monographs; approximately 120 serial titles. |
| Special collections, unpublished scripts: | Robert J. Flaherty papers, including correspondence, journals, and manuscripts. The Oral History Collection "Popular Arts Project," which includes interviews with people involved in the development of motion pictures from early days to the present. Epstean Collection in The History and Science of Photography, which includes books and periodicals, and early and rare works on cinematography. Eleanor Belmont correspondence to the Motion Picture Research Council. The Eric Barnouw papers, which include correspondence, scripts, manuscripts, and reports. |
| Nonprint and other library material: | The Dramatic Library Portrait Collection (Rare Book and Manuscript Library) includes portraits and stills of movie stars from the 1920s through the 1950s. |
| Interlibrary loan policy summary: | Books are lent for four weeks. Some bound periodicals are lent for two weeks. Photocopies are available for a fee. |

CORNELL UNIVERSITY LIBRARY
Ithaca, N.Y. 14850

Although no information was supplied on the scope of the monograph collection of the library, special collections are shown in Young, William L., *American Theatrical Arts*. These include materials on Jean Cocteau, Irving R. Levine, Miklos Rosza, and others, as well as a collection of materials in the motion picture industry in Ithaca in the 1920s.

WILLIAM B. MEREDITH LIBRARY
Dartmouth College Library
Hanover, N.H. 03755
Details appear in the chapter on U.S. Archives.

DENISON UNIVERSITY LIBRARY
Granville, Ohio 43023

| | |
|---|---|
| Size of film studies collection: | 100 monographs; 12 serial titles, 10 currently received. |
| Special collections, unpublished scripts: | None. |
| Nonprint and other library material: | None. |
| Interlibrary loan policy summary: | Books are lent, and articles from journals and government documents will be copied for a fee. |

EASTERN MICHIGAN UNIVERSITY
Center of Educational Resources
Ypsilanti, Mich. 48197

| | |
|---|---|
| Size of film studies collection: | 1,000 monographs; 22 serial titles, 16 currently received. |
| Special collections, unpublished scripts: | None. |
| Nonprint and other library material: | 13 stills, 18 films on film study, 16 feature films on 16mm. |
| Interlibrary loan policy summary: | Monographs are lent. |

EMERSON COLLEGE
Abbot Memorial Library
303 Berkeley St.
Boston, Mass. 02116

| | |
|---|---|
| Size of film studies collection: | 825 monographs; serials not estimated. |
| Special collections, unpublished scripts: | None. |

Nonprint and other library material: 50 16mm feature films.
Interlibrary loan policy summary: Books are lent.

### EVERGREEN STATE COLLEGE
Library 1316
Olympia, Wash. 98505

Other locations: Nonprint materials for self-instruction are housed in Laboratory Building I.

Size of film studies collection: 1,050 monographs; 18 serial titles, 17 currently received. There are substantial or complete holdings of *Film Comment, Film Journal, Film Quarterly,* and *Society of Motion Picture Engineers.*

Special collections, unpublished scripts: None.

Nonprint and other library material: 50 films in film study, 1 video cassette, 8 feature films on 16mm, 3 instructional media packages.

Interlibrary loan policy summary: Books and film loops are lent. Photocopies of articles from periodicals and microfilm are provided.

### FLORIDA STATE UNIVERSITY
Robert Manning Strozier Library
Tallahassee, Fla. 32306

Size of film studies collection: 1,320 monographs; 41 periodicals.
Special collections, unpublished scripts: None.
Nonprint and other library material: None.
Interlibrary loan policy summary: Books are lent.

### FORDHAM UNIVERSITY LIBRARY
Bronx, N.Y. 10458

Other Locations: Monographs, including reference material are housed at Fordham University Library at the Lincoln Center.

Size of film studies collection: 775 monographs; 20 currently received periodicals.

Special collections, unpublished scripts: None.
Nonprint and other library material: 12 16mm feature films.
Interlibrary loan policy summary: Monographs are lent for four weeks. Pre-1962 theses are lent, and microfilm is lent.

HAMPSHIRE COLLEGE
Harold F. Johnson Library Center
Amherst, Mass. 01002

| | |
|---|---|
| Size of film studies collection: | 1,250 monographs, with emphasis on theory, history, and criticism, 28 serial titles, most currently received. |
| Special collections, unpublished scripts: | None. |
| Nonprint and other library material: | 65 8mm films; 370 16mm films, which includes films on film study; and over 80 documentaries. |
| Interlibrary loan policy summary: | American Library Association code is followed. |

HOFSTRA UNIVERSITY LIBRARY
1000 Fulton Ave.
Hempstead, N.Y. 11550

| | |
|---|---|
| Other locations: | Film, filmstrips, and videotapes are located at the University Technical and Media Services. |
| Size of film studies collection: | 14 bibliographies; 1,250 theory, history, and criticism monographs; 100 cinematography and filmmaking technical titles; 3 active; 1 inactive serial titles, 9 currently received periodicals. |
| Special collections, unpublished scripts: | Some theatrical materials on Harold Pinter. |
| Nonprint and other library material: | 2,300 stills. |
| Interlibrary loan policy summary: | Books are lent for four weeks. Copies provided from current, bound, and microfilm journals. Circulating theses are lent. Some stills may be lent. |

HOLLINS COLLEGE
Fishburn Library
Hollins College, Va. 24020

| | |
|---|---|
| Other locations: | 16mm sound films are housed in the Theatre Arts Department. |
| Size of film studies collection: | Approximately 300 monographs; 18 serial titles. |
| Special collections, unpublished scripts: | None. |
| Nonprint and other library material: | 11 8mm feature films, 21 16mm films. |

Interlibrary loan policy summary: American Library Association code is followed and photocopies of journal articles are provided.

**HOWARD UNIVERSITY LIBRARIES**
Channing Pollock Theatre Collection
500 Howard Place, N.W.
Washington, D.C. 20059

Size of film studies collection: 420 monographs, with emphasis on theory, criticism, and biography; 8 annuals; 26 currently received periodicals, of which 21 are substantially complete.
Special collections, unpublished scripts: The shooting script of John Cromwell's *Since You Went Away* (1944).
Nonprint and other library material: 12,377 Cabinet photos, 6,603 Carte de Visite photographs, 168 posters.
Interlibrary loan policy summary: Not given.

**HUMBOLDT STATE UNIVERSITY LIBRARY**
Arcata, Cal. 95521

Other locations: Films are housed at the Instructional Media Center.
Size of film studies collection: 1,250 monographs, with emphasis on theory, history, and criticism; 35 serial titles, 16 currently received, 9 of which are substantially complete.
Special collections, unpublished scripts: None.
Nonprint and other library materials: None.
Interlibrary loan policy summary: Books, theses, and some microfilm are lent. Copies of journal articles are available.

**HUNTER COLLEGE**
Hunter Arts Library
695 Park Avenue
New York, N.Y. 10021

Size of film studies collection: 1,350 monographs, with 500 filmmaking titles; 20 serial titles, 11 currently received, 6 substantially complete back sets.
Special collections, unpublished scripts: None.
Nonprint and other library material: None.
Interlibrary loan policy summary: Books are lent for four weeks; copies up to 25 pages free, 10¢ per page

after 25 pages; four weeks for MA theses only.

**INDIANA UNIVERSITY LIBRARY**
**Bloomington, Ind. 47401**

| | |
|---|---|
| Other locations: | The Fine Arts Library houses books, periodicals, and clipping files. The Institute for Sex Research Library houses some books, the Lilly Library houses the Welles Collection and other books, and the Media Center of the Undergraduate Library houses video tapes. |
| Size of film studies collection: | 2,500 monographs, with emphasis on theory, criticism, and history; 135 serial titles in the main collections, 69 of which are currently received periodicals, 36 of which have substantially complete back sets. |
| Special collections, unpublished scripts: | The John McGreevey (screenwriter) Collection; a substantial collection of source novels; the Welles Collection (a total of approximately 40 cartons—5 feet of recordings, 4 feet of film scripts, one half-carton of financial records and papers, 2½ cartons of correspondence, 10 cartons of radio scripts, several cartons of Mercury Theatre and other theater work); and approximately 500 other scripts and 600 pressbooks. |
| Nonprint and other library material: | 20 videotapes. |
| Interlibrary loan policy summary: | Monographs (except reference) and microfilm are lent; single copies are provided. |

**INDIANA UNIVERSITY LIBRARY AT SOUTH BEND**
**1700 Mishawaka Ave.**
**South Bend, Ind. 46615**

| | |
|---|---|
| Size of film studies collection: | 450 monographs; a few serial titles. |
| Special collections, unpublished scripts: | None. |
| Nonprint and other library material: | 49 16mm feature films. |
| Interlibrary loan policy summary: | Books are lent for three weeks; current periodicals and microfilm are lent for one week; bound periodicals are lent for three-day use. |

**INDIANA UNIVERSITY, NORTHWEST**
Library
3400 Broadway
Gary, Ind. 46408

| | |
|---|---|
| Size of film studies collection: | Approximately 50 monographs; 5 serials. |
| Special collections, unpublished scripts: | None. |
| Nonprint and other library material: | 6 16mm films on film study. |
| Interlibrary loan policy summary: | Books are lent for two weeks. |

**IOWA STATE UNIVERSITY LIBRARY**
Ames, Iowa 50011

| | |
|---|---|
| Other locations: | Films are housed at the Media Resources Center. |
| Size of film studies collection: | 1,400 monographs, with emphasis on theory and criticism; 62 series titles, 32 currently received, 25 back sets. |
| Special collections, unpublished scripts: | The American Archives of Factual Film houses 2,500–3,000 films (all nontheatrical), and is beginning an oral history program. There are approximately 50 feet of promotional materials, scripts, and other documents in the American Archives of Factual Film. |
| Nonprint and other library material: | None. |
| Interlibrary loan policy summary: | Books and theses are lent, and photocopies of articles are provided. |

**ITHACA COLLEGE LIBRARY**
Ithaca, N.Y. 14850

| | |
|---|---|
| Other locations: | Nonprint material is housed at the Film Library, Instructional Resources Center, and Dillingham Performing Arts Center. |
| Size of film studies collection: | 800 monographs; 25 serial titles. |
| Special collections, unpublished scripts: | None. |
| Nonprint and other library material: | None. |
| Interlibrary loan policy summary: | Books are lent for three weeks; duplicate theses are lent; copies of articles are available for a fee. |

**JACKSON STATE UNIVERSITY**
Henry T. Sampson Library
1325 John R. Lynch Street
Jackson, Miss. 39217

| | |
|---|---|
| Other locations: | Approximately 100 classical films and student-produced films are housed at the Department of Mass Communications. |
| Size of film studies collection: | 750 monographs; a few periodicals. |
| Special collections, unpublished scripts: | None. |
| Nonprint and other library material: | 350 stills, 25 posters, 2 16mm films. |
| Interlibrary loan policy summary: | Books are lent; copies of articles are made. |

JERSEY CITY STATE COLLEGE
Center for Media Technology and Communication Art
2039 Kennedy Blvd.
Jersey City, N.J. 07305

| | |
|---|---|
| Other locations: | Film criticism material is housed in the Forest A. Irwin Library; film technology material is housed in the Reference Room; and journals are housed in the Periodicals and Documents Library. |
| Size of film studies collection: | 530 monographs; 20 serial titles, 15 of which are currently received. |
| Special collections, unpublished scripts: | None. |
| Nonprint and other library material: | None. |
| Interlibrary loan policy summary: | Monographs, theses, and photocopies of journal articles are lent. |

JUNIATA COLLEGE
Beeghly Library
Huntington, Pa. 16652

| | |
|---|---|
| Size of film studies collection: | 200 monographs; a few journals. |
| Special collections, unpublished scripts: | None. |
| Nonprint and other library material: | 91 8 and 16mm films, 56 Super-8 cartridges. |
| Interlibrary loan policy summary: | Monographs are lent for four weeks. Photocopies of journal articles are made for a fee. |

KANSAS CITY ART INSTITUTE
Jessie Burnham Dowing Library
4421 Warwick Blvd.
Box 10360
Kansas City, Mo. 64111

| | |
|---|---|
| Size of film studies collection: | 385 monographs; a few journals. |

| | |
|---|---|
| Special collections, unpublished scripts: | None. |
| Nonprint and other library material: | 5 16mm feature films, 5 video cassettes. The Media Center, a separate department, has nonprint material. |
| Interlibrary loan policy summary: | Not given. |

**LOYOLA MARYMOUNT UNIVERSITY**
Van Der Ahe Library
Los Angeles, Cal. 90045

| | |
|---|---|
| Other locations: | Some nonprint material is housed in the Communications Arts Department. |
| Size of film studies collection: | 2,100 monographs, with emphasis on theory, criticism, and history; 12 journals. |
| Special collections, unpublished scripts: | 400 scripts, with collections of Arthur O'Connell material and television scripts. |
| Nonprint and other library material: | 300 stills, 200 posters, 5,000 slides, 200 films on film study, 15 16mm feature films, 2 35mm films, 20 videotapes. |
| Interlibrary loan policy summary: | Not given. |

**MASSACHUSETTS COLLEGE OF ART LIBRARY**
364 Brookline Ave.
Boston, Mass. 02215

| | |
|---|---|
| Size of film studies collection: | 750 monographs; 13 periodicals. |
| Special collections, unpublished scripts: | None. |
| Nonprint and other library material: | A few slides, 16 educational films on film study, 17 8mm feature films, 30 16mm feature films. |
| Interlibrary loan policy summary: | Books are lent. |

**MASSACHUSETTS INSTITUTE OF TECHNOLOGY**
Rotch Library
Cambridge, Mass. 02139

| | |
|---|---|
| Other locations: | Student productions and some reference material are housed in the Department of Architecture Film Section. |
| Size of film studies collection: | 500 monographs; 18 currently received periodicals, 7 of which are substantially complete. |
| Special collections, unpublished scripts: | None. |

*Survey of Film Study Libraries* 143

| | |
|---|---|
| Nonprint and other library material: | 3 8mm and 20 16mm feature films. |
| Interlibrary loan policy summary: | Monographs are lent. |

MEMPHIS STATE UNIVERSITY LIBRARIES
Memphis, Tenn. 38152

| | |
|---|---|
| Other locations: | Films are housed in the Learning Media Center, which is not part of the Memphis State University Library system. Stills and photos are housed in Special Collections. |
| Size of film studies collection: | 1,800 monographs, with emphasis on theory and criticism; 38 serial titles, 26 of which are currently received, 12 substantially complete runs. |
| Special collections, unpublished scripts: | None. |
| Nonprint and other library material: | Approximately 1,000 stills, 50 8mm feature films, 50 16mm feature films. |
| Interlibrary loan policy summary: | Books, theses, and microfilm are lent. Photocopies of journal articles are supplied for a fee. |

MINNEAPOLIS COLLEGE OF ART AND DESIGN LIBRARY AND MEDIA CENTER
200 East 25th St.
Minneapolis, Minn. 55404

| | |
|---|---|
| Size of film studies collection: | Approximately 350 monographs; 17 serials, 16 currently received periodicals. |
| Special collections, unpublished scripts: | Approximately 200 presskits. |
| Nonprint and other library material: | Stills and photos from presskits, 315 slides, 35 videotapes. |
| Interlibrary loan policy summary: | Books are lent only through MINITEX; photocopies of periodical articles are made only through MINITEX. |

MONTANA STATE UNIVERSITY LIBRARY
Bozeman, Mont. 49717

| | |
|---|---|
| Size of film studies collection: | Approximately 250 monographs; 16 currently received periodicals. |
| Special collections, unpublished scripts: | None. |
| Nonprint and other library material: | None. |
| Interlibrary loan policy summary: | Monographs, microfilms, and theses are lent. |

**MOORHEAD STATE UNIVERSITY LIBRARY**
Moorhead, Minn. 56560
Size of film studies collection: Approximately 550 monographs; 6 currently received periodicals, 3 back sets.

Special collections, unpublished scripts: None.
Nonprint and other library material: None.
Interlibrary loan policy summary: Monographs are lent.

**MOUNT VERNON COLLEGE LIBRARY**
2000 Foxhall Road, N.W.
Washington, D.C. 20007
Size of film studies collection: Approximately 360 monographs; 15 currently received periodicals.

Special collections, unpublished scripts: None.
Nonprint and other library material: 300 slides, 10 filmstrips, 5 educational films, 20 video recordings.
Interlibrary loan policy summary: No materials available for interlibrary loan.

**MOUNT ST. VINCENT UNIVERSITY LIBRARY**
Bedford Highway
Halifax, Nova Scotia B3M 2J6
Other locations: Films and video recordings are housed at Audio Visual Services.
Size of film studies collection: Approximately 150 monographs; 9 serials, 5 currently received periodicals, 7 back sets.

Special collections, unpublished scripts: None.
Nonprint and other library material: None.
Interlibrary loan policy summary: Monographs are lent. Photocopies of serial articles and microfilms are available. Microfilm copies of theses are lent.

**NEW YORK UNIVERSITY**
Bobst Library
70 Washington Square, South
New York, N.Y. 10012
Size of film studies collection: Not given.
Special collections, unpublished scripts: 300 scripts, including a complete set of all scripts of telecasts of *U.S. Steel Hour: Theatre Guild on the Air*.

Survey of Film Study Libraries    145

Nonprint and other library material: Approximately 20 videotapes.
Interlibrary loan policy summary: Books are lent for four weeks. Copies of journal articles are made for a fee. Theses available through University Microfilms are not lent.

**NORTH TEXAS STATE UNIVERSITY MEDIA LIBRARY**
Denton, Texas 76201
Other locations: 16mm films are housed in the Radio/TV/Film Division, and 16mm and super-8 films are housed in the Art Department; noncirculating.
Size of film studies collection: 500 monographs; 30 serial titles, 25 of which are currently received; housed in Main Library.
Special collections, unpublished scripts: Several hundred scripts, not part of a special subject collection; housed in Radio/TV/Film Division; noncirculating.
Nonprint and other library material: 10 films on film study in Media Library.
Interlibrary loan policy summary: Print material requests to Interlibrary Loan, NTSU Libraries. Media Library does not lend off-campus.

**NORTHWESTERN UNIVERSITY LIBRARY**
Evanston, Ill. 60201
Size of film studies collection: 1500 monographs; no estimate of serials.
Special collections, unpublished scripts: None.
Nonprint and other library material: None.
Interlibrary loan policy summary: Books and microfilms are lent. Photocopies of journal articles are available for a fee.

**OCCIDENTAL COLLEGE LIBRARY**
1600 Campus Rd.
Los Angeles, Cal. 90041
Size of film studies collection: Not given.
Special collections, unpublished scripts: Correspondence from film personalities to Bill Henry, and Barret Kushing (MGM publicist) Collection.
Nonprint and other library material: None.
Interlibrary loan policy summary: Not given.

146   FILM STUDY COLLECTIONS

**OHIO STATE UNIVERSITY LIBRARIES**
1858 Neil Ave. Mall
Columbus, Ohio 43210

Other locations: Most material is housed in the Milton Caniff Library, 100 Journalism Building, 242 West 18th Ave.

Size of film studies collection: Not estimated.

Special collections, unpublished scripts: 650 scripts are housed in the Department of Special Collection, and the Howard Lindsay-Walter Hampden collection of early materials on the history of U.S. theater and film.

Nonprint and other library material: 3,200 stills and photos; an extensive collection of posters which is not part of the Library, and which is awaiting transfer to the Milton Caniff Research Room, 145 Journalism Bldg.

Interlibrary loan policy summary: Monographs and theses are lent.

**OKLAHOMA STATE UNIVERSITY**
Edmon Low Library
Stillwater, Okla. 74074

Other locations: Films and other audiovisual material are housed at the University's Audiovisual Center.

Size of film studies collection: Approximately 1,900 monographs, with emphasis on theory, criticism, and scripts; 22 serials, 15 currently received, 6 back sets.

Special collections, unpublished scripts: None.

Nonprint and other library material: Films, feature films, and video recordings are housed in the University's Audiovisual Center.

Interlibrary loan policy summary: Monographs, microfilms, and theses are lent.

**PENNSYLVANIA STATE UNIVERSITY**
Fred Lewis Pattee Library
University Park, Pa. 16802

Other locations: 500 films and some nonprint materials are housed also at the University's Audiovisual Department.

Size of film studies collection: Over 1,500 monographs, with emphasis on theory, criticism, and scripts;

Survey of Film Study Libraries    147

|  |  |
|---|---|
|  | 67 serials, 27 currently received periodicals, 40 back sets. |
| Special collections, unpublished scripts: | John O'Hara books and manuscripts. |
| Nonprint and other library material: | 5 John O'Hara film posters, which are part of the library's John O'Hara Collection. |
| Interlibrary loan policy summary: | Monographs, microfilms, and theses are lent. |

PHILADELPHIA COLLEGE OF ART LIBRARY
Broad and Spruce
Philadelphia, Pa. 19102

|  |  |
|---|---|
| Other locations: | 275 16mm films are housed in the Audiovisual Department, and 400–500 relevant slides are housed in the Slide Library. |
| Size of film studies collection: | Approximately 1,380 monographs; 19 serials, 8 currently received periodicals. |
| Special collections, unpublished scripts: | None. |
| Nonprint and other library material: | Some 16mm films are housed in the Audiovisual Department; stills and photographs are found in the general picture files in the Main Library. |
| Interlibrary loan policy summary: | Monographs, microfilms, and photographs/stills are lent. |

PRATT INSTITUTE LIBRARY
215 Ryerson St.
Brooklyn, N.Y. 11025

|  |  |
|---|---|
| Size of film studies collection: | Approximately 800 monographs; approximately 15 serials, 11 currently received periodicals, 11 back sets. |
| Special collections, unpublished scripts: | None. |
| Nonprint and other library material: | None. |
| Interlibrary loan policy summary: | Monographs are lent. |

QUEENS COLLEGE
City University of New York
Paul Klapper Library
65-30 Kessina Blvd.
Flushing, N.Y. 11367

|  |  |
|---|---|
| Size of film studies collection: | 1,625 monographs, with emphasis on theory, criticism, and history; 41 |

| | |
|---|---|
| | serial titles, 27 currently received, 17 sets of substantially complete sets 10 or more years old. |
| Special collections, unpublished scripts: | Approximately 50 scripts of various films. |
| Nonprint and other library material: | 5,000 stills, 100 posters, 1,500 slides (housed at Multimedia Services), 59 films for film study, 20 videotapes. |
| Interlibrary loan policy summary: | Books and theses are lent. Periodical articles are copied. |

**RHODE ISLAND SCHOOL OF DESIGN LIBRARY**
2 College St.
Providence, R.I.

| | |
|---|---|
| Other locations: | Materials are also housed in the Department of Film Studies. |
| Size of film studies collection: | Approximately 200 monographs; 10 serial titles, 6 curently received periodicals, 3 back sets. |
| Special collections, unpublished scripts: | None. |
| Nonprint and other library material: | 1,200 stills, 16 posters, and 47 slides. |
| Interlibrary loan policy summary: | Monographs are lent. |

**ROCHESTER INSTITUTE OF TECHNOLOGY**
Wallace Memorial Library
Rochester, N.Y. 14623

| | |
|---|---|
| Size of film studies collection: | 650 monographs; over 50 currently received periodials. |
| Special collections, unpublished scripts: | None. |
| Nonprint and other library material: | 24 films on film study, a small number of filmstrips and 16mm feature films. |
| Interlibrary loan policy summary: | Monographs and microfilms are lent; photocopies of serial articles are available; and theses are photocopied with author's permission. |

**ROGER WILLIAMS COLLEGE LIBRARY**
Old Ferry Rd.
Bristol, R.I. 02809

| | |
|---|---|
| Size of film studies collection: | Over 500 monographs; 14 serials, 11 currently received periodicals. |
| Special collections, unpublished scripts: | None. |
| Nonprint and other library material: | None. |
| Interlibrary loan policy summary: | Monographs are lent. Photocopies of periodical articles are supplied. |

SAN DIEGO STATE UNIVERSITY LIBRARY
San Diego, Cal. 92182

| | |
|---|---|
| Other Locations: | Curriculum-oriented materials are also housed in the Learning Resources Center. Some TV tapes and films are housed in the Telecommunications & Film Department. |
| Size of film studies collection: | Over 5,000 monographs; 172 serials, numerous back sets, and over 700 reference books. |
| Special collections, unpublished scripts: | Desi Arnaz Collection (films, TV tapes, scripts) and miscellaneous film production material (correspondence, celluloids, storyboards, animation designs, and drawings) especially on *The Incredible Mr. Limpet*. |
| Nonprint and other library material: | 1,000 stills and photographs; 500 posters, etc.; 146 16mm classic film titles. |
| Interlibrary loan policy summary: | Monographs, microfilms, and theses are lent. |

SAN FRANCISCO ART INSTITUTE
Anne Bremer Memorial Library
800 Chestnut St.
San Francisco, Cal. 94133

| | |
|---|---|
| Size of film studies collection: | Approximately 400 monographs; 18 currently received periodicals. |
| Special collections, unpublished scripts: | None. |
| Nonprint and other library material: | 190 slides; 22 feature films, of which there are 21 16mm. |
| Interlibrary loan policy summary: | Materials not available for interlibrary loan. |

SAN FRANCISCO STATE UNIVERSITY
J. Paul Leonard Library
1630 Holloway Ave.
San Francisco, Cal. 94132

| | |
|---|---|
| Size of collection: | 3,150 monographs; 65 serials, 51 of which are currently received periodicals (43 of these titles are substantially complete). |
| Special collections, unpublished scripts: | 182 scripts in a general collection of scripts. |

150     FILM STUDY COLLECTIONS

Nonprint or other library material: An estimated 200 stills, 9 8mm silent films, 54 complete 16mm feature films, 9 16mm excerpts, a collection of videocassettes for film and video studies, and overhead transparencies.

Interlibrary loan policy summary: Monographs and theses are lent for four weeks with renewal.

SAN JOSE STATE UNIVERSITY LIBRARY
250 S. Fourth St.
San Jose, Cal. 95192

Special collections, unpublished scripts: The John Steinbeck Research Center has a screenplay collection written by or based on works by Steinbeck. See Mehr[2] for details.

SARAH LAWRENCE COLLEGE
Glen Washington Rd.
Bronxville, N.Y. 10708

Other locations: Films and audio cassettes are housed at the Audiovisual Office.

Size of film studies collection: Approximately 900 monographs; 23 serials, including 9 currently received periodicals, 8 back sets.

Special collections, unpublished scripts: None.
Nonprint and other library material: None.
Interlibrary loan policy summary: Monographs are lent; photocopies of serial articles are available.

SCHOOL OF THEOLOGY AT CLAREMONT
1325 N. College Ave.
Claremont, Cal. 91711

Special collections, unpublished scripts: The Robert and Frances Flaherty Study Center holds a collection of works by and on Robert Flaherty. see Mehr[2] for details.

SCHOOL OF VISUAL ARTS LIBRARY
380 Second Ave.
New York, N.Y. 10010

Other locations: The film archive is housed in the Film Department.

Size of film studies collection: Approximately 800 monographs; 15 currently received periodicals.

Special collections, unpublished scripts: None.
Nonprint and other library material: None.

Interlibrary loan policy summary: No materials are available on interlibrary loan.

**SOUTH DAKOTA STATE UNIVERSITY**
Hilton M. Briggs Library
Brookings, S.D. 57007
Size of film studies collection: Approximately 275 monographs, with emphasis on theory, criticism, and scripts; 4 currently received periodicals, 4 back sets.

Special collections, unpublished scripts: None.
Nonprint and other library material: None.
Interlibrary loan policy summary: Monographs and theses are lent. Photocopies of serial articles and microfilms are available.

**SOUTHERN ILLINOIS UNIVERSITY**
Morris Library
Carbondale, Ill. 62901
Other locations: Some feature films and periodicals are housed in the Department of Cinema and Photography.
Size of film studies collection: Approximately 2,500 monographs, with emphasis on theory, criticism, scripts, and cinematographic technique. Approximately 50 serials, approximately 25 currently received, approximately 25 back sets.

Special collections, unpublished scripts: John Howard Lawson (screenwriter) papers—111 boxes, Archives of Library Affairs Film Production Unit—includes papers and 440 16mm reels of film, Katherine Dunham (choreographer) Collection, Mordecai Gorelick (director, scene designer) Collection.

Nonprint and other library material: None.
Interlibrary loan policy summary: Monographs, serials, microfilms, unpublished scripts, and theses are lent.

**SOUTHERN METHODIST UNIVERSITY**
Fondren Library
Dallas, Texas 75275
Other locations: Stills, photographs, posters, books, screenplays, clippings, and slides

152 FILM STUDY COLLECTIONS

|   |   |
|---|---|
| | are housed at the McCord Theatre Collection. Films are housed at Media Services. |
| Size of film studies collection: | Number of monographs not given; 25 current periodical subscriptions. |
| Special collections, unpublished scripts: | L. Stoddard Taylor Collection of photos of show business personalities. |
| Nonprint and other library material: | 10,000 stills, 4,200 photographs, 750 posters (including theater posters), 220 slides (including theater slides), 10 16mm films. |
| Interlibrary loan policy summary: | Monographs are lent. Other materials are not available for interlibrary loan. |

**SPRING HILL COLLEGE**
Thomas Byrne Library
Mobile, Ala. 36608

|   |   |
|---|---|
| Size of film studies collection: | 100 monographs; a few periodicals. |
| Special collections, unpublished scripts: | None. |
| Nonprint and other library material: | None. |
| Interlibrary loan policy summary: | Monographs are lent for two weeks. Photocopies are provided. |

**STANFORD UNIVERSITY LIBRARIES**
Cecil H. Green Library
Stanford, Cal. 94305

|   |   |
|---|---|
| Other locations: | Department of Special Collections houses photographs, promotional material, scripts and screenplays, and the Steinbeck Collection. The Stanford University Museum of Art houses the Eadweard J. Muybridge Collection, and precinema devices showing motion. The J. Henry Meyer Memorial Library houses a representative undergraduate book collection. |
| Size of film studies collection: | 2,900 monographs, with emphasis on theory and criticism, but with a large number of monographs on technique; 70 serial titles, 30 currently received periodicals. |
| Special collections, unpublished scripts: | Approximately 100 unpublished scripts, including film titles from |

|  |  |
|---|---|
|  | 1930 and from all major studios; the Delmar Lawrence Davis (1904–1977) papers (83 boxes); The Steinbeck Collection, 1926–1968, (25 feet); the Muybridge Collection (25 items); and over 600 television scripts from 1950 to the present. |
| Nonprint and other library material: | 7,500 stills and photos, 1,200 items of promotional material, 11 films on film study, 74 16mm feature films. |
| Interlibrary loan policy summary: | Books, theses, dissertations, and some microfilm are lent. Journal articles are copied for a fee. |

STATE UNIVERSITY OF NEW YORK—BINGHAMTON
Fine Arts Library/Library North
Vestal Parkway East
Binghamton, N.Y. 13901

|  |  |
|---|---|
| Other locations: | Film reels are located at the Film Archive, Department of Special Collections, and general reference materials are located in Bartle Library. |
| Size of film studies collection: | 1,700 monographs; 50 serial titles, 40 of which are currently received periodicals. |
| Special collections, unpublished scripts: | None. |
| Nonprint and other library material: | 13 8mm feature films, 100 16mm feature films. |
| Interlibrary loan policy summary: | Books and microfilms are lent. |

STATE UNIVERSITY OF NEW YORK—BUFFALO
Lockwood Library
Amherst Campus
Buffalo, N.Y. 14260

|  |  |
|---|---|
| Other locations: | The Undergraduate Library also houses print material, and the Educational Communication Center and the Center for Media Studies house films and print material. |
| Size of film studies collection: | 2,050 monographs at the Library and 1,500 monographs at the Center for Media Study; 60 currently received periodicals at the Library, 15–20 at the Center for Media Study. |
| Special collections, unpublished scripts: | None. |

154    FILM STUDY COLLECTIONS

| | |
|---|---|
| Nonprint and other library material: | Some stills at the Center for Media Study; some slides, films, and filmstrips at the Educational Communication Center. |
| Interlibrary loan policy summary: | Monographs are lent; photocopies of articles are made for a fee. |

## STATE UNIVERSITY OF NEW YORK—CORTLAND
Memorial Library
Prospect Terrace
Cortland, N.Y. 13045

| | |
|---|---|
| Other locations: | Film catalogs, 40 training films, and a few feature films are housed at Sperry Learning Resources Center. |
| Size of film studies collection: | 700 monographs, with emphasis on theory, criticism, and history. Number of serial titles not given. |
| Special collections, unpublished scripts: | None. |
| Nonprint and other library material: | 9,335 pieces, including phono discs, film loops, filmstrips, cassette tapes, a-v kits, maps, charts, and slides, in all subjects. |
| Interlibrary loan policy summary: | Monographs, recorded cassettes, microforms, and theses are lent; photocopies of serials articles are available; other materials are generally not available on ILL. |

## STEPHEN F. AUSTIN STATE UNIVERSITY
Ralph W. Stein Library
Nacogdoches, Texas 75962

| | |
|---|---|
| Size of film studies collection: | 850 monographs; 17 serial titles, 12 of which are currently received periodicals. |
| Special collections, unpublished scripts: | None. |
| Non-print and other library material: | 5 films on film study. |
| Interlibrary loan policy summary: | Monographs and theses are lent. |

## STEPHENS COLLEGE
Hugh Stephens Library
Columbia, Mo. 65201

| | |
|---|---|
| Other locations: | Video cassettes and films are housed at Instructional Services. |
| Size of film studies collection: | Approximately 600 monographs; 4 currently received periodicals, 3 back sets. |

| | |
|---|---|
| Special collections, unpublished scripts: | None. |
| Nonprint and other library material: | None. |
| Interlibrary loan policy summary: | Monographs are lent. Other materials are not available for interlibrary loan. |

UNIVERSITY OF BRIDGEPORT
Magnus Wahlstrom Library
126 Park Ave.
Bridgeport, Conn. 06602

| | |
|---|---|
| Size of film studies collection: | 400 monographs; 25 serials, 22 currently received, 20 sets of back runs. |
| Special collections, unpublished scripts: | None. |
| Nonprint and other library material: | None. |
| Interlibrary loan policy summary: | Books are lent. Photocopies are made for a fee. Theses, microforms, and periodicals are not lent. |

UNIVERSITY OF CALIFORNIA—BERKELEY
University Library
Berkelely, Cal. 94720

| | |
|---|---|
| Special collections, unpublished scripts: | Among others, Dane Collidge, *Greed* (stills and photos), Sidney Coe Howard, Robert Allerton Parker, and Harry Wilson. See Mehr[2] for further information. |

UNIVERSITY OF CALIFORNIA—LOS ANGELES
Los Angeles, Cal. 90024
Details appear in the chapter on U.S. Archives

UNIVERSITY OF CALIFORNIA—SANTA BARBARA
Library
Santa Barbara, Cal. 93106

| | |
|---|---|
| Size of film studies collection: | 120 serials, 103 currently received, 17 back sets. |
| Special collections, unpublished scripts: | Some director and cinematographer interviews. Dame Judith Anderson Collection. |
| Nonprint and other library material: | None. |
| Interlibrary loan policy summary: | Books, bound periodicals, microfilm, and theses will be lent. |

## UNIVERSITY OF CALIFORNIA—SANTA CRUZ
Library
Santa Cruz, Cal. 95060

| | |
|---|---|
| Other locations: | Films are housed at Instructional Services. |
| Size of film studies collection: | No estimate available; approximately 25 serial titles. |
| Special collections, unpublished scripts: | Motion Picture Photograph Collection, 1911–1975, including stills, portraits, lobby cards, and other photographs. |
| Nonprint and other library material: | See "Special collections." |
| Interlibrary loan policy summary: | Materials are not lent. |

## UNIVERSITY OF GEORGIA LIBRARY
Athens, Ga. 30602

| | |
|---|---|
| Other locations: | Some materials are housed at the Instructional Resources Center and at the Center for Continuing Education. |
| Size of film studies collection: | 2,250 monographs; 85 serial titles, 35 of which are currently received periodicals, 25 of which are substantially complete. |
| Special collections, unpublished scripts: | 10 film scripts, including *Gone With the Wind* material and scripts pertaining to the state of Georgia. The George Foster Peabody Radio-TV Awards Collection. |
| Nonprint and other library material: | 63,000 stills, 100 posters, 4,500 16mm feature films. |
| Interlibrary loan policy summary: | Monographs, pre-1956 dissertations, and duplicate theses are lent; microfilm is lent for one week; and photocopies of articles are provided for a fee. |

## UNIVERSITY OF ILLINOIS—URBANA
Undergraduate Library
Urbana, Ill. 61801

| | |
|---|---|
| Other locations: | Foreign language monographs and serials are housed in the main library bookstacks. The Communications Library, Modern Languages Library, Engineering |

| | |
|---|---|
| | Library, Art and Architecture Library, and Rare Book Room all hold some film study material. |
| Size of film study collection: | An estimated 6,000 monographs; 250 serials, 150 of which are currently received periodicals, with a strong collection of foreign titles. |
| Special collections, unpublished scripts: | 300 shooting scripts from all major studios, with special holdings of Samson Raphaelson, Ben Hecht, and Preston Sturges scripts. |
| Nonprint and other library material: | 300 stills and several stillbooks, 1,760 slides, several microfiche sets; microfilm holdings of *Variety*, the indexes to British Film Institute holdings, *Motion Picture Herald*, *Hollywood Reporter;* a few filmstrips; 100 video cassettes of feature films. A collection of films is held by the Unit for Cinema Studies. |
| Interlibrary loan policy summary: | Books, pre-1954 dissertations, circulating theses, circulating microforms, and some older bound periodicals are lent. Circulating government documents are lent, and copies of articles are made for a fee. |

UNIVERSITY OF IOWA LIBRARIES
Iowa City, Iowa 52242

| | |
|---|---|
| Other locations: | Most material is housed in the Department of Special Collections. Films are housed in the Department of Broadcasting and Film, Old Armory. |
| Size of film studies collection: | 2,650 monographs, with emphasis on theory and criticism; 320 serial titles, 220 periodicals, 117 of which are currently received, 103 ceased titles. |
| Special collections, unpublished scripts: | Substantial collections of Robert Blees, Luis Buñuel, Albert Cohen, Norman Felton, and Twentieth Century-Fox Film Corporation scripts. For details, see chapter on U.S. Archives. |

158    FILM STUDY COLLECTIONS

Nonprint and other library material: Significant holdings of posters in the Department of Special Collections.
Interlibrary loan policy summary: Books and theses are lent for four weeks; photocopies are made from current issues, bound copies, or microfilm for a fee.

### UNIVERSITY OF KANSAS LIBRARIES
Watson Library
Lawrence, Kans. 66045

Other locations: Films are housed at the Audiovisual Center, 746 Massachusetts Ave., Lawrence, Kans., and at the University Archives, Spencer Library.
Size of film studies collection: 1,250 monographs; 40 serial titles, 10 of which are substantially complete.
Special collections, unpublished scripts: William Inge Collection.
Nonprint and other library material: The Audiovisual Center (not the library) owns about 30 films on film study. The library has none.
Interlibrary loan policy summary: Monographs and theses are lent. Photocopies of journal articles are available. The American Library Association code is followed.

### UNIVERSITY OF MARYLAND—BALTIMORE COUNTY
Library
5401 Wilkins Ave.
Baltimore, Md. 21228

Size of film studies collection: 1,500 monographs; 46 currently received serial titles.
Special collections, unpublished scripts: 675 scripts, with no special subject.
Nonprint and other library material: 970 slides, 5 films on film study, approximately 300 feature films on 16mm, a few videotapes.
Interlibrary loan policy summary: Books and some microfilms are lent.

### UNIVERSITY OF MARYLAND—COLLEGE PARK
Library
College Park, Md. 20742

Other locations: Most nonprint material is housed in the Non-print Media Services Unit, although some films are housed by the Department of English, and some films, video, and audio re-

*Survey of Film Study Libraries* 159

| | |
|---|---|
| | cordings are housed by the Radio, TV, and Film Department. |
| Special collections, unpublished scripts: | None. |
| Nonprint and other library material: | 7 feature films in video, 15 video units on film study. |
| Interlibrary loan policy summary: | Books are lent. |

**UNIVERSITY OF MIAMI LIBRARY**
Coral Gables, Fla. 33124

| | |
|---|---|
| Other locations: | Films are housed in the Communications Services Division. |
| Size of film studies collection: | Approximately 1,000 monographs, with emphasis on criticism and history; 9 serial titles, 7 currently received. |
| Special collections, unpublished scripts: | None. |
| Nonprint and other library material: | 10 feature or film study films on 16mm. |
| Interlibrary loan policy summary: | Books, theses, and most microfilms are lent. Photocopies are made of journal articles. |

**UNIVERSITY OF MICHIGAN**
Harlan Hatcher Graduate Library
Ann Arbor, Mich. 48109

| | |
|---|---|
| Other locations: | A number of monographs and serials on theory, criticism, and history are housed in the Undergraduate Library; monographs on cinematography and technique are housed in the Architecture Library; and bibliographies, directories, and indexes are housed in the Library Science Library. |
| Size of film studies collection: | Approximately 3,900 monographs, with emphasis on theory and history and a good collection of cinematography. Approximately 90 serial titles, 75 of which are currently received. |
| Special collections, unpublished scripts: | None. |
| Nonprint and other library material: | None. |
| Interlibrary loan policy summary: | Books are lent for two weeks; most microfilm is also lent for two weeks. |

## UNIVERSITY OF MINNESOTA
Audio Visual Library Service
Continuing Education and Extension
3300 University Ave., S.E.
Minneapolis, Minn. 55414

| | |
|---|---|
| Size of film studies collection: | Approximately 450 monographs; 33 currently received periodicals. |
| Special collections, unpublished scripts: | Unknown number of scripts from University of Minnesota productions; 16 mm out-takes from Robert Flaherty's *Louisiana Story* and Mary Ellen Bute's *Finnegan's Wake*. |
| Nonprint and other library material: | Miscellaneous film title files contain reviews, clippings, and promotional material; 150 films on film study, 18 16mm feature films. |
| Interlibrary loan policy summary: | Print materials are available for building use. Nonprint media is loaned on a service-fee basis. |

## UNIVERSITY OF MISSOURI—KANSAS CITY
General Library
5100 Rockhill Rd.
Kansas City, Mo. 64110

| | |
|---|---|
| Size of film studies collection: | Approximately 1,250 monographs. Number of serial titles not reported. |
| Special collections, unpublished scripts: | Leith Stevens scores for films. |
| Nonprint and other library material: | Some music scores for films. |
| Interlibrary loan policy summary: | Monographs are lent. |

## UNIVERSITY OF NEW ORLEANS
Earl K. Long Library
Lakefront
New Orleans, La. 70122

| | |
|---|---|
| Other locations: | 2 35mm films on filmmaking are housed at Audiovisual Center. |
| Size of film studies collection: | Approximately 750 monographs; 94 serials, 58 currently received periodicals, 7 back sets. |
| Special collections, unpublished scripts: | None. |
| Nonprint and other library material: | 700 stills. |
| Interlibrary loan policy summary: | Monographs, microfilms, and theses are lent. |

UNIVERSITY OF NORTH CAROLINA AT CHARLOTTE
J. Murray Atkins Library
UNCC Station
Charlotte, N.C. 28223

| | |
|---|---|
| Other locations: | Films are housed at the Learning Resources Center. |
| Size of film studies collection: | Approximately 375 monographs; 10 serials, 7 currently received periodicals, 6 back sets. |
| Special collections, unpublished scripts: | None. |
| Nonprint and other library material: | Small number of films on film study. |
| Interlibrary loan policy summary: | Monographs, monographs in microform, and theses are lent. |

UNIVERSITY OF NOTRE DAME
Memorial Library
Notre Dame, Ind. 46556

| | |
|---|---|
| Other locations: | Material is also housed in the Audiovisual Center. |
| Size of film studies collection: | Approximately 650 monographs; 44 serials, 20 currently received periodicals, 10 back sets. |
| Special collections, unpublished scripts: | None. |
| Nonprint and other library material: | None. |
| Interlibrary loan policy summary: | Monographs, microfilms, and theses are lent. Photocopies of bound serials are available. |

UNIVERSITY OF OKLAHOMA
Bizzell Memorial Library
Norman, Okla. 73069

| | |
|---|---|
| Size of film studies collection: | Approximately 900 monographs; 15 currently received periodicals. |
| Special collections, unpublished scripts: | Material on *The Passing of the Oklahoma Outlaws,* a film by William Tilghman, U.S. Marshall. |
| Nonprint and other library material: | None. |
| Interlibrary loan policy summary: | Monographs, microfilms, and theses are lent. |

UNIVERSITY OF OREGON LIBRARY
Eugene, Ore. 97403

| | |
|---|---|
| Special collections, unpublished scripts: | Papers from many writers, including Frank Adams, Willis Ballard, Harry |

Behn, Houston Branch, Lowell Brentano, Richard Collins, William Cox, Thomas Curry, Michael Fessier, John and Ward Hawkins, and Charles Warren. Also some collections of TV writers, and radio and TV composers. See Young[1] and Mehr[2] for details.

**UNIVERSITY OF THE DISTRICT OF COLUMBIA**
Fine Arts Library
916 G St., N.W.
Washington, D.C.

| | |
|---|---|
| Other locations: | Technical books are housed at 724 9th St., N.W., and theory and history books are at 425 2nd St., N.W. |
| Size of film studies collection: | 350 monographs; 6 serial titles. |
| Special collections, unpublished scripts: | None. |
| Nonprint and other library material: | None. |
| Interlibrary loan policy summary: | Not given. |

**UNIVERSITY OF SOUTHERN CALIFORNIA—DEPARTMENT OF SPECIAL COLLECTIONS**
Doheny Library
Details appear in the chapter on U.S. Archives.

**UNIVERSITY OF TEXAS—AUSTIN**
Hoblitzelle Theatre Arts Library
Humanities Research Center
P. O. Box 7219
Austin, Texas 78712

| | |
|---|---|
| Other locations: | The Perry-Castenada Library, General Libraries, holds monographs, and the Radio/TV/Film and Drama Departments hold some material. Film, portraits, and videotapes are housed in the Photography Collections. |
| Size of film study collection: | 1,850 monographs; 40 serials, 5 of which are currently received periodicals. The Perry-Castenada Library holds 5,300 monographs. |
| Special collections, unpublished scripts: | 50 scripts from the collections of Edward Carrick and Robert Downing. The Carrick scripts are of British films from 1925–1940. The Alfred Junge collection of designs from |

## UNIVERSITY OF NORTH CAROLINA AT CHARLOTTE
J. Murray Atkins Library
UNCC Station
Charlotte, N.C. 28223

| | |
|---|---|
| Other locations: | Films are housed at the Learning Resources Center. |
| Size of film studies collection: | Approximately 375 monographs; 10 serials, 7 currently received periodicals, 6 back sets. |
| Special collections, unpublished scripts: | None. |
| Nonprint and other library material: | Small number of films on film study. |
| Interlibrary loan policy summary: | Monographs, monographs in microform, and theses are lent. |

## UNIVERSITY OF NOTRE DAME
Memorial Library
Notre Dame, Ind. 46556

| | |
|---|---|
| Other locations: | Material is also housed in the Audiovisual Center. |
| Size of film studies collection: | Approximately 650 monographs; 44 serials, 20 currently received periodicals, 10 back sets. |
| Special collections, unpublished scripts: | None. |
| Nonprint and other library material: | None. |
| Interlibrary loan policy summary: | Monographs, microfilms, and theses are lent. Photocopies of bound serials are available. |

## UNIVERSITY OF OKLAHOMA
Bizzell Memorial Library
Norman, Okla. 73069

| | |
|---|---|
| Size of film studies collection: | Approximately 900 monographs; 15 currently received periodicals. |
| Special collections, unpublished scripts: | Material on *The Passing of the Oklahoma Outlaws*, a film by William Tilghman, U.S. Marshall. |
| Nonprint and other library material: | None. |
| Interlibrary loan policy summary: | Monographs, microfilms, and theses are lent. |

## UNIVERSITY OF OREGON LIBRARY
Eugene, Ore. 97403

| | |
|---|---|
| Special collections, unpublished scripts: | Papers from many writers, including Frank Adams, Willis Ballard, Harry |

Behn, Houston Branch, Lowell Brentano, Richard Collins, William Cox, Thomas Curry, Michael Fessier, John and Ward Hawkins, and Charles Warren. Also some collections of TV writers, and radio and TV composers. See Young[1] and Mehr[2] for details.

UNIVERSITY OF THE DISTRICT OF COLUMBIA
Fine Arts Library
916 G St., N.W.
Washington, D.C.

| | |
|---|---|
| Other locations: | Technical books are housed at 724 9th St., N.W., and theory and history books are at 425 2nd St., N.W. |
| Size of film studies collection: | 350 monographs; 6 serial titles. |
| Special collections, unpublished scripts: | None. |
| Nonprint and other library material: | None. |
| Interlibrary loan policy summary: | Not given. |

UNIVERSITY OF SOUTHERN CALIFORNIA—DEPARTMENT OF SPECIAL COLLECTIONS
Doheny Library
Details appear in the chapter on U.S. Archives.

UNIVERSITY OF TEXAS—AUSTIN
Hoblitzelle Theatre Arts Library
Humanities Research Center
P. O. Box 7219
Austin, Texas 78712

| | |
|---|---|
| Other locations: | The Perry-Castenada Library, General Libraries, holds monographs, and the Radio/TV/Film and Drama Departments hold some material. Film, portraits, and videotapes are housed in the Photography Collections. |
| Size of film study collection: | 1,850 monographs; 40 serials, 5 of which are currently received periodicals. The Perry-Castenada Library holds 5,300 monographs. |
| Special collections, unpublished scripts: | 50 scripts from the collections of Edward Carrick and Robert Downing. The Carrick scripts are of British films from 1925–1940. The Alfred Junge collection of designs from |

American, British, and German films from 1927–1957 includes 2,765 photos of scenic locations used in designing sets for films, 385 original designs, 1,841 photos, and 56 negatives of original designs, and manuscript material on Junge's notes. The Edward Carrick collection of British film designs from 1925–1945 includes 1,452 original designs and 122 costume designs by Carrick and others, campaign books from the 1930s, clipping files and stills with notes on art direction. The W. H. Crain Collection contains Paul Rotha's manuscript on Robert Flaherty, along with stills from most of Flaherty's films and photos during the filming of most of these films. In addition, the Crain Collection has full biographical still collections of Cary Grant and Carole Lombard. The E. V. Richards Collection concerning the Saenger Theatre Chain in the Southeast U.S. contains photos, standees, pressbooks, and stills. The King Vidor Collection holds set models, costume and set renderings from the MGM Art Department for *H.M. Pulham, Esq.* and a file for the makeup for aging. The Ernest Lehman Collection contains approximately 350 manuscript filmscripts. Some are series of revisions for particular titles; for example, there are 65 for *Sound of Music* alone, following the screenplay from its inception to final draft. In addition, there are thousands of pages of individual changes of dialogue, location, shooting schedules, treatment ideas, character notes, etc. Hundreds of pages of photos, song lyrics in manuscript form, i.e., *West Side Story*, etc., are also included. The collection dates from 1953–1965. The Maurice Zolotow Collection of interviews includes material on Marilyn Monroe, John Wayne, and others. The Messmore Kendall/Harry Houdini Collection has approximately 5,000 hand-lettered hand-drawn title cards for films from 1915–1922. The Albert Davis Collection has 300 rare playbills for films from 1896–1920 and some souvenir books. The Burnes Hollyman Collection contains location and time sheets and shooting schedules for *Serpico*.

Nonprint and other library material: 650,000 stills and photos, and 200,000 posters.

Interlibrary loan policy summary: All material in the Hoblitzelle Theatre Arts Library is for building use only.

**UNIVERSITY OF TOLEDO**
Carlson Library
Toledo, Ohio 43606

Size of film studies collection: 500 monographs. Serials not estimated.

Special collections, unpublished scripts: None.
Nonprint and other library material: 15 16mm feature films
Interlibrary loan policy summary: Monographs are lent; journal articles are copied.

**UNIVERSITY OF TULSA**
McFarlin Library
600 South College
Tulsa, Okla. 74129

Size of film studies collection: Approximately 850 monographs, with emphasis on theory, criticism, and scripts; 14 currently received periodicals, 10 back sets.

Special collections, unpublished scripts: None.
Nonprint and other library material: 4 8mm and 12 16mm feature films.
Interlibrary loan policy summary: Monographs, microfilms, and theses are lent. Other materials are not available for interlibrary loan.

**UNIVERSITY OF VIRGINIA**
Alderman Library
Charlottesville, Va. 22901

Special collections, unpublished scripts: William Faulkner manuscripts and papers include screenplays such as

*The Big Sleep* and several television scripts. In addition, the library has acquired from MGM and Twentieth Century-Fox numerous scripts authored or partially authored by Faulkner.

UNIVERSITY OF WISCONSIN—MADISON
Memorial Library
728 State Street
Madison, Wis. 53706

| | |
|---|---|
| Other locations: | The Wisconsin Center for Film and Theater Research holds special collections. |
| Size of film studies collection: | Over 5,000 monographs, with a very strong collection of theory, criticism, and history. Approximately 150 serial titles, 70 of which are currently received periodicals. |
| Special collections, unpublished scripts: | None. See Wisconsin Center for Film and Theater Research, in the chapter on U.S. Archives. |
| Nonprint and other library material: | None. See Wisconsin Center for Film and Theater Research. The Bureau of Audiovisual Instruction, and the Instructional Media Distribution Center, College Library, hold educational films. |
| Interlibrary loan policy summary: | Books and some dissertations and microfilms are lent for two weeks. Copies of journal articles are provided for a fee. |

UNIVERSITY OF WISCONSIN—MILWAUKEE
Library
P. O. Box 604
Milwaukee, Wis. 53201

| | |
|---|---|
| Size of film studies collection: | 2,000 monographs, with emphasis on theory, criticism, and history; 41 serial titles, 33 of which are currently received periodicals. |
| Special collections, unpublished scripts: | None. |
| Nonprint and other library material: | 12 videotapes, and a few films on film study. |
| Interlibrary loan policy summary: | Books are lent. |

## UNIVERSITY OF WISCONSIN—OSHKOSH
Polk Library
800 Algoma Blvd.
Oshkosh, Wis. 54901

| | |
|---|---|
| Size of film studies collection: | Approximately 900 monographs, with emphasis on theory, criticism, and scripts. Approximately 30 serials, 10 currently received, 13 back sets. |
| Special collections, unpublished scripts: | Pare Lorentz Collection of tapes, films, and books. |
| Nonprint and other library material: | 29 films on film study, 20 16mm feature films, small number of video recordings and filmstrips. |
| Interlibrary loan policy summary: | Monographs, government documents, and some microfilms are lent; theses are lent within Wisconsin; other materials are not available for interlibrary loan. |

## UNIVERSITY OF WISCONSIN—STEVENS POINT
Learning Resources Center
Stevens Point, Wis. 54481

| | |
|---|---|
| Other locations: | 16mm films are housed in the Learning Resources Center. |
| Size of film studies collection: | 91 monographs. Approximately 20 serials, 9 currently received. |
| Special collections, unpublished scripts: | None. |
| Nonprint and other library material: | 112 16mm feature films, 17 8mm feature films, and a small number of video recordings. |
| Interlibrary loan policy summary: | Monographs and theses are lent. Other materials are not available for interlibrary loan. |

## WASHINGTON STATE UNIVERSITY
Holland Library
Pullman, Wash. 99163

| | |
|---|---|
| Size of film studies collection: | 1,100 monographs; 9 currently received periodicals. |
| Special collections, unpublished scripts: | None. |
| Nonprint and other library material: | 16 films on film study, 2 8mm and 13 16mm feature films. |
| Interlibrary loan policy summary: | Books are lent, photocopies are made for a fee. |

## WESLEYAN UNIVERSITY
Olin Memorial Library
Middletown, Conn. 06457

| | |
|---|---|
| Other locations: | Monographs on theory and scripts are housed in the Art Library. |
| Size of film studies collection: | Approximately 1,300 monographs, with emphasis on theory, criticism, and scripts; 20 serials, 15 currently received periodicals. |
| Special collections, unpublished scripts: | None. |
| Nonprint and other library material: | None. |
| Interlibrary loan policy summary: | Monographs are lent. Other materials are not available for interlibrary loan. |

## WILLIAM PATERSON COLLEGE OF NEW JERSEY
Sarah Byrd Askew Library
300 Pompton Rd.
Wayne, N.J. 07470

| | |
|---|---|
| Other locations: | Some materials are housed in faculty offices. |
| Size of film studies collection: | Approximately 400 monographs; 30 serials, 29 currently received. |
| Special collections, unpublished scripts: | None. |
| Nonprint and other library material: | Small number of films. |
| Interlibrary loan policy summary: | Duplicate copies of microforms and cataloged theses are lent. Other materials are not available for interlibrary loan. |

## WRIGHT STATE UNIVERSITY LIBRARY
Colonel Glenn Highway
Dayton, Ohio 45435

| | |
|---|---|
| Other locations: | Print material on the theater arts is housed in the Creative Arts Library, Millett Hall. |
| Size of film studies collection: | 754 monographs, with emphasis on theory, criticism, and scripts; 88 serial titles, 36 currently received. |
| Special collections, unpublished scripts: | None. |
| Nonprint and other library material: | 50 8mm feature films and a small |

Interlibrary loan policy summary: number of other nonprint materials.
Monographs and theses are lent. Other materials are not available for interlibrary loan.

# Appendix A: Publishers' Addresses

Academic Media
Affiliate of Marquis Who's Who
4300 W. 62nd St.
Indianapolis, Ind. 46268

Academy of Motion Picture Arts and Sciences
8949 Wilshire Blvd.
Beverly Hills, Cal. 90211

Acropolis Books, Ltd.
Colortone Building
2400 17th St., N.W.
Washington, D.C. 20009

*Action*
See Directors Guild of America

*Afterimage*
See Visual Studies Workshop

*American Cinematographer*
See American Society of Cinematographers

American Film Institute
John F. Kennedy Center for The Performing Arts
Washington, D.C. 20566

American Library Association
50 E. Huron St.
Chicago, Ill. 60611

American Society for Information Science
1155 16th St., N.W., Suite 210
Washington, D.C. 20036

American Society of Cinematographers
1782 N. Orange Dr.
Los Angeles, Cal. 90028

American Federation of Film Societies
144 Bleecker St.
New York, N.Y. 10012

Appleton Century Crofts
Division of Prentice-Hall, Inc.
292 Madison Ave.
New York, N.Y. 10017

Archiva Nationala de Filme
Casuta Postale 126
Bucharest 1, Rumania

Arco Publishing Co., Inc.
219 Park Ave. S.
New York, N.Y. 10003

Arizona Jim Co-op.
Old Hope Schoolhouse
Cottage Grove, Wis. 53527

Arlington House, Inc.
165 Huguenot St.
New Rochelle, N.Y. 10801

Arno Press, Inc.
A New York Times Company
3 Park Ave.
New York, N.Y. 10016

Association for Educational Communications and Technology
1126 16th St., N.W.
Washington, D.C. 20036

Association Press
291 Broadway
New York, N.Y. 10007

*Audiovisual Instruction*
See Association for Educational Communications and Technology

Avon Books
The Hearst Corporation
959 Eighth Ave.
New York, N.Y. 10019

Bantam Books, Inc.
666 Fifth Ave.
New York, N.Y. 10019

A. S. Barnes & Co., Inc.
Forsgate Drive
Cranbury, N.J. 08512

Barnes and Noble Books
Division of Harper & Row Publishers
10 East 53rd St.
New York, N.Y. 10022

Basic Books, Inc., Publishers
10 East 53rd St.
New York, N.Y. 10022

Bonanza Books
See Crown Publishers, Inc.

*Booklist*
See American Library Association

Booklegger Press
555 29th St.
San Francisco, Cal. 94131

R. R. Bowker Company
A Xerox Publishing Company
1180 Avenue of the Americas
New York, N.Y. 10036

   Orders to:
Subscription Service Department
Box 67
Whitinsville, Maine 01588

British and American Film Holdings, Ltd.
Brook House
Park Lane
London W1
ENGLAND

British Federation of Film Societies
81 Dean Street
London W1
ENGLAND

British Film Institute
81 Dean Street
London W1V AA
ENGLAND

OR
155 West 15th St.
New York, N.Y. 10001

William C. Brown Company, Publishers
2460 Kerper Blvd.
Dubuque, Iowa 52001

*Cahiers du Cinéma in English*
635 Madison Ave.
New York, N.Y. 10022

Capelli
Via Marsili, 9
40100 Bologna
ITALY

Center for The Information Services
LeHigh University
Bethlehem, Pa. 18015

Center for The Study of Popular Culture
Bowling Green Popular Press
Bowling Green State University
101 University Hall
Bowling Green, Ohio 43403

Il Centro
Centro Sperimentale du Cinematografia
Via Tuscolana 1524
Rome
ITALY

Century House Publishing, Inc.
Watkins Glen
N.Y. 14891

Chelsea-Lee Books
P.O. Box 66273
Los Angeles, Cal. 90066

Chicorel Library Publishing Corporation
275 Central Park West
New York, N.Y. 10024

*Choice*
100 Riverview Center
Middletown, Connecticut 06457

*Cineaste*
333 6th Ave.
New York, N.Y. 10014

*Cinema*
See Spectator International, Inc.

*Cinema Journal*
See Society for Cinema Studies

Cinematica Nacional
Palacio Fox Restauradors
Lisbon
PORTUGAL

Citadel Press
Wholly Owned Subsidiary of Lyle Stuart, Inc.
120 Enterprise Ave.
Secaucus, N.J. 07094

Thomas Y. Crowell Company, Inc.
Division Harper & Row, Publishers
10 East 53rd St.
New York, N.Y. 10022

Crown Publishers, Inc.
1 Park Ave.
New York, N.Y. 10016

DaCapo Press, Inc.
Subsidiary of Plenum Publishing Corporation
227 West 17th St.
New York, N.Y. 10011

Det Danske Filmmuseum
Store Søndervoldstraede
1419, København K.
DENMARK

Dell Publishing Co., Inc.
Subsidiary of Doubleday & Co., Inc.
One Dag Hammarskjold Plaza
New York, N.Y. 10017

André Deutsch, Ltd.
105 Great Russell Street
London WC1B 3LJ
ENGLAND

The Dial Press
Wholly Owned Subsidiary of Dell Publishing Co., Inc.
One Dag Hammarskjold Plaza
New York, N.Y. 10017

Dickenson Publishing Company, Inc.
Subsidiary of Wadsworth Publishing Co., Inc.
16250 Ventura Blvd.
Encino, Cal. 91436

Directors Guild of America, Inc.
7950 Sunset Blvd.
Hollywood, Cal. 90046

Doubleday & Company, Inc.
245 Park Ave.
New York, N.Y. 10017

Dover Publications, Inc.
180 Varick St.
New York, N.Y. 10014

Drama Book Specialists (Publishers)
150 West 52nd St.
New York, N.Y. 10019

E. P. Dutton
Division of Sequoia-Elsevier Publishing Co., Inc.
2 Park Ave.
New York, N.Y. 10016

E. Story-Scientia
Address not available

Eastman Kodak Company
343 State St.
Rochester, N.Y. 14650

Edizioni di Bianco e Nero
(Centro Sperimentale di Cinematografia)
Via S. Dorotea, 6
Roma
ITALY

Edizioni Mostra Cinema
Address not available

Educational Film Library Association, Inc.
43 West 61st St.
New York, N.Y. 10023

*EFLA Evaluations*
See Educational Film Library Association

Fairleigh Dickinson University Press
285 Madison Ave.
Madison, N.J. 07940

*Film*
See British Federation of Film Societies

*Film Comment*
See Film Society of Lincoln Center

*Film Culture*
Box 1499 GPO
New York, N.Y. 10001

*Film Journal*
% Thomas R. Atkins
Box 9602
Hollins College, Va. 24020 (Temporarily Suspended)

Film Library Information Council
Box 348
Radio City Station
New York, N.Y. 10019

*Film Library Quarterly*
See Film Library Information Council

*Film Literature Index*
See Filmdex, Inc.

*Film News: The International Review of AV Materials and Equipment*
Film News Co.
250 West 57th St.
New York, N.Y. 10019

*Film Review Digest*
See Kraus-Thomson Organization Ltd. (Ceased)

*Film Quarterly*
See University of California Press

Film Society of Lincoln Center
1865 Broadway
New York, N.Y. 10023

*Film Society Review*
See American Federation of Film Societies

*Film TV Daily Yearbook of Motion Pictures and Television*
Wid's Films and Film Folk, Inc.
A Division of DFI Communications, Inc.
330 West 58th St.
New York, N.Y. 10019 (Distributed by Arno Press)

Filmdex, Inc.
Box 22672
State University of New York, Albany
1400 Washington Ave.
Albany, N.Y. 12222

*Filmmaker's Newsletter*
See Suncraft International Corporation

*Films and Filming*
See Hansom Books

*Films in Review*
See National Board of Review of Motion Pictures, Inc.

Burt Franklin & Co., Inc.
235 East 44th St.
New York, N.Y. 10017

Friedrich-Ebert-Stiftung
53 Bonn-Bad Godesberg
Kolner-Strasse 149
Federal Republic of Germany

Gale Research Company
Book Tower
Detroit, Mich. 48226

Garland Publishing, Inc.
545 Madison Ave.
New York, N.Y. 10022

Gordon Press Publishers
P.O. Box 459
Bowling Green Station
New York, N.Y. 10004

Government Printing Office
North Capitol and H. Sts., N.W.
Washington, D.C. 20401

Grafton Books
See André Deutsch, Ltd.

Granada Publishing, Ltd.
1221 Avenue of the Americas
New York, N.Y. 10020

   OR
P.O. Box 9
29 Frogmore
St. Albans, Hertfordshire AL22NF
ENGLAND

Grossman Publishers, Inc.
% Viking Penguin
625 Madison Ave.
New York, N.Y. 10022

Grove Press, Inc.
196 West Houston St.
New York, N.Y. 10014

G. K. Hall & Company
70 Lincoln St.
Boston, Mass. 02111

Hansom Books
Artillery Mansions
75 Victoria Street
London SW1H OHZ
ENGLAND

# Appendix A 173

Harcourt Brace Jovanovich, Inc.
757 Third Ave.
New York, N.Y. 10017

Harper & Row, Publishers, Inc.
10 East 53rd St.
New York, N.Y. 10022

Hart-Davis MacGibbon
See Granada Publishing, Ltd.

Hastings House Publishers, Inc.
10 East 40th St.
New York, N.Y. 10016

James H. Heineman, Inc. Publishers
475 Park Ave.
New York, N.Y. 10022

Hill and Wang
Division of Farrar, Straus, & Giroux, Inc.
19 Union Square West
New York, N.Y. 10003

Historical Films
P.O. Box 46505
Los Angeles, California 90046

Hollywood Film Archive
8344 Melrose Ave.
Hollywood, Cal. 90069

Holt, Rinehart and Winston
CBS, Inc.
383 Madison Ave.
New York, N.Y. 10017

Hopkinson & Blake, Inc.
185 Madison Ave.
New York, N.Y. 10016

Indiana University Press
Tenth and Morton Sts.
Bloomington, Ind. 47401

Institute des Hautes Études Cinématographiques
Biblioteque Nationale, Département des Periodiques
Rue Richelieu
Paris
FRANCE

*International Index to Film Periodicals*
See St. Martins Press

*Journal of Popular Film*
See Center for the Study of Popular Culture

Kemp's Group, Ltd.
1-5 Bath Street
London, EC1V 9QA
ENGLAND

Kent State University Press
Kent, Ohio 44242

Kraus-Thomson Organization, Ltd.
RTE. 100
Millwood, N.Y. 10546

*Learning Directory*
See Westinghouse Learning Corporation

*Library Journal*
See R. R. Bowker Company

Library of Congress
Edition Information:
Catalog Maintenance and Catalog Publication Division
Library of Congress
Washington, D.C. 20540
Subscriptions:
Cataloging Distribution, Inc.
Library of Congress
Washington, D.C. 20541

Little, Brown & Company
34 Beacon St.
Boston, Mass. 02106

McGraw-Hill Book & Educational Services Group
McGraw-Hill, Inc.
1221 Avenue of the Americas
New York, N.Y. 10020

Macmillan Publishing Co., Inc.
866 Third Ave.
New York, N.Y.

Peter Martin Associates, Ltd.
280 Bloor Street West
Suite 305
Toronto, Ontario M5S 1W1
CANADA

*Media and Methods; Exploration in Education*
See North American Publishing Company

*Media Review Digest*
See Pierian Press

Morgan & Morgan, Inc.
145 Palisade St.
Dobbs Ferry, N.Y. 10522

William Morrow & Co., Inc.
Wholly owned Subsidiary of Scott,
   Foresman & Co.
105 Madison Ave.
New York, N.Y. 10016

*Movie*
See Movie Magazine, Ltd.

*Movie Magazine, Ltd.*
3 Cork Street
London, W1
ENGLAND

*MS: The New Magazine for Women*
See Ms. Magazine Corporation

MS. Magazine Corporation
370 Lexington Ave.
New York, N.Y. 10017

National Board of Review of Motion
   Pictures, Inc.
210 East 68th St.
New York, N.Y. 10021

National Information Center for Edu-
   cational Media (NICEM)
University of Southern California
University Park
Los Angeles, Cal. 90007

Netherlands Information Service
Netherlands, Rijksvoorlichtingsdienst
2513 AA
's-Gravenhage (The Hague)
Binnenhof 20
HOLLAND

The New American Library, Inc.
Subsidiary of The Times Mirror Co.
1301 Avenue of the Americas
New York, N.Y. 10019

*New York Review of Books*
See N. Y. R. E. V., Inc.

New York Zoetrope
31 East 12th St.
New York, N.Y. 10003

Newsbank, Inc.
P.O. Box 645
Greenwich, Conn. 06830
   OR
P.O. Box 10047
741 Main St.
Stamford, Conn. 06904

North American Publishing Company
401 North Broad St.
Philadelphia, Pa. 19108

Northwestern University Library
Evanston, Ill. 60211

N. Y. R. E. V., Inc.
250 West 57th St.
New York, N.Y. 10019

Ohara Publications, Inc.
1847 West Empire Ave.
Burbank, Cal. 91504

Oxford University Press, Inc.
Division of William H. Sadler, Inc.
11 Park Place
New York, N.Y. 10007

Jerome S. Ozer, Publisher, Inc.
340 Tenafly Rd.
Englewood Cliffs, N.J. 07631

Pacific Coast Publishers
4085 Campbell Ave.
Menlo Park, Cal. 94025

Jean-Jacques Pauvert
8 Rue de Nesle
75006 Paris
FRANCE

Penguin
Division of Viking Penguin, Inc.
625 Madison Ave.
New York, N.Y. 10022

Peterson's Guides, Inc.
228 Alexander St.
Princeton, N.J. 08540

The Pierian Press
Box 1808
Ann Arbor, Mich. 48106

Praeger Publishers, Inc.
Division of Holt, Rinehart & Win-
   ston/CBS, Inc.
383 Madison Ave.
New York, N.Y. 10017

Prentice-Hall, Inc.
Englewood Cliffs, N.J. 07632

*Previews: News and Reviews of Non-
   print Media*
See R. R. Bowker Co.

*Publishers Weekly*
See R. R. Bowker Company

Pyramid Publications
See Harcourt Brace Jovanovich

Quadrangle Books
3 Park Ave.
New York, N.Y. 10016

Quigley Publishing Company
1270 Avenue of the Americas
New York, N.Y. 10020

Random House, Inc.
Subsidiary of RCS Corporation
201 East 50th St.
New York, N.Y. 10022

Reel Research
P.O. Box 6037
Albany, Cal. 94706

Revisionist Press
P.O. Box 2009
Brooklyn, N.Y. 11202

Verlag Hans Rohr
Oberdorfstrasse 5
8024 Zurich
SWITZERLAND

Royal Film Archive of Belgium
Palais des Beaux-Arts
23 Rue Ravenstein
Brussels 1
BELGIUM

St. Martin's Press
175 Fifth Ave.
New York, N.Y. 10010

San Diego State Library
5300 Capanile Drive
San Diego, Cal. 92182

San Francisco Community Press
Address not available

Scarecrow Press, Inc.
Subsidiary of Grolier, Inc.
52 Liberty St.
Metuchen, N.J. 08840

*Screen*
See Society for Education in Film and Television

Seven Arts Press
6605 Hollywood Blvd., No. 215
Hollywood, Cal. 90028

*Sight and Sound*
See British Film Institute

*Sightlines*
See Educational Film Library Association, Inc.

Simon and Schuster, Inc.
The Simon & Schuster Building
1230 Avenue of the Americas
New York, N.Y. 10020

Society for Cinema Studies
% Gerald Noxon
Department of Radio-TV-Film
Temple University
Philadelphia, Pa. 19122

Society for Education in Film and Television
29 Old Compton Street
London W1V 5PL
ENGLAND

Southern Illinois University Press
Box 3697
Carbondale, Ill. 62901

Spectator International Inc.
9667 Wilshire Blvd.
Beverly Hills, Cal. 90212

Lyle Stuart, Inc.
120 Enterprise Ave.
Secaucus, N.J. 07094

Studio Vista
Cassell & Collier Macmillan Publications, Ltd.
35 Red Lion Square
London WC1R 4SG
ENGLAND

Suncraft International Corporation
Box 115
Ward Hill, Maine 01830

TAB Books
Blue Ridge Summit, Pa. 17214

*Take One*
See Unicorn Publishing Corporation

Teachers College
Columbia University
1234 Amsterdam Ave.
New York, N.Y. 10027

Time, Inc.
Time & Life Building
New York, N.Y.

  Subscriptions to:
Time, Inc.
591 North Fairbanks Ct.
Chicago, Ill. 60611

*Time: The Weekly News Magazine*
See Time, Inc.

Turtle Island Foundation
2845 Buena Vista Way
Berkeley, Cal. 94708

Twayne Publishers
Division of G. K. Hall, Inc.
70 Lincoln St.
Boston, Mass. 02111

Frederick Ungar Publishing Co., Inc.
250 Park Ave. S.
New York, N.Y. 10003

Unicorn Publishing Corporation
Box 1778, Station B
Montreal H3B 3L3
CANADA

University of California Press
2223 Fulton St.
Berkeley, Cal. 94720

University of Illinois Press
Urbana, Ill. 61801

University of Southern California
  Press
Student Union 400
University of Southern California
Los Angeles, Cal. 90007

Van Nostrand Reinhold Company
Division of Litton Educational Publishing, Inc.
450 West 33rd St.
New York, N.Y. 10001

Variety, Inc.
154 West 46th St.
New York, N.Y. 10036

*Velvet Light Trap*
See Arizona Jim Co-op.

The Viking Press
625 Madison Ave.
New York, N.Y. 10022

*Village Voice*
80 University St.
New York, N.Y. 10003

Visual Studies Workshop
4 Elton St.
Rochester, N.Y. 14607

Watson-Guptill Publications
Division of Billboard Publications,
  Inc.
1215 Broadway
New York, N.Y. 10036

Wayside Press
P.O. Box 475
Cottonwood, Ariz. 86326

Bruce Webster
426 N.W. 20th St.
Oklahoma City, Okla. 73103

*Weekly Record*
See R. R. Bowker Company

*Weekly Variety*
See Variety, Inc.

Westinghouse Learning Corporation
100 Park Ave.
New York, N.Y. 10017

White Lion Publishers
138 Park Lane
London W1
ENGLAND

Whitston Publishing Company
Box 322
Troy, N.Y. 12181

Who's Who in Show Business, Inc.
1780 Broadway
New York, N.Y. 10019

The H. W. Wilson Company
950 University Ave.
Bronx, N.Y. 10452

World Microfilms Publications
62 Queen's Grove
London NW8 6ER
ENGLAND

Yale University Library Publications
P.O. Box 1603A
Yale Station
New Haven, Conn. 06520

A. Zwemmer Ltd.
26 Litchfield Street
London WC2H 9NJ
ENGLAND

# Appendix B: Libraries Holding Screenplays

Academy of Motion Picture Arts and Sciences Margaret Herrick Library
American Film Institute Charles K. Feldman Library
Boston University Library
Brigham Young University Library
California Lutheran College Library
California State University at Fullerton, Library
California State University at Los Angeles, Library
Carleton College Library
City College Library
Columbia University Library
Cornell University Library
Dartmouth College Library
George Eastman House
Howard University Library
Indiana University—Bloomington, Library
Iowa State University Library
Library of Congress
Loyola Marymount University Library
New York University Library
North Texas State University Library
Ohio State University Library
Queens College Library
San Diego State University Library
San Francisco State University Library
San Jose State University Library
School of Theology at Claremont Library
Southern Illinois University Library
Stanford University Library
University of California at Berkeley, Library
University of California at Los Angeles, Library
University of Georgia Library
University of Illinois Library
University of Iowa Library
University of Kansas Library
University of Maryland—Baltimore County, Library
University of Minnesota Library
University of Oregon Library
University of Southern California Library
University of Texas at Austin, Library
University of Virginia Library
Wisconsin Center for Film and Theater Research

# Topics Index

Academy of Motion Picture Arts and Sciences
 collections, 71
 reference services, 102
Acquisitions sources, 22ff
Adrienson and Post, 54
American Film Institute
 collections, 72
 reference services, 101
*American Film Institute Series* (Little, Brown), 14
Anchor Bookshop, 68
*Anglo-American Cataloguing Rules.* 2nd ed., 113, 116
Archives, 71ff
Art Institute of Chicago Film Center, 105
At the Sign of the Dancing Bear, 66
Audiovisual materials: cataloging, 115, 117
Autoren Buchhandlung, 69

BRS (Bibliographic Retrieval System), 95, 98ff
Bibliographic networks, 93ff
Bibliographies
 evaluative criteria, 41
 listing, 17ff
Biographical materials: evaluative criteria, 42
Birns and Sawyer, Inc., 64
Black Sun Books, 62, 64
Bond Street Book Store, 54, 64
Book City, 68
Book review sources, 23ff
Bookstores
 international, 68
 scripts, 62
 United States, 64-67
 visual or advertising material, 54
Boston Film/Video Foundation, 105
Brandt's (Eddie) Saturday Matinee, 65
Budgets, 5, 127
Buchhandlung Walther Konig, 69

Card catalog
 entries for scripts, 111
 filing, 109-110
 motion picture entries, 109
Cataloging, *see* Descriptive cataloging
Catalogs of films: evaluative criteria, 42
Cherokee Bookshop, 54
Cine Books, 69
The Cinema Bookshop, 68
Cinema City, 54, 64
*Cinéma d'Aujourd'hui in English* (Crown), 13
*Cinema One* (Indiana University Press), 14
*Cinema One* (Viking Press), 16
*Cinema Series* (Revisionist Press), 15
*Cinema Studies Series* (Hopkinson & Blake), 14
*Cinema Two* (Indiana University Press), 14
*Cinema World* (Doubleday), 13
Cinemabilia, 54, 64
*Classic Film Scripts* (Simon & Schuster), 15
Classifications, 121
Clipping files, 34
Collection development sources, 17ff, 22ff
Collectors Book Store, 54, 62, 64
Computer-based information networks, 95, 97ff
Continuities, 59
 cutting, 59
 dialogue, 59
Copyright
 for preservation, 57
 format change, 56
 videotaping, 57
Corner Book Shop, 65
Cox (A. E.), 68
Creative Film Society, 54
Credits
 indexes: evaluative criteria, 42
Critical works
 indexes: evaluative criteria, 43
Curricula for film study, 3, 4
Cutting continuity, 59

Dancing Bear (At the Sign of the), 66
Dartmouth College Library collections, 76
Data bases for film study, 97ff
Decimal classification, 122
Descriptive cataloging
  audiovisual materials, 115, 117
  manuscripts, 114, 117, 118
  photographs, 115
  stills, 115
Dewey Decimal Classification, 122
Dialogue continuity, 59
Dictionaries: evaluative criteria, 41
*Dissertations on Film Series* (Arno Press), 13
Document delivery networks, 93-96
*Dover Film Series*, 14
Drama Book Shop, 65
Duffy (Martin) and Sons, 65
Duncan Poster Service, 65

Eastman (George) House collections, 77
Edmunds (Larry), 54, 65
Educational Film Library Association: reference services, 102
Einhorn (M. M. Maxwell), 66
Encyclopedias: evaluative criteria, 41
Enrollments in film courses, 7
*Essandess World of Film Series* (Simon & Schuster), 15
Evaluation criteria, 39ff

Fee-based information services, 101
Fédération Internationale des Archives du Film
  *Guidelines for Describing Unpublished Script Materials*, 118
Les Feux de la Rampe, 69
Filing rules, 110
Film courses
  materials used, 8-10
  statistics, 6-8
Film study materials: faculty use, 8-10
*Film Focus Series* (Prentice-Hall), 15
*Film in Sweden* (A. S. Barnes), 13
Film in the Cities, Inc., 105
The Film Library, 68
*Film Script Series* (Appleton-Century-Crofts), 13
Film study archives, 71ff
Film study librarians: number of, 126
Filmbuchhandlung Hans Rohr, 69
*Filmguide Series* (Indiana University Press), 14
*Films of — Series* (Citadel Press), 13

Genre criticism: evaluative criteria, 47
George Eastman House collections, 77
Gielow (Wolfgang), 69
Global Village, 105
*Gordon Press Film Series*, 14
Gotham Book Mart, 66
Graduate film courses, 6
*Grove Press Film Book Series*, 14

H and H Bookstore, 54
Hamilton (Jack), 66
Hampton Books, 66
Historical works: evaluative criteria, 45
Hollywood Book Service, 54
*Hollywood Professionals* (A. S. Barnes), 13
The Hollywood Review, 54, 66

*Illustrated History of Movies Series* (Pyramid Publications), 15
Indexes
  evaluative criteria of, 42, 43-44
  to reviews of nonprint materials, 51
  to serials: evaluative criteria, 43-44
  listing, 38
Interlibrary loan, 93-96
*International Film Guide Series* (A. S. Barnes), 13

The Kitchen, 105

Larry Edmunds, 54, 65
"Il Leuto," 70
Librairie Contacts, 69
Librairie de la Fontaine, 69
Library budgets for film study, 127
Library filing rules, 110
Library instruction
  basic concepts, 107
  sample presentation, 108-112
Library materials: shelving of, 123
Library of Congress
  *Classification Scheme*, 122
  collections, 35, 75
  *List of Subject Headings*, 109, 120ff
  reference services, 102
  screenplay deposits, 58
*Library of Film and Television Practice* (Hastings House), 14
Libreria Editrice Bonacci, 70
Limelight Bookstore, 66
*Literature and Film Series* (Dickinson Publishing Co.), 13

Topics Index 181

Lobby cards, 53
Lockheed, 95, 97ff

*MGM Library of Film Scripts* (Viking Press), 16
Manuscripts: cataloging, 114, 117, 119
*Masterworks Film Series* (Harper & Row), 14
Maxwell (M. M. Einhorn), 66
Media Centers, *see* Regional Film Study Centers
Media Study, Inc., 105
Memorabilia dealers
  international, 68-70
  United States, 64-67
Le Minotaure, 69
*Modern Film Scripts* (Simon & Schuster), 15
Monarch Film Series, 15
Monograph: definition, xii
Monograph series, 11ff
The Motion Picture Bookshop at the National Film Theatre, 68
Motley Books, 68
*Movie Editions* (University of California Press), 15
*Movie Makers* (Doubleday), 13
Movie Poster Service, 66
Movie Star News, 54, 67
*Moving Pictures—Their Impact on Society* (Jerome S. Ozer), 14
Museum of Modern Art Film Department, 105
  *Classification Scheme*, 123
  collections, 76

National Film Information Service, 102
New York Zoetrope, 67
Nonprint material
  copyright, 55
  definition, xii
  indexes, 51
  review journals, 51
  selection, 51
  uses, 52-53
Northwest Film Study Center, 105

Ohlinger's (Jerry) Movie Material Store, 54, 62, 67
Oral history, 54

Pacific Film Archive, 105
  reference services, 103
*Paperback Film Scripts* (Viking Press), 16

Periodicals
  areas related to film, 37
  definition, xii
  frequently indexed, 28-33
  indexes, 38
  international: listing, 35-37
  selection criteria, 27
Photographs: descriptive cataloging, 115
*Pictorial Treasury of Film Stars Series* (William C. Brown Co.), 13
Pittsburgh Film-makers, Inc., 105
Posters, 54
*Praeger Film Books*, 15
*Praeger Film Library*, 15
Premiere booklets, 54
Press-sheets, 54
Pressbooks, 54
Primary resources: definition, xii
Production stills, 53
Production studies: evaluative criteria, 48
Publishers: film studies, 25-26

Reference materials
  definition, 40
  listing, 81-92
  subject index to, 81
*A Reference Publication in Film Series* (G. K. Hall), 14
Reference referral, 93
  national resources, 101
  question categories, 94
Regional film study centers
  definition, 104
  listing, 105
Reviewing journals, 22-25
Rocky Mountain Film Center, 105

SDC (Systems Development Corporation), 95, 97ff
Sally (Stephen), 54, 67
Sandbergs (A. B.) Bokhandel, 70
Sautter & Lackmann, 69
Schoeller (Marga), 69
*Screen Series* (A. S. Barnes), 13
*Screenplay Library Series* (Southern Illinois University Press), 15
Screenplays
  forms of, 59
  evaluative criteria, 47-49
  published, 13, 14, 15, 16, 59-60
  sources, 60, 62
  uses, 58, 59
The Scriptorium, 67

Scripts, *see* Screenplays
Secondary sources: definition, xii
Selection and scheduling of films, 51-52, 126-127
Selection of film study material: responsibilities, 126
Selection tools for books, 22
Serial: definition, xii
Series
  definition, xii
  monograph, 11-16
Shelving of library materials, 123
Shooting scripts, 59; *see also* Screenplays
The Silver Screen, 54, 67
16 mm films: selection, 51
Smith (Bob) Poster Service, 54
South Carolina Arts Commission, 105
Southwest Alternate Media Project, 105
Souvenir Programs, 54
Space Age Books, 68
Sterling Books, 62, 67
Stills, 53, 54
  descriptive cataloging, 115
  sources, 64-70
Stoddard (Richard), 67
Subject headings, 119
  for film study, 109, 119
Survey of film study collections, 124ff

Technical works: evaluative criteria, 46-47
*Theater, Film and the Performing Arts Series* (DaCapo Press), 13

*Theatrical Arts Series* (Twayne Publishers), 15
Trade magazines, 33-34
Treasures and Pleasures, 68
Trivia questions, 80

Undergraduate film courses, 6
*Ungar Film Library*, 15
University Film Study Center, 105
  reference services, 104
University of California - Los Angeles. Theatre Arts Library
  collections, 74
  reference services, 103
University of Iowa collections, 75
University of Southern California Library
  collections, 74
  reference services, 103

Velde (Donald L.) Inc., 67
Videotaping, 57

Walker Art Center, 105
Wisconsin/Warner Bros. Screenplay Series (University of Wisconsin Press), 15
Wood (Peter), 68

Le Zinzin d'Hollywood, 69
Zoetrope, 67
Zwemmer, Ltd., 68

# Collections Index

Academy of Motion Picture Arts and Sciences, 71
Adams, Frank, 161
*Adventure Tomorrow*, 131
Allied Artists (studios), 76
Altman, Robert, 78
American Archives of Factual Film, 140
American Film Institute, 72
    Center for Advanced Film Studies Seminars, 73
American University, 127
Anderson, Judtih, 155
Andy Hardy Series, 73
Anhalt, Edward, 74
Animation, 73, 149
Arnaz, Desi, 149
Art direction, 74
Asian cinema, 74
Astor, Mary, 129
Auburn University, 128

Ballard, Willis, 161
Ballin, Hugo, 73
Bard College, 128
Barnouw, Eric, 134
Barret, Tony, 74
Barrymore, Lionel, 73
Behn, Harry, 162
Belmont, Eleanor, 134
Benchley, Nathaniel, 129
Benny, Jack, 73
Biograph (studios), 76
Bitzer, Billy, 76
Blees, Robert, 75, 157
Bob Jones University, 128
Boston University, 129
Branch, Houston, 162
Braverman, Barnet, 76
Brentano, Lowell, 162
Bridgeport, University of, 155
Brigham Young University, 129
Brooklyn College, 129

Buñuel, Luis, 157
Bute, Mary Ellen, 160

California-Berkeley, University of, 155
California-Los Angeles, University of, *see* University of California-Los Angeles
California-Santa Barbara, University of, 155
California-Santa Cruz, University of, 156
California College of Arts and Crafts, 130
California Institute of the Arts, 130
California Lutheran College, 130
California State University at Fresno, 130
California State University at Fullerton, 131
California State University at Los Angeles, 131
California State University at Northridge, 131
Cantor, Eddie, 73
Carleton College, 131
Carrick, Edward, 162-163
Case Western Reserve University, 132
Center for Advanced Film Studies Seminars, 73
Central Michigan University, 132
Central Missouri State University, 132
Chandler, George, 73
Chandler, Raymond, 73
Chayefsky, Paddy, 78
City College, 132
Cleveland Institute of Art, 133
Cocteau, Jean, 135
Cohen, Albert J., 75, 157
College of Staten Island, 133
Collidge, Dane, 155
Collins, Richard, 162
Columbia (studios), 72, 73
Columbia College Library, 134
Columbia University, 134
Cooper, Gladys, 74
Cornell University, 135
Cotton, Joseph, 74
Cox, William, 162

183

Crain, W. H., 163
Crawford, Merritt, 76
*Crime Does Not Pay*, 133
Cromwell, John, 138
Cukor, George, 73
Curry, Thomas, 162
Curtis, Tony, 73

Dartmouth College, 76
Davis, Albert, 164
Davis, Bette, 129
Davis, Delmar Lawrence, 153
DeMille, Cecil B., 129
Dempster, Carol, 76
Denison University, 135
Devine, Andy, 129
Dieterle, William, 74
Disney, Walter, 61, 74
District of Columbia, University of the, 162
Doheny Library, University of Southern California, 74
Douglas, Kirk, 78
Douglas, Melvin, 78
Downing, Robert, 162
Dunham, Katherine, 151
Dunne, Philip, 74
Duryea, Dan, 74
Dwan, Allan, 73

Eastern Michigan University, 135
Eastman (George) House, 77
Eddy, Nelson, 74
Edens, Roger, 74
Edison Company, 61, 76
Emerson College, 135
Evans, Mark, 129
Evergreen State College, 136

Faulkner, William, 164
Feldman (Charles K.) Library, American Film Institute, 72
Felton, Norman, 157
Fessier, Michael, 162
Flaherty, Robert, 76, 93, 150, 160, 163
Fleischer, Max, 73
Fleischer, Richard, 74
Florida State University, 136
Fordham University, 136
Fox Film Corporation, 74, 76
Frankenheimer, John, 78
Freed, Arthur, 74

Gable, Clark, 74
General Music Corporation, 74

George Eastman House, 77
Georgia, University of, 156
Glazer, Benjamin, 73
Goldwyn, Samuel, 72
*Gone With The Wind*, 156
Gorelick, Mordecai, 151
Grant, Cary, 163
*The Great Race*, 75
*Greed*, 155
Griffith, D. W., 76

*H. M. Pulham, Esq.*, 163
Hampden, Walter, 146
Hampshire College, 137
Hardy (Andy) Series, 73
Hathaway, Henry, 73
Hawkins, John and Ward, 162
Hawks, Howard, 129
Head, Edith, 78
Hecht, Ben, 157
Henry, Bill, 145
Herrick (Margaret) Library-Academy of Motion Picture Arts and Sciences, 71
Hoblitzelle Theatre Arts Library, 162-164
Hofstra University, 137
Holbrook, Hal, 78
Hollins College, 137
Hollyman, Burnes, 164
Hollywood Studio Strike, 73
Hollywood Ten, 78
Horner, Harry, 73
Houdini, Harry, 164
Houseman, John, 73
Howard, Sidney Coe, 155
Howard University, 138
Humboldt State University, 138
Hunter, Evan, 129
Hunter College, 138

Illinois-Urbana, University of, 156
Ince, Thomas, 72, 73, 76
*The Incredible Mr. Limpet*, 149
Indiana University-Bloomington, 139
Indiana University-Northwest, 140
Indiana University-South Bend, 139
Inge, William, 158
*International Index to Film Periodicals* (cards), 76
Iowa, University of, 75, 157
Iowa State University Library, 140
Ithaca College Library, 140

Jackson State University, 140
Jagger, Dean, 129

## Collections Index 185

Jersey City State College, 141
Jewison, Norman, 78
Johnson, George P. (Negro Film Collection), 73
Junge, Alfred, 162-163
Juniata College, 141
Junkin, Ralph, 75

Kansas, University of, 158
Kansas City Art Institute, 141
Kantor, Hal, 78
Kelly, Gene, 129
Kendall, Messmore, 164
Kerr, Walter and Jean, 78
Koch, Howard, 73
Kovacs, Ernie, 73
Kramer, Stanley, 73
Kushing, Barret, 145

Laszlo, Ernest, 74
Laughton, Charles, 73
Lawson, John Howard, 151
Lehman, Ernest, 163
Leisen, Mitchell, 73
Lesser, Sol, 74
Levine, Irving R., 135
Lewin, Albert, 74
Lewis, Jerry, 74
Library Affairs Film Production Unit, 151
Library of Congress, 35, 75
Lindsay, Howard, 146
Lombard, Carole, 163
Lorentz, Pare, 166
*Los Angeles Daily News* Morgue File on Films, 73
Loyola Marymount University, 142

MGM Studios, see Metro-Goldwyn-Mayer
MTM Enterprises, 78
McCarey, Leo, 73
McDowall, Roddy, 129
McGreevey, John, 139
Mancini, Henry, 74
Mann, Abby, 74
March, Fredrick, 78
Marion, Ira, 133
Martin, Ray, 131
Maryland-Baltimore County, University of, 158
Maryland-College Park, University of, 158
Massachusetts College of Art, 142
Massachusetts Institute of Technology, 142
Memphis State University, 143
Mercury Theatre, 139

Metro-Goldwyn-Mayer, 73, 74, 76, 77, 133, 145, 163, 165
Miami, University of, 159
Michigan, University of, 159
Minneapolis College of Art and Design, 143
Minnesota, University of, 160
Mintz, Jack, 73
Mirisch, Walter, 78
Mirisch Productions, 73
Missouri-Kansas City, University of, 160
Monogram Films, 61
Monroe, Marilyn, 164
Montana State University, 143
Moore, Mary Tyler, 78
Moorhead State University, 144
Motion Picture Photograph Collection 1911-1975, 156
Motion Picture Research Council, 134
Mount St. Vincent University, 144
Mount Vernon College, 144
Museum of Modern Art, 77
Muybridge, Eadweard J., 152, 153

NBC Matinee Theater, 73
National Association of Theatre Owners, 129
New Orleans, University of, 160
New York University, 144
Newley, Anthony, 129
Newman, Alfred, 74
Nichols, Dudley, 73
North, Alex, 74
North Carolina-Carlotte, University of, 161
North Texas State University, 145
Northwestern University, 145
Notre Dame, University of, 161
Nugent, Frank, 129

Occidental College, 145
O'Connell, Arthur, 142
O'Hara, John, 147
Ohio State University, 146
Oklahoma, University of, 161
Oklahoma State University, 146
Oral history, 54, 73, 74, 134
Oregon, University of, 161
*Our Gang*, 131

Paramount (studios), 61, 72, 73, 74
Parker, Robert Allerton, 155
Pasternak, Joe, 74
Pathé (studios), 72
Peabody, George Foster, 156
Peckinpah, Sam, 73

## COLLECTIONS INDEX

Pennsylvania State University, 146
Philadelphia College of Art, 147
*Photoplay*, index to, 51
Pinter, Harold, 137
Poe, James, 73
Polonsky, Abraham, 73
Pratt Institute, 147

Queens College, 147

RKO (studios), 61, 72, 78
Radio scripts, 74
Rains, Claude, 129
Raphaelson, Samson, 157
Republic Studios, 61, 73, 76, 77, 129
Rhode Island School of Design, 148
Richards, E. V., 163
Roach, Hal, 61, 131
Robinson, Edward G., 74
Rochester Institute of Technology, 148
Roger Williams College, 148
Ross, Arthur A., 75
Rosza, Miklos, 135
Rotha, Paul, 73, 163
Roxy Theater, 76

Saenger Theatre Chain, 163
San Diego State University, 149
San Francisco Art Institute, 149
San Jose State University, 150
Sapinsley, Alvin, 128
Sarah Lawrence College, 150
Schary, Dore, 78
Schneider, Alan, 78
School of Theology at Claremont, 150
School of Visual Arts, 150
Seaton, George, 73
Seitz, George B., 73
Selig, William, 72
Sennett, Mack, 72
Serling, Rod, 73, 78
*Serpico*, 164
Shearer, Norma, 76
Shorts (Jules White Collection), 72
Shulman, Max, 129
Sisk, Robert, 74
Small, Edward, 74
*Sound of Music*, 163
South Dakota State University, 151
Southern California, University of, 35, 74
Southern Illinois University, 151
Southern Methodist University, 151
Spigelgass, Leonard, 129

Spring Hill College, 152
Stahl, John, 74
Stanford University, 152
*Star Trek*, 131
State Historical Society of Wisconsin, 77
State University of New York-Binghamton, 153
State University of New York-Buffalo, 153
State University of New York-Cortland, 154
Steinbeck, John, 150, 153
Stephen F. Austin State University, 154
Stephens College, 154
Stevens, Leith, 160
*Streets of San Francisco*, 129
Sturges, Preston, 73, 74, 157
Sunset Music Corporation, 74
Susskind, David, 78
Swift, David (Productions), 75

Taylor, L. Stoddard, 152
Texas-Austin, University of, 162
Thalberg, Irving, 76
Tilghman, William, 161
Tiomkin, Dimitri, 74
Toledo, University of, 164
Trade publications, 72
Trumbo, Dalton, 78
Tulsa, University of, 164
Twentieth Century Fox (studios), 61, 73, 74, 76, 157, 165

U.S. Steel Hour: Theatre Guild on the Air, 144
United Artists (studios), 61, 72, 77, 78
Universal Studios, 61, 72, 75, 77
University of Bridgeport, 155
University of California-Berkeley, 155
University of California-Los Angeles, 73
   Department of Special Collections, 73
   Film-Television Archive, 73
   Music Library, 74
   Oral History Program, 73
   Theater Arts Library, 74
University of California-Santa Barbara, 155
University of California-Santa Cruz, 156
University of Georgia, 156
University of Illinois-Urbana, 156
University of Iowa, 75, 157
University of Kansas, 158
University of Maryland-Baltimore County, 158
University of Maryland-College Park, 159
University of Miami, 159

University of Michigan, 159
University of Minnesota, 160
University of Missouri-Kansas City, 160
University of New Orleans, 160
University of North Carolina at Charlotte, 161
University of Notre Dame, 161
University of Oklahoma, 161
University of Oregon, 161
University of Southern California, 35, 74
University of Texas-Austin, 162
University of the District of Columbia, 162
University of Toledo, 164
University of Tulsa, 164
University of Virginia, 164
University of Wisconsin at Madison, 77, 165
University of Wisconsin-Milwaukee, 165
University of Wisconsin-Oshkosh, 166
University of Wisconsin-Stevens Point, 166

Victor Animatograph Company, 75
Vidal, Gore, 78
Vidor, King, 73, 74, 163
Virginia, University of, 164
von Sternberg, Joseph, 73
von Stroheim, Erich, 73

Walt Disney Studios, see Disney, Walter
Wanamaker, Sam, 129
Wanger, Walter, 76
Warner Brothers (studios), 61, 75, 76, 77
Warren, Charles, 162
Warren, Harry, 73
Washington State University, 166
Wayne, John, 164
Welles, Orson, 139
Wesleyan University, 167
*West Side Story*, 163
Wexler, Haskell, 74
White (Jules) Collection of Shorts, 72
William Paterson College of New Jersey, 167
Wilson, Harry, 155
Wisconsin-Madison, University of, 77, 165
Wisconsin-Milwaukee, University of, 165
Wisconsin-Oshkosh, University of, 166
Wisconsin-Stevens Point, University of, 166
Wisconsin Center for Film & Theatre Research, 77–78
Wisconsin State Historical Society, 77
Wise, Robert, 74
Wolper, David, 74
Wray, Fay, 74
Wright State University, 167

Zolotow, Maurice, 163
Zugsmith, Albert, 75

# Works Cited Index

Academy Awards, 91
Academy of Motion Picture Arts and Sciences
  Academy Players Directory, 81
  Screen Players Directory, 81
  Who Wrote the Movie, and What Else Did He Write?, 82
Action, 23, 38
An Actor Guide to the Talkies, 82, 84
Afterimage, 28
An Alphabetical Guide to Motion Pictures, Television and Videotape Production, 87
The American Cinema: Directors and Directions, 90
American Cinematographer, 23, 38
American Film, 23
American Film Directors, 86
American Film-Index, 87
American Film Institute
  Catalog of Motion Pictures Produced in the United States, 82
  National Survey of Film and Television Higher Education. Report of Finding, 8
  Guide to College Courses in Film and Television, xi, 6-8, 125
American Library Association. Catalog Use Study, 121
The American Movies Reference Book: the Sound Era, 88
The American Musical, 92
American Theatrical Arts: A Guide to Manuscripts and Special Collections in the United States and Canada, 60, 92, 124, 129ff
An Analysis of Questions and Answers in Libraries, 94
Anglo-American Cataloguing Rules, 113ff
Annotated Bibliography of New Publications in the Performing Arts, 65
An Approach to Film Study: A Selected Booklist, 18

Armes, Roy. French Cinema Since 1946, 82
Armour, Robert. "A Survey: The Teaching of Film in English Departments," 3
Aros, Andrew A.
  An Actor Guide to the Talkies, 1965-1974, 82
  A Title Guide to the Talkies, 1964-1974, 82
Artel, Linda. Film Programmers' Guide to 16mm Rentals, 82
Audiovisual Instruction, 51
Avant-Scéne Cinéma, 36

Baer, D. Richard
  The Film Buff's Bible of Motion Pictures, 1915-1972, 82
  The Film Buff's Checklist of Motion Pictures, 1912-1979, 82
Baer, Eleanora A. Titles in Series: A Handbook for Librarians and Students, 12
Basic Books in the Mass Media, 17
Batty, Linda. Retrospective Index to Film Periodicals, 1930-1971, 28ff, 38, 82
Bawden, Liz-Anne. The Oxford Companion to Film, 82
Beattie, Eleanor. Handbook of Canadian Film, 83
Bianco e Nero, 36
Bibliografie Internationala Cinema / Bibliographie Internationale Cinema, 20
Bibliographic Guide to Theatre Arts, 18
Bibliographie Internationale du Cinéma et de la Télévision, 21
Bild and Ton: Zeitschrift für Film und Fototechnik, 36
Billings, Pat. Hollywood Today, 83
A Biographical Dictionary of Film, 91
Biographical Encyclopedia and Who's Who of the American Theater, 90
Blacks in American Movies, 90
The Blue Book of Hollywood Musicals, 83
Blum, Eleanor. Basic Books in the Mass Media, 17

Bohler, Betty. *Seen Through the Dark: A Guide to Film Reference Sources*, 80
*Booklist*, 22, 51
*Books About Film: A Bibliographical Checklist*, 19
*Books in Print*, 25
*Books in Series in the United States 1966-1975*, 12
Bowles, Stephen E.
  *An Approach to Film Study: A Selected Booklist*, 18
  *Index to Critical Film Reviews in British and American Film Periodicals together with Index to Critical Reviews of Books About Film*, 18, 28ff, 38, 83
Bowser, Eileen. "Guidelines for Describing Unpublished Script Materials," 118
*Boxoffice*, 34
*British Cinema*, 85
*British Film and Television Yearbook*, 83
*British Film Catalogue*, 85
British Film Institute, London
  *The British Film Institute Film Title Index*, 18
  *The British Film Institute Personality and General Subject Index*, 18
  *Catalogue of the Book Library of the British Film Institute*, 18, 60
Bucher, Felix. *Germany*, 83
Bukalski, Peter J. *Film Research: A Critical Bibliography with Annotations and Essay*, 18
Burton, Jack. *The Blue Book of Hollywood Musicals*, 83

*Cahiers du Cinéma*, 36
*Cahiers du Cinéma in English*, 28
*Catalog of Motion Pictures Produced in the United States, Feature Films*, 82
*Catalog of the Library of the Museum of Modern Art, New York City*, 18
*Catalog Use Study*, 121
*Catalogo Biblioteca de Cinematica Nacional*, 60
*Catalogue Collectif des Livres et Periodiques Publiés Avant 1914*, 20
*Catalogue of the Book Library of the British Film Institute*, 18, 60
Cawkwell, Tim. *The World Encyclopedia of the Film*, 83
Centro Sperimentale de Cinemotografia. Biblioteca *Catalogo Della Biblioteca*, 20

Chaneler, Sol. *Collecting Movie Memorabilia*, 54
Chicorel, Marietta. *Chicorel Index to Film Literature*, 18
*Choice*, 22
*Cineaste*, 23, 28
*Cineforum; Rivista di Cultura Cinematografica*, 36
*Cinema*, 28
*Cinema Booklist*, 19
*Cinema Journal*, 23, 29
*Cinema Nuovo*, 36
*Cinema—The Magic Vehicle*, 85
*Cinema: Unabhängige Schweizerische Filmzeitschrift/Revue Cinématographique Indépendent Suisse*, 37
*Ciné—Revue*, 35
*Cinetheque*, 36
*Classic Film Collector*, 23
*Classification*, 122
*Classification Scheme for Literature, Film, and Television*, 124
*Collecting Movie Memorabilia*, 54
*Computer-Readable Bibliographic Data Bases*, 97
*A Copyright Guide for Educators and Librarians*, 57
Corliss, Richard. *The Hollywood Screenwriters*, 83
Costner, Tom. *Motion Picture Market Place*, 83
Cowie, Peter. *Sweden*, 83
*The Critical Index: a Bibliography of Articles on Film In English*, 28ff, 38, 85
*Cut! Print!*, 88
*Czechoslovak Film*, 35

*Daily Variety*, 34
Daisne, Johan, see Thiery, Herman
Dawson, Bonnie. *Women's Films in Print*, 84
*Dewey Decimal Classification and Relative Index*, 122
*Dictionnaire Filmographique de la Littérature Mondiale*, 91
*The Directory of Fee-Based Information Services*, 101
*Dictionary of Film Makers*, 90
*Dictionary of Films*, 90
*Dictionary of 1000 Best Films*, 89
*A Dictionary of the Cinema*, 85

Dimmitt, Richard B.
 An Actor Guide to the Talkies, 84
 A Title Guide to the Talkies, 84
The Drama Scholar's Index to Plays and Filmscripts, 90
Druxman, Michael B. Make It Again, Sam: A Survey of Movie Remakes, 84
Dyment, Alan R. The Literature of the Film, 18

EFLA Review Cards, 51
Eastern Europe, 86
Écran, 36
Edera, Bruno. Full Length Animated Feature Films, 84
Ekran, 37
Emmons, Carol A. Famous People on Film, 84
Encyclopedia of Information Systems and Services, 97
Enser, Carol A. Filmed Books and Plays, 84

FIAF, see Fédération Internationale des Archives du Film
Famous People on Film, 84
Feature Films on 8mm, 16mm, and Videotape, 51, 87
Fédération Internationale des Archives du Film
 Catalogue Collectif des Livres et Periodiques Publiés Avant 1914, 20
 Guidelines for Describing Unpublished Script Materials, 118
Film (London), 29
Film (Warsaw), 37
Film a Doba, 35
Film Actors Guide: Western Europe, 89
The Film Buff's Bible of Motion Pictures, 82
The Film Buff's Catalog, 88
The Film Buff's Checklist of Motion Pictures, 82
Film Comment, 23, 29
Film Copyright Reference Book: Films in the Public Domain from June 1940-June 1946, 92
Film Criticism: An Index to Critics' Anthologies, 86
Film Culture, 24, 29
Film Daily Yearbook, 84
Film Directors: A Guide to Their American Films, 89
Film Heritage, 29
Film: How and Where to Find Out What You Want to Know, 80

The Film Index, 20, 92
Film Journal (Carlton, Victoria, Australia), 30
The Film Journal (Hollins College, Va.), 29
Film Library Quarterly, 30
Film Library Techniques: Principles of Administration, 52
Film Literature Index, 28ff, 38, 84
Film Music: From Violins to Video, 88
Film News, 51
Film Programmers' Guide to 16mm Rentals, 82
Film Quarterly, 24, 30
Film Research: A Critical Bibliography with Annotations and Essay, 18
Film Review, 24
Film Review Digest, 28ff, 38, 84
Film Society Review, 30
Film Study: A Resource Guide, 19
Film Superlist, 86
Film und Ton-Magazin, 37
Filmarama, 91
Filmcritica, 36
Il Filme la Sua Storia, 21
Filmed Books and Plays, 84
Filmfacts, 84
Filmgoer's Book of Quotes, 85
Filmgoer's Companion, 85
Filmjournalen, 36
Filmkritik, 37
Filmkunst: Zeitschrift für Filmkultur and Wissenschaft, 35
Filmlexicon Degli Autori e Delli Opere, 85
Filmmaker's Newsletter, 24, 30
Films and Filming, 24, 30
Films Illustrated, 24
Films in Review, 24, 31
Filmska Kultura: Jugoslavenski casopis za Filmski Pitania, 37
Focal Encyclopedia of Film and TV Techniques, 85
Focus on Film, 24, 31
Forty Years of Screen Credits, 92
The Fox Girls, 89
France, 88
French Cinema Since 1946, 82
Full Length Animated Feature Films, 84

Garbicz, Adam. Cinema, The Magic Vehicle, 85
Geduld, Harry. An Illustrated Glossary of Film Terms, 85
General Bibliography of Motion Pictures, 20

Gerlach, John C. *The Critical Index: A Bibliography of Articles on Film in English, 1946-1973,* 28ff, 38, 85
Germany, 83
Gifford, Denis
 *British Cinema,* 85
 *British Film Catalogue, 1895-1970,* 85
Gill, Samuel. *Paramount Collection Inventory,* 72
*Glossary of Motion Picture Terminology,* 87
Gottesman, Ronald. *Guidebook to Film,* 85
Graham, Peter John, *A Dictionary of the Cinema,* 85
*The Great Movie Stars,* 91
*Great Spy Pictures,* 89
*The Great Western Pictures,* 89
Grogg, Sam L., Jr. "Where Do Film Teachers Come From?", 4
*Guide to College Courses in Film and Television,* xi, 6-8, 125
*A Guide to Critical Reviews, pt. IV: The Screenplay,* 90
*Guidebook to Film,* 85
*Guidelines for Describing Unpublished Script Materials,* 118

Halliwell, Leslie
 *Filmgoer's Book of Quotes,* 85
 *Filmgoer's Companion,* 85
 *Halliwell's Filmguide,* 86
*Handbook of Canadian Film,* 83
Harrison, Helen P. *Film Library Techniques: Principles of Administration,* 52
Heinzkill, Richard. *Film Criticism: An Index to Critics' Anthologies,* 86
Hibbin, Nina. *Eastern Europe,* 86
Hieber, C. E. "An Analysis of Questions and Answers in Libraries," 94
Hochman, Stanley. *American Film Directors,* 86
Hodgkinson, Anthony W. "Film— A Central Discipline?", 3
*Hollywood on Record,* 89
*Hollywood Quarterly,* 31
*Hollywood Reporter,* 34
*The Hollywood Screenwriter,* 83
*Hollywood Today,* 83
*Horror and Science Fiction Films,* 92
*How to Locate Criticism and Reviews of Plays and Films,* 80
Humphrys, Barbara. "Information Sources: Programmers' Tools," 52
Hurst, Walter. *Film Superlist,* 86

*An Illustrated Glossary of Film Terms,* 85
*Index to Critical Film Reviews in British and American Film Periodicals,* 18, 28ff, 38, 83
*Index to 16mm Educational Films,* 51
*International Encyclopedia of Film,* 86
International Federation of Film Archives, see Fédération Internationale des Archives du Film.
*International Film Guide,* 86
*International Index to Film Periodicals,* 28ff, 38, 76, 86
*International Index to Multi-Media Information,* 51
*International Motion Picture Almanac,* 86
*Internationale Filmbibliographie,* 21
*Iskusstvo Kino,* 37

Japan, 91
Jones, Karen. *Nye Boger on Film/New Books on Film,* 20
Jordan, Thurston C. *Glossary of Motion Picture Terminology,* 87
*The Journal* (Producers' Guide of America), 31
*Journal of Popular Film,* 24, 31
*Journal of the University Film Association,* 25

*Kemp's Film and Television Yearbook,* 87
*Kosmarama,* 36
Koszarski, Richard. *The Men with the Movie Cameras,* 87
Kowalski, Rosemary Ribich. *Women and Film; a Bibliography,* 87
Kruzas, Anthony Thomas. *Encyclopedia of Information Systems and Services,* 97

Lamparski, Richard. *Whatever Became of . . . ,* 87
Lauritzen, Einar. *American Film-Index, 1908-1915,* 87
*Learning Directory,* 51
*Learning Resources,* 51
LeClercq, Angie. "Collecting Non-Print Media in Academic Libraries," 52
Lee, Walter. *Reference Guide to Fantastic Films: Science Fiction, Fantasy, and Horror,* 87
Levitan, Eli L. *An Alphabetical Guide to Motion Pictures, Television, and Videotape Production,* 87
*Library Journal,* 22
Library of Congress
 *Classification,* 122

Library of Congress (continued)
*Monographic Series*, 12
*Moving Pictures in the United States and Foreign Countries: a Selected List of Recent Writings*, 19
*Subject Headings*, 109, 110, 119ff
Likeness, George. *The Oscar People*, 87
Limbacher, James L.
*Feature Films on 8mm, 16mm, and Videotape*, 51, 87
*Film Music: From Violins to Video*, 88
*Remakes, Series, and Sequels on Film and Television*, 87
*Literature/Film Quarterly*, 25
*The Literature of the Film: A Bibliographical Guide to the Film as Art and Entertainment*, 18

*The MGM Stock Company*, 89
MacCann, Richard Dyer. *The New Film Index: A Bibliography of Magazine Articles in English*, 28ff, 38, 88
McCarty, Clifford. *Published Screenplays: A Checklist*, 19, 60, 88, 112
*Make It Again, Sam: a Survey of Movie Remakes*, 84
Manchell, Frank. *Film Study: A Resource Guide*, 19
Manvell, Roger. *International Encyclopedia of Film*, 86
Manz, H. P. *Internationale Filmbibliographie*, 21
Martin, Marcel, *France*, 88
*Mass Media Booknotes*, 25
*Media and Methods*, 51
*Media Review Digest*, 51
Mehr, Linda Harris. *Motion Pictures, Television, and Radio: a Union Catalogue of Manuscript Collections in the Western United States*, 60, 72, 73, 88, 124, 130ff
*The Men With The Movie Cameras*, 87
Meyer, William R. *The Film Buff's Catalog*, 88

Michael, Paul. *The American Movies Reference Book: The Sound Era*, 88
Miller, Jerome, K. *A Copyright Guide for Educators and Librarians*, 57
Miller, Tony. *Cut! Print!*, 88
Minus, Johnny. *Film Superlist*, 86
Mitry, Jean. *Bibliographie Internationale du Cinéma et de la Télévision*, 21

Monaco, James
*Books About Film: A Bibliographical Checklist*, 19
*Film: How and Where to Find Out What You Want to Know*, 80
*Monographic Series*, 12
Mostra Internazionale del Libro e del Periodico Cinematografico, Televisivo e Fotografico. *Catalogo*, 21
*Motion Picture Directors*, 28ff, 38, 91
*Motion Picture Market Place*, 83
*Motion Picture Performers*, 28ff, 38, 91
*Motion Pictures: A Catalog of Books, Periodicals, Screenplays, Television Scripts, and Production Stills*, 60
*Motion Pictures from the Library of Congress Paper Print Collection*, 89
*Motion Pictures, Television, and Radio: A Union Catalogue of Manuscript Collections in the Western United States*, 60, 72, 73, 88, 124, 130ff
Moulds, Michael. *Classification Scheme for Literature, Film, and Television*, 123
*Movie*, 32
*Moving Pictures*, 19
*Moving Pictures in the United States and Foreign Countries*, 19
*Ms. The New Magazine for Women*, 32

NICEM. *Index to 16mm Educational Films*, 51
Nachbar, John G. *Western Films: An Annotated Critical Bibliography*, 88
*The New Film Index: A Bibliography of Magazine Articles in English*, 28ff, 38, 88
*New York Review of Books*, 32
*New York Times Film Reviews*, 88
*Newsbank: Review of the Arts: Film and Television*, 89
Niver, Kemp. *Motion Pictures from the Library of Congress Paper Print Collection*, 89
*North American Film and Video Directory*, 52
*Nye Boger on Film*, 20

*The Oscar People*, 87
*The Oxford Companion to Film*, 82

*Paramount Collection Inventory*, 72
*The Paramount Pretties*, 89

Parish, James Robert
  *Film Actors Guide: Western Europe,* 89
  *Film Directors: A Guide to Their American Films,* 89
  *The Fox Girls,* 89
  *Great Spy Pictures,* 89
  *Great Western Pictures,* 89
  *The MGM Stock Company,* 89
  *The Paramount Pretties,* 89
  *The RKO Gals,* 89
*Performing Arts Books in Print,* 19
*Performing Arts Research: A Guide to Information Sources,* 20
*Performing Arts Resources,* 19
Perry, Ted. *Performing Arts Resources,* 19
Pickard, R. A. E. *Dictionary of 1000 Best Films,* 89
Pitts, Michael. *Hollywood on Record: The Film Stars' Discography,* 89
Plotkin, Richard. "Approaches to Film Study at the University of Illinois," 3
*Positif,* 36
Poteet, G. Howard. *Published Radio, Television, and Film Scripts,* 19, 60, 90, 112
Powers, Anne, *Blacks in American Movies,* 90
*Premier Plan. Hommes, Oeuvres, Problèmes du Cinéma,* 36
*Previews,* 51
*Primary Cinema Resources: An Index to Screenplays, Interviews, and Special Collections at the University of Southern California,* 60, 74
Producers' Guild of America. *The Journal,* 31
*Published Radio, Television, and Film Scripts,* 19, 60, 90, 112
*Published Screenplays: A Checklist,* 19, 60, 88, 112
*Publishers' Trade List Annual,* 12
*Publishers' Weekly,* 22

*Quarterly of Film, Radio, and Television,* 32
*Quarterly Review of Film Studies,* 25

*The RKO Gals,* 89
Ragan, David. *Who's Who in Hollywood. 1900-1976,* 90
*Reference Guide to Fantastic Films,* 87
Rehrauer, George
  *Cinema Booklist,* 19
  *The Film User's Handbook,* 52

*Remakes, Series, and Sequels on Film and Television,* 88
*Repertoriu Mondiale al Filmografiilor Nationale,* 21
*Retrospective Index to Film Periodicals,* 28ff, 38, 82
*Revue du Cinéma/Image et Son,* 36
Ridgon, Walter. *Biographical Encyclopedia and Who's Who of the American Theater,* 90
Rose, Ernest. D. *World Film and Television Study Resources,* 90

Sadoul, George
  *Dictionary of Film Makers,* 90
  *Dictionary of Films,* 90
Salem, James M. *A Guide to Critical Reviews, Part IV, The Screenplay,* 90
Samples, Gordon
  *The Drama Scholars' Index to Plays and Filmscripts,* 90
  *How to Locate Criticism and Reviews of Plays and Films,* 80
Sarris, Andrew. *The American Cinema: Directors and Directions,* 90
Schneider, Harold W. "Literature and Film: Marking out some Boundaries," 3
Schoolcraft, Ralph N.
  *Annotated Bibliography of New Publications in the Performing Arts,* 65
  *Performing Arts Books in Print,* 19
Schuster, Mel
  *Motion Picture Directors,* 28ff, 38, 91
  *Motion Picture Performers,* 28ff, 38, 91
*Screen,* 32
*Screen Achievements Records Bulletin,* 81
*Screen International,* 34
*Screen World,* 91
*Seen Through the Dark: A Guide to Film Reference Sources,* 80
Shale, Richard, *Academy Awards,* 91
Sheahan, Eileen. *Moving Pictures,* 19
Shipman, David. *The Great Movie Stars,* 91
*Sight and Sound,* 25, 32
*Sightlines,* 51
*Skrien,* 36
*Soviet Film,* 37
Stewart, John. *Filmarama,* 91
*Subject Guide to Books in Print,* 25
*Supplement to Books in Print,* 25
Svensson, Arne. *Japan,* 91
*Sweden,* 83

Take One, 25, 33
Thiery, Herman. *Dictionnaire Filmographique de la Littérature Mondiale*, 91
Thomson, David. *A Biographical Dictionary of Film*, 91
*Time: the Weekly Newsmagazine*, 33
*Title Guide to the Talkies*, 82, 84
*Titles in Series*, 12
Truitt, Evelyn Mack. *Who Was Who on Screen*, 92
Turconi, Davide. *Il Film e la Sua Storia*, 21
*Twenty Years of Silents*, 92

University Film Association. *Journal*, 25
University of California at Los Angeles Library. *Motion Pictures: A Catalog of Books, Periodicals, Screenplays, Television Scripts, and Productions*, 20, 60

Vallance, Tom. *The American Musical*, 92
*Variety*, 25, 34
*The Velvet Light Trap*, 33
*Village Voice*, 33
Vincent, Carl. *General Bibliography of Motion Pictures*, 20
Vioculescu, Ervin. *Repertoriu Mondiale al Filmografiilor Nationale*, 21

Warnken, Kelly. *The Directory of Fee-Based Information Services*, 101
Weaver, John T.
  *Forty Years of Screen Credits*, 92
  *Twenty Years of Silents*, 92
Weaver, Kathleen. *Film Programmers' Guide to 16mm Rentals*, 2nd ed., 82

Weber, Olga. *North American Film and Video Directory*, 52
Webster, Bruce. *Film Copyright Reference Book: Films in the Public Domain from June 1940-June 1946*, 92
*Weekly Record*, 22
*Western Films: An Annotated Critical Bibliography*, 88
Whalon, Marion K. *Performing Arts Research*, 20
*Whatever Became of . . .* , 87
Wheaton, Christopher. *Primary Cinema Resources*, 60, 74
*Who Was Who on Screen*, 92
*Who Wrote the Movie and What Else Did He Write?*, 82
*Who's Who in Hollywood*, 90
*Who's Who in Show Business*, 92
*Wide Angle*, 25
Williams, Martha. *Computer-Readable Bibliographic Data Bases*, 97
Willis, Donald. *Horror and Science Fiction Films*, 92
*Women and Film: a Bibliography*, 87
*Women's Films in Print: An Annotated Guide to 800 Films by Women*, 84
*The World Encyclopedia of the Film*, 83
*World Film and Television Study Resources*, 90
*World Filmography*, 92
*Writers' Program The Film Index*, 20, 92

Young, William C. *American Theatrical Arts: A Guide to Manuscripts and Special Collections in the United States and Canada*, 60, 92, 124, 129ff

NANCY ALLEN is Communications Librarian at the University of Illinois, Urbana. A native of Illinois, she has her M.S. in Library Science from the University of Illinois (1973) and is the author of several articles of library interest. She published a bibliography, "Film Books for Students and Teachers," in *Film Library Quarterly* (under the name Nancy Manley) and organized and chaired a discussion group for cinema librarians in the American Library Association.

MICHAEL GORMAN, who contributed the chapter "Cataloging and Classification," was Head of the Bibliographic Standards Office, British Library, 1974–1977. Now Director of Technical Services and Professor at the University of Illinois at Urbana-Champaign, he is co-editor of *Anglo-American Cataloguing Rules,* published by the American Library Association.